WISDOM
WALK

WISDOM WALK

Nine Practices *for* Creating Peace and Balance *from the* World's Spiritual Traditions

Sage Bennet, PhD

New World Library
Novato, California

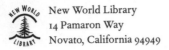 New World Library
14 Pamaron Way
Novato, California 94949

Passage by Thich Nhat Hanh on page 34 is reprinted from *Touching Peace* (1992)
by Thich Nhat Hanh, page 1. Thich Nhat Hanh's poem on page 37 is reprinted
from *The Long Road Turns to Joy: A Guide to Walking Meditation* (1996) by Thich
Nhat Hanh, page 27. Both are reprinted with permission of Parallax Press, Berkeley, California, www.parallax.org.

Text design and typography by Tona Pearce-Myers

Library of Congress Cataloging-in-Publication Data
Bennet, Sage.
Wisdom walk : 9 practices for creating peace and balance from the world's spiri-
tual traditions / Sage Bennet.
    p.   cm.
Includes bibliographical references.
ISBN 978-1-57731-582-7 (pbk. : alk. paper)
1. Spiritual life. 2. Religions. I. Title.
BL624.B397 2007
204'.4—dc22   2006101687

First printing, April 2007
ISBN-10: 1-57731-582-0
ISBN-13: 978-1-57731-582-7

Printed in Canada on acid-free, partially recycled paper

g New World Library is a proud member of the Green Press Initiative.

10 9 8 7 6 5 4 3 2 1

To the memory of my parents, Jack and Rachel,
with love and gratitude for their legacy

Life is the gift of nature,
But beautiful living is the gift of wisdom.

— ANCIENT GREEK ADAGE

CONTENTS

ACKNOWLEDGMENTS   xi

INTRODUCTION   xiii

CHAPTER 1. HINDUISM: *Create a Home Altar*   1

CHAPTER 2. BUDDHISM: *Meditate and Find Peace*   21

CHAPTER 3. ISLAM: *Surrender to Prayer*   47

CHAPTER 4. CHRISTIANITY: *Forgive Yourself and Others*   75

CHAPTER 5. JUDAISM: *Make Time for the Sabbath*   99

CHAPTER 6. NATIVE AMERICAN SPIRITUALITY:
Let Nature Be Your Teacher   123

CHAPTER 7. TAOISM: *Go with the Flow*   151

CHAPTER 8. NEW THOUGHT:
  Catch God's Vision of Your Life   183

CHAPTER 9. ALL TRADITIONS:
  Offer Yourself in Service to Others   207

EPILOGUE. ACQUIRING A TASTE FOR WISDOM   235

APPENDIX 1. TOOLS FOR THE JOURNEY   245

APPENDIX 2. REFLECTIONS ON YOUR
  WISDOM WALK   263

APPENDIX 3. WISDOM WALK CHECKLIST   265

NOTES   269

BIBLIOGRAPHY   275

ABOUT THE AUTHOR   281

ACKNOWLEDGMENTS

Endless thanks to Terry Wolverton, my writing mentor and founder of Writers at Work in Los Angeles, for her amazing, creative guidance during all the phases of this project. I'm grateful to Barbara Moulton, my literary agent, for her clarity, integrity, and enthusiasm for this work, and Jason Gardner, senior editor at New World Library, for his gentle, respectful editorial style, keen eye, and compassionate heart.

Thanks to my spiritual mentors: Dr. Brugh Joy, for his insights into the mystery and his support of my intuitive nature; Dr. Carolyn Conger, for her generous, practical mentoring; and Dr. Linda Garnets, for her brilliant insights over many years. Thanks to Dr. Michael Bernard Beckwith for the opportunities of ministry and teaching Wisdom Walk at Agape International Spiritual Center. Abundant thanks to my friends, colleagues, and prayer partners in the ministry: Rev. Janet Garvey-Stangvik, Dr. Juanita Dunn, Rev. Greta Sesheta, Rev. Mary Murray Shelton, Rev. Diane Harmony, and Lorene Belisama.

I am blessed to feel the harbor of community that has been my sanctuary during the writing of this book. Special acknowledgments to my partner, Sandy Viall, and dog, Beau, whom I love beyond measure; my birth family for our warm connection, especially my Aunt Dottie, and my ancestors — Dr. Michael Mands, and my grandmothers, Esther and Molly — for their wisdom and guidance; our family of friends, Helene Zuckerman, Scott Marr, Marsha and Larry Sheldon, Donald and Fang Doyle, for our frequent dinners and holiday celebrations; the community members of Joy's Jubilation, affectionately called JJ2, for their unforgettable companionship on the transformational path; and my lifelong friends Charlene Shildmyer, Robin Johnson, and Helen Siegel.

Lastly, I thank the students in my classes with whom I've had the pleasure of taking a wisdom walk. To protect their privacy I've changed their names. In a few cases some characters are a composite of several students I've known. I've kept the names of family, friends, and colleagues when I could obtain their permission; otherwise I've changed these.

INTRODUCTION

Welcome to *Wisdom Walk*. In picking up this book you begin an adventure: the exploration of the world's great spiritual traditions. Along the way you will gather wisdom from each of these paths, and you will be invited to engage in a specific practice from each tradition that will enrich your daily life.

Ancient wisdom indicates, "Wisdom is better than rubies." The prevailing message of our time is different and encourages us to seek external riches instead. We may do this by acquiring products, climbing the corporate ladder, attaining degrees, and following other pursuits. Oftentimes we get lost along the way. We lose touch with ourselves and find ourselves overworking, overspending, feeling stressed, even depressed, wondering how we lost our balance. We think, "If I just reach my goals I'll get back in balance. I'll work harder, get a better job, buy a house, get out of debt." It is hard to say whether it is the seeking of external riches that causes us to lose our equilibrium or whether being out of balance provokes us to seek external solutions. Either way we find ourselves on a perpetual treadmill, endlessly running and achieving, yet not knowing exactly how to find our way home to a place of rest inside, where we can be quiet, satisfied, and serene. Even those of us who feel fairly content may still not claim the riches of the path of wisdom. Yet the diamonds of inner peace and the emeralds of a loving heart can be ours. If we follow the guidance of *Wisdom Walk* we can attain these riches.

Benefits of This Book

Wisdom Walk contains nine chapters. Each of the first eight chapters introduces you to a different spiritual tradition — Hinduism, Buddhism, Islam, Christianity, Judaism, Native American spirituality, Taoism, and New Thought — and offers an easy-to-do wisdom practice from which you can benefit. The ninth chapter departs from this format by focusing on all traditions and their views about service as a spiritual practice. At the end of each chapter you will find Wisdom Steps; these suggested actions contain how-to directions that will assist you in applying the wisdom practices in your daily life. You will learn how to:

- Create a home altar. Establish a reminder in your home that you are linked to a larger spiritual presence that adds richness and wisdom to your life.

- Meditate and find peace. Learn the skill of turning within and practice the art of stillness that brings peace of mind and bodily health, and leads you to uncover your authentic self.

- Surrender to prayer. Cultivate the art of directing reverent words of request, praise, and thanksgiving to a higher power as an alternative to worry and fear.

- Forgive yourself and others. Improve the quality of everyday living by dissolving the negativity of past resentments and opening your heart to more love.

- Make time for the Sabbath. By designating one day per week as a respite from work, you can deepen your connection with God, become more aware of the blessings in your life, and create more intimacy with family and friends.

- Let nature be your teacher. Connect to and learn from nature, and establish an awareness that you are part of the grand matrix of life.

- Go with the flow. Become at one with the universal flow of life, and spend less time and energy resisting its movement.

- Catch God's vision of your life. Practice the art of visioning, which links you to inner and universal wisdom, allowing you to discover your true life purpose.

- Offer yourself in service to others. Assist others in your family, community, and the world, and reap the satisfaction of selfless service.

I have experienced these benefits over and over as I write about and teach the material contained in *Wisdom Walk*. Thousands of students have experienced the rewards over the two decades in which I have taught classes on this subject. I have included many of their stories of successes and challenges, and how they overcame their difficulties using the wisdom practices and ideas contained in these pages. In addition to the particular benefits associated with the wisdom practices, this book allows you to:

- Encounter the world's great spiritual traditions as expressed through specific wisdom practices.

- Recognize the wisdom in traditions different from the one in which you were brought up.

- Appreciate the interrelatedness among people of different cultures and religious orientations, perhaps thereby knocking down the barriers in consciousness that separate people from one another.

- Participate in the "beloved community," a term Martin Luther King used to describe a world unspoiled by racial or religious prejudice.

- Heal old wounds from your own religion of origin.

- Overcome prejudices and misunderstandings about other religions. (To help you explore this further, in the appendixes I have included a list of leading questions that you can answer.)

- Develop a wisdom practice that will assist you in achieving serenity of soul.

How to Read This Book

Just as there are many paths to the same summit, there are several ways you can read this book. In writing *Wisdom Walk* I envisioned you reading each chapter, reflecting on the wisdom offered, and engaging in one or more of the Wisdom Steps at the end of the chapter. For example, chapter 1 draws from Hinduism. The wisdom practice is "Create a Home Altar." The Wisdom Steps at the end of the chapter are: *Locate a place in your home for your altar. Assemble objects for your own unique altar. Light a candle on your altar.* After gaining a sense of the benefit of the wisdom practice, I imagined that you would turn to the next chapters in the sequence they are presented. The order of the chapters reflects a development of the wisdom practices from simple to more complex, rather than a chronology of the spiritual traditions.

However, if you prefer to read the chapters in random order, based on attraction or intuition, you can do so without missing essential parts. For example, you can make time for a Sabbath in your week before you create a home altar with no loss of benefit.

You will also gain insights from reading *Wisdom Walk* in a small group or class. Undertaking a wisdom walk in community helps to provide support for integrating the wisdom practices into your daily lives. You may start your own wisdom-walk circle with friends and family taking turns to help facilitate small group discussions. You may also find like-minded people who live in your area on the *Wisdom Walk* website: www.sagebennet.com. Or you can join one of the *Wisdom Walk* teleclasses. You can find dates and times on the website.

Whether you are working in a wisdom-walk circle or on your own, if these practices are new to you, it may be helpful to give yourself at least two weeks with a particular set of Wisdom Steps before moving on to a new set.

Some readers will prefer to accentuate the healing journey. Others will enjoy the path of knowledge and learning about the eight spiritual traditions. Still others who are passionate about practice may prefer to spend time perfecting the wisdom practices. Embarking on a wisdom walk does not mean you are abandoning a spiritual tradition to which you hold a cherished allegiance. You may learn about and benefit from the wisdom of various traditions and still remain faithful to the teachings prescribed by your own faith. Your journey may even serve to strengthen your appreciation of your own unique path as well as widen your understanding of other ways to wisdom. This introduction may also

pave the way to more substantial study. You can make your journey through *Wisdom Walk* your own. With whatever focus you
read this book, you will develop skills for living wisely and reap
the benefits with which wisdom graces us.

How My Wisdom Walk Began

Nineteen eighty-four was a year of crisis for me. The Chinese
pictograph for "crisis" is composed of two characters: *danger* and
opportunity. My life mirrored both of these. I was an itinerant college professor moving from city to city, securing one teaching
contract after another. There was a shortage of teaching jobs in
the humanities during those years, and I was grateful, despite the
stress involved, to undergo the big life changes I had to make in
order to accept these teaching positions.

I had just moved, after finishing two years at the University
of Kentucky, to the University of Wisconsin. Because my new
husband had left his job in Kentucky to move with me, we agreed
that I would be the sole wage earner until he could find a new
position. The transition was harder than expected, and he could
not find work. My stepdaughter was having trouble in the more
advanced Wisconsin school system, and we were adjusting to
being a stepfamily. After a year of working full-time in a new job,
learning to be a stepparent, and feeling the financial pressure of
supporting a family, I entered my second winter in Wisconsin.
We had a stretch of thirty-below-zero temperatures. Something
inside of me was screaming, *No more. Stop.* But I still could not
decipher this internal message. Instead, clueless, I fell into an
abyss of raging fevers and double pneumonia.

For a month I slept poorly, sitting up in a brown-tweed re-
cliner. Often I was awake for long periods, staring into the quiet

of 4:00 AM. My life loomed large before me. *Surely not being able to breathe was a sign of something. What?* I had achieved many of my goals: a PhD in philosophy, a teaching position at a good university when jobs were scarce, a new family to appease the ticking of my biological clock. My life had all the trimmings of success, but I was sick, stressed, and emptier than I had realized. As the sleepless nights continued, I recognized I was completely out of balance. Overwork had become a normal lifestyle — six years of intensity on the PhD fast track, the daily adrenaline rush of living in New York City, career moves to Kentucky and Wisconsin, and now — splat! I'd hit a wall. My life had come to a halt, and I was sitting up at night feeling like a lion was lying atop my chest. With each breath, I felt pain deeper than pneumonia.

On one particularly restless night I lit a candle and stared into the flame. The candlelight soothed me. Comforted by the silence, I felt my breathing slow down. For short periods my normally incessant coughing stopped. This was as close to meditation as I had experienced for many years. *Why wasn't I practicing meditation when I loved it?* A voice in the darkness within me asked the question and gave the answer: *You've been too busy with the external parts of life.* I thought about this for a long while. That night became a turning point in my life. It took several more weeks of sitting up at night to regain my strength to breathe so that I could resume my teaching schedule. I emerged from the illness knowing that I had to change something in my life. I didn't know that my marriage would end.

I am awed by the turns in life that seem to happen beyond our human doing. Shortly after my divorce, I got a call out of the blue to visit a meditation center near where I lived. Up until that time I hadn't known the center existed. The meditation teacher in charge of weekend retreats had seen my card on a bulletin board at the local food co-op and called to invite me to attend a meditation weekend. I accepted the offer. I loved sitting in meditation. I felt as if I had found myself that weekend, and I intuitively knew that I was supposed to live at the center. I asked if this was possible, and the answer was yes. I was also able to consolidate my teaching schedule at the university to two or three days a week, which made commuting an hour each way manageable. Living in spiritual community felt like home, something I sorely needed at that time.

At the Christine Center, a haven of hermitages dotted in snow-covered woods, I was exposed to an eclectic array of spiritual practices from various traditions: Buddhist meditation, Sufi poetry and dancing, Native American sweat lodges and medicine wheels, Hindu *pujas*, and a mystical approach to the teachings of Jesus and the Catholic mass. I was assigned to work in the library, where I explored the rich selection of books from these traditions. I read the pages of Rumi, Saint John of the Cross, and other spiritual authors from diverse traditions, and drank in their wisdom like a thirsty traveler. Then I applied various practices from these pages — meditation, prayer, mindful walking, and forgiveness — to my own spiritual practice. My wisdom walk opened before me like a clearing in the forest. These practices brought me closer and closer to an inexplicable joy and peace I had only heard about but had never experienced until this time.

My life was transforming. My pace seemed slower from the inside out. I felt in contact with a spiritual dimension within myself that was radiant and wise. I felt more connected to my heart and body, and was happier than I had been in a long time. It was as if I'd found my way. I had taken a wisdom walk, step by step, and it had led me back to myself, my essential self — the part of me that is connected with the infinite.

When I left the Christine Center, Sister Virginia, the founder and teacher at the center, reminded me that the mystic map inside of me would guide me to where I needed to go. I was led to Southern California, where I taught at a community college on a one-year sabbatical replacement. At Rancho Santiago College I was asked to teach a course in world religions, which was a wonderful synchronicity.

For the past twenty years I have been teaching classes about spiritual traditions combined with the wisdom practices that comprise the rich journey of spiritual transformation. During this time I have continued to deepen my practice, restore more balance in my life, heal my life from the inside out. Today I bless those dark nights in Wisconsin when I sat up alone looking at the face of death. I realize now that my life was reflecting the insight of Saint John of the Cross. The dark night of the soul is a time when our familiar structures of life crumble — in my case, a conceptual framework of success that included a busy lifestyle and productive work life. After the death of the old structures in the dark-night experience, we have to rely more and more on the spiritual, our true foundation. We turn to Spirit, God, the Beloved, the One — whatever we want to call it — because that is all we have left.

Whether you have had a dark night of the soul, are overly busy, desire more peace and balance in your life, or want to learn more about yourself, spirituality, and the world's great spiritual traditions, I am happy to bring you the possibilities contained in the pages of this book.

The wisdom walk awaits us. Many blessings to you on the journey.

CHAPTER ONE

∽⟤

HINDUISM: *Create a Home Altar*

Build a temple in your heart.
Install the Lord Krishna in it;
Offer him a flower of love.

— PERIYALVAR, EIGHTH-CENTURY POET

In the spring of 2002, I attended an eight-day retreat in Kauai facilitated by Brugh Joy. As part of our spiritual explorations, we visited a Hindu temple one balmy afternoon in March. Kumar, a witty monk dressed in a traditional saffron robe, told us, "When making our vows, monks receive three things: an orange robe, a cell phone, and a laptop." Our small group laughed at this enigma of ancient and modern blending. We could see a cell phone in plain sight on his waistband. "In Hinduism," he continued, "we also believe in one God or Presence, and that every person and thing in this world is sacred. That goes for someone even like Bin Laden. In Hinduism we believe in reincarnation and that people take more than one lifetime to realize certain lessons to discover the light within. It is as if each person is a furnace and his or her job is to keep the surface clean so the light can shine through — and this is the responsibility of each person. If someone's furnace is black on the outside, it appears dark and absent of light. But the light is still there just the same. Also we believe that everyone must work on cleansing the outside of the furnace. You cannot do this for another person. If you put your hand in someone else's furnace, you will get burned. We also believe that hell is a state of mind, and you can get out, or stay in, as you choose."

After the tour ended I approached Kumar, who was standing outside the main temple getting ready for another group. His brown face glowed against his orange robe, revealing almost perfectly formed white teeth. I looked into his brown eyes. They reminded me of a patch of earth in a forest where I'd feel comfortable taking off my shoes and walking barefoot. "What wisdom message from Hinduism would you recommend to those who wanted to take one practice with them from this tradition?" I asked.

He answered quickly, "Tell them to create a home altar."

As I walked back to rejoin my group I thought, *Yes, that would be a wonderful place to begin our wisdom walk — setting up a home altar, a place where we could begin creating a connection with the divine and our own inner sanctuary.*

❧

We begin our wisdom walk by establishing a sanctuary within our homes and also within our hearts. Here we can learn the art of devotion, which opens us to an inner peace and better acquaintance with ourselves.

The predominant religion of India, Hinduism is one of the oldest known spiritual philosophies, dating back more than six thousand years, preceding recorded history. The beginning of Hinduism does not rely on a single founder. Rather, a variety of sacred texts written by enlightened teachers makes up the rich and sacred history of Hindus' many millennia of spiritual traditions.

Students in Wisdom Walk classes are surprised to learn that

many contemporary teachers and movements they've heard of are Hindu: Yogananda and the Self-Realization Fellowship, Sai Baba, Maharishi Yogi and Transcendental Meditation (TM), A. C. Bhaktivedanta Prabhupada and the Hare Krishna movement, Gurumayi and the Siddha Yoga movement, Sri Aurobindo and the East-West Cultural Center, and the widely known Deepak Chopra, who has popularized Ayurvedic medicine.

Getting Our Bearings: Hinduism

NATURE OF THE DEITY. Early Hindus worshipped gods that represented powers in nature, such as the sun and rain. Over time Hindus believed that, although these divinities appeared in separate form, they were part of the universal spirit called *Brahman*. Many divinities make up Brahman, the most important of which are *Brahma*, creator of the universe; *Vishnu*, its preserver; and *Shiva*, its destroyer. Hindus believe that the universe undergoes endless cycles of creation, preservation, and destruction.

RELATIONSHIP OF INDIVIDUAL TO THE DIVINE. Brahman, the one all-pervasive Supreme or Absolute, is not only within each being and each object in the universe, but transcends them as well. The divine within each individual is called the *atman* presence. The many forms of worship, ritual, and meditation in Hinduism are intended to lead the soul toward direct experience of God. Four paths are available to the seeker — through love and adoration, work and service, the mind and study, or a combination of these, including psycho-spiritual exercises.

HOW TO WORSHIP. When followers worship in temples, they do so as individuals rather than as congregations. Most Hindu temples have many shrines, each of which is devoted to a particular divinity. Home is also an important site of worship, centered around a home altar.

ETHICAL BELIEFS. Hindus believe in *karma*, the law of cause and effect by which individuals create their destiny through thoughts, words, and deeds. The law of karma states that every action influences how the soul will be reborn in the next incarnation. Hindus believe in the necessity of having a *guru*, or enlightened teacher, in order to awaken to the absolute truth. They also believe that all life is sacred and is to be loved and revered; therefore they practice *ahimsa*, or nonviolence, in action, word, and deed. Hindus believe that no one religion teaches the way to salvation above all others; each spiritual path deserves tolerance and understanding.

THE SOUL AND BELIEFS ABOUT DEATH. The essence of each soul is divine, and the purpose of life is to become aware of that divine essence. All souls are evolving toward liberation, or *moksha*. Hindus believe that the soul never dies. When the body dies, the soul is reborn, or reincarnated. When all karmas are resolved and moksha is attained, all beings are guaranteed the destiny of liberation from the cycle of rebirth.

What Is a Home Altar?

Ancient Hindus designated a sacred place in every home as a sanctuary, a place where home dwellers could rise in the early morning and commune with the divine. This center of spiritual force, *devatarchanam*, is the "place for honoring divinity." The home shrine provides a fortress of purity for the family and sets a sacred tone for the home. Every prominent devout Hindu home has a holy shrine room, which, like a miniature temple, radiates blessings throughout the home dwelling and the community.

At the center of the shrine is the altar, an area designated for the sacred act of devotion. As in the temple, images and icons of divinities are the central focus of the altar. An icon is more than a clay or metal ornament; its image is seen as actually embodying the God in one's own home. All icons possess one of the following qualities:

- Anthropomorphic, meaning human in appearance
- Theriomorphic, having animal characteristics, like Lord Hanuman, the monkey god, or Ganesh, the elephant god
- Aniconic, meaning without representational likeness, such as the element of fire or the smooth Shaligrama stone worshipped as Vishnu

A home altar in the Hindu tradition may include a replica of a deity, prayer beads to count while praying, and spiritual literature intended for inspiration, all of which create a sacred context for common spiritual practices at home altars: meditating, chanting, burning incense, and offering flowers and food to the deity or teacher to whom one is devoted.

Creating and using home altars is a tradition that anyone can follow, regardless of spiritual orientation. Altars can serve many functions. They bring a sense of the sacred into our living spaces and provide a focus for our communication with inner and spiritual realms. A home altar can assist us in our own healing or transformational journey as well as provide a starting point for cultivating spiritual practice. Altars can also strengthen family relationships when activities such as holidays, seasonal changes, birthdays, and graduations are observed in this sacred space.

Creating Sacred Space

Even if we don't claim the Hindu tradition as our own, we can still enjoy the benefits of creating a home altar. This sanctuary within our own home acts as a meeting place for us to rendezvous with ourselves as well as the divine, however we may conceive of it.

Let's start with ourselves. Many of us may not know the sense of peace that is at our center. We may be scurrying about at a fast pace throughout most of the day, unaware of the bands of gold hidden beneath the surface self. The home altar gives us a chance to sit down and greet this peaceful, inner center. As we continue to sit we may find our way to a larger sense of ourselves, the part of us that is connected to the infinite.

How do we create the sacred space of the home altar? First, what we mean by *sacred space* is an environment that is peaceful, beautiful, and reflective of the spiritual, unseen reality that imbues all things.

FINDING A LOCATION. You may not have the luxury of an entire room that can be devoted to your altar, but you can find a place within a room where you can go regularly every morning, afternoon, or evening to be quiet and contemplative. You can select a corner of a bedroom or living room, and set up a separate table or cover an existing one with colored fabric that you enjoy. You can set up your sacred home shrine on a patio overlooking a yard, or even near the bathtub, where you can light several candles and soak in peace.

PURIFICATION. It is best to prepare the altar space with sparkling cleanliness. Sweep the floors, wipe surfaces, and burn incense or smudge with sage to purify the altar space. It is also important to prepare ourselves by coming to our sacred space with fresh clothes and clear thoughts. We may also use sage or water to create a ceremonial purification, for example, spraying our face and hands with fresh water or brushing the smoke of sage around our head, arms, torso, and feet with a feather.

WHAT TO PUT ON THE ALTAR. A great way to start creating your altar is to drape the surface of the area you have designated. This covering might be a cranberry-velvet cloth, antique white lace, earth-toned scarves, or whatever pleases you. You may prefer to not have a cloth but rather keep the altar on a wooden or glass surface. Candles are another favorite item for altar building, as they are not only a source of light but a powerful symbol of spirit. Other possibilities include sandalwood incense, fresh daffodils, photos of loved ones, shells, and feathers. Additionally, icons from various spiritual traditions can form a wonderful central focus for the altar. The Hindu gods Ganesh or Hanuman, or the goddess Sarasvati, may offer you a rich experience. You may also choose a statue from another spiritual tradition that is meaningful to you.

MAKING AN OFFERING. An offering is a way to acknowledge and honor the deity by presenting a gift — usually food and flowers — as an act of worship or sacrifice. The word *sacrifice*, meaning "to make holy," indicates that it is a holy act to make offerings at the altar. You may choose to bring an offering of fresh flowers to your altar or place bowls filled with water as a symbol of gratitude for the fullness of your life.

CREATING A RITUAL. Developing a ritual that you can repeat allows you to have a regular way to enter the state of consciousness that an altar provides: a peaceful, receptive place where you can begin your spiritual practice. The ritual you create may be as simple as lighting a candle and placing a rose on your altar. The act of cleaning your altar may provide a daily ritual and will allow you to preserve its freshness and your awareness of the honored guest you have invited into your home. Another activity that is common at altars is reading inspirational literature. Keep some pages next to you that uplift your spirit and inspire peace and balance.

PORTABLE ALTARS. When you travel away from home you can take a portable altar with you. A red candle in a votive glass surrounded by a necklace, a small statue of the Buddha, or a picture of Mary placed on a small piece of silk can begin to transform any tabletop into a sacred space. Whether arriving at a hotel room in an unfamiliar city, visiting a relative, or moving your work space outside, a portable altar can open the portal to the sacred wherever you go.

Even though we may desire to create an altar, have already chosen a location, and even have gathered some objects to place upon the altar, we may still feel awkward actually doing so. We may even feel a slight aversion to creating an altar. At least, this was the case for me. Since walking through my own resistance led to such a satisfying experience with creating altars, I offer my story.

When Altars Come Alive

To tell the truth, I didn't start out with an affinity for altars. I didn't resonate with icons from a culture that was not my own. I was accustomed to living so fast that I felt impatient with taking time to set up things in a designated place. I didn't collect many things and the ones I did accumulate I could rarely find again. Quite frankly, it seemed like a bother, more a waste of time than a sacred act. However, I did notice that when I saw an altar that was already set up, I felt an inner stirring in connection with its beauty. I was somehow moved by what I could not name.

What opened me to the power of altars was teaching a class with my friend Lorene. After some meditation and discussion, we called the class "Prayer, Ritual, and the Sacred: Living in the Presence of God." One of our topics was cultivating the consciousness of sacred space. Of course, we needed to model this by creating such an environment for our students to experience. Since this wasn't my strength at the time, I was glad when Lorene took the lead.

Watching her and participating with her inducted me into the sacred practice of creating an altar. First, we cleansed the classroom by sweeping the smoke of burning sage throughout its four corners. We then took turns smudging each other from head to toe with broad strokes of feather and smoke. Next, we meditated and offered prayers that our class and altar would be the reflection of sacred presence. We prayed that our hands and hearts would be guided by divine grace in building the altar. After about fifteen minutes of sitting in the silence, bathed by the pungent smell of sage, we felt ready to begin.

I watched Lorene spread a white, velvety cloth over the round tabletop we had placed on a cardboard box. The fabric folded gracefully on all sides and around the gray carpet. Lorene draped earth-toned scarves around the table, interspersing shells, pinecones, feathers, and candles to bring in the four elements. By this time I joined in, arranging a mixed bouquet of flowers in the center of the altar, spreading red and pink rose petals throughout the altar's surface and around the altar table. We lit the candles and took a step back to receive the altar. It was beautiful, more alive and greater than the collection of items we'd placed upon the table. The experience opened me, and I realized that slowing down and experiencing the consciousness of the sacred through purification, meditation, prayer, and intention were all part of creating the altar. I saw that consciousness was as important as the items placed upon the surface.

I like to bring fresh flowers to my altar. When I sit in my meditation chair near the altar, I feel peaceful. I notice that whenever I see my altar I am reminded about my spiritual practice. It's as if the energy of the altar helps to bring me into a spiritually uplifted space and encourages me to connect with my spiritual practice, even during times when I don't feel like meditating or being still.

Recently during a difficult time in my marriage, I created a marriage altar for our living room. I carefully placed magenta orchids in a vase that we'd used at our wedding. I bowed before two small bronze statues of Ganesh, the Hindu god that removes obstacles, and prayed that the barriers of our marriage would be removed so that we could remember the love that brought us together and our commitments. We had said our vows in front of beloved witnesses just one year earlier. Over the next few weeks I placed fresh flowers in the vase, alternately replenishing them with white gardenias, red roses, yellow daffodils, and white daisies with yellow centers. At times I looked deeply at the two rose-quartz hearts that also adorned the altar. To help us remember the sanctity of our marriage, I invited my partner to also say prayers that I believed would be answered. They were.

Creating the marriage altar was not a quick fix. We still had to walk through our inner turbulence and embrace our own and each other's shadows. We needed to really listen to each other, refrain from blaming, and look instead at our own dark sides that were more easily projected onto each other. I noticed that as we did this the altar created a gentle atmosphere for our inner work. In the same way that flowers extended a sweet fragrance, the altar radiated peaceful blessings through our home and marriage.

We found our way back from the darkness and learned a great deal from the journey. One insight I gained was that, no matter what was going on in my life, I still had to feed the relationship. Otherwise, like the flowers on the altar, the relationship would wither without a fresh supply of love and attention. Creating and tending the altar provided a focus that allowed such insights to occur.

The Art of Devotion

For Hindus, the home altar and shrine room involve the entire family, who gather, often in the early morning but also in the afternoon and evening, through the devotional act of *puja*, meaning "adoration" or "worship." Many people believe the best time for puja is before dawn. To prepare, the whole family bathes and dresses in clean clothing. In presenting oneself before the deity, one wants to look and be one's best. At other times the altar is covered.

It is common to not eat anything for at least an hour or more before the puja. Each worshipper brings an offering of flowers or fruit, which is prepared before the bath. Worship rites can be as simple as placing a flower at the deity's feet or lighting a lamp. Or they can be more elaborate, with many Sanskrit chants and offerings. The food for the deity is called *prasad*.

The essential aspect to any puja is devotion. For Hindus, altars are not only a place of tranquil beauty that inspires recognition of divinity, but also the ritual location where individuals actually communicate with the deity. Developing a relationship with the deity is considered a great blessing and continues throughout one's lifetime.

I once previewed a film from the library about a Hindu family gathering in worship at their home shrine to celebrate the birthday of Ganesh, the elephant-headed deity, remover of obstacles. The young boy in the film spoke of his worship experience with such excitement you'd think it was his birthday and he'd received a pony he'd always wanted. I was so struck by the devotion of such a young one speaking about a spiritual experience that I felt inspired to write his story.

Before Dawn

Sanjaya, a ten-year-old boy, the eldest in his family, is the first to rise on this special occasion of Ganesh's birthday. This is his favorite puja of the year. For a whole week the family will honor the deity to celebrate the occasion. Sanjaya has chosen grapes and apricots for his offering this morning, which he places on a golden offering bowl given to him by his grandmother for such festivities. His brown fingers cup each grape as he carefully arranges them in a circle around the apricots. The fruit smells sweet on his slightly sticky fingers, which stirs his hunger. He wants to pop a few grapes into his mouth but puts the thought out of his mind. *This offering is for Ganesh.* He remembers his grandmother's words: "Never taste the fruit you are offering our lord. Sacrifice satisfying your desire and give your offering with love. Then you will be graced with a special blessing, and your prayers will be answered." Sanjaya misses his grandmother, who died when he was seven. But remembering her words brings her closer to him. This is not a time to get lost in daydreams. He has to hurry to bathe and dress before the puja begins. His younger brother still sleeps on a cot on the other side of the room. His parents have not yet come to awaken them, so he must have plenty of time before the puja begins.

Sanjaya wants so much to have a special talk with the deity, as his parents have done. He has tried to hear the deity's words, but strain as he does, nothing happens. "Open your heart with more love and the deity will see that you are sincere," his mother has counseled.

"But I am trying to be loving, yet still nothing happens," he's complained to his mother.

"Let your love be in every act of devotion — the preparation of your offering, your bathing and dressing, and your prayers. Then the deity will know your love, shower you with blessings, and come alive before your eyes."

In the still morning darkness, Sanjaya comes from his bath and prepares to dress. He closes his eyes, trying to concentrate on love as he puts on saffron *dhoti*, which look like pleated pants, and *kurta*, a traditional collarless shirt that his mother laid out the night before. His brother is now in the bath, and Sanjaya can hear the footsteps of his family, their opening and closing doors, as they prepare for the puja.

His father rings the first bell at the altar, the signal that the puja is ready to begin. Sanjaya enters the family shrine room, prostrates himself on the floor in the back of the room, then moves closer to the altar where his mother, father, and two aunts and uncles are already laying their offerings. While his father passes a flame in front of the deity to welcome him into their home, Sanjaya carries his offering of fruit up to the altar. By this time Sanjaya knows that the altar doors will be open. He is glad he is wearing his formal clothes so the deity will see him at his best.

Kneeling before the altar, Sanjaya breathes in the fragrance of jasmine incense that has already filled the room. Still on his knees, Sanjaya faces Ganesh, whose elephant head, raised arms, and dancing feet are familiar images Sanjaya has come to love. Sanjaya touches his head to the ground, then places his fruit on the altar at Ganesh's feet. He closes his eyes and whispers very low, "Ganesh, I bring these grapes and apricots to you. They are my favorite fruit. Even though I was hungry this morning, I didn't eat them. Please bless my parents, aunts, and uncles. Help me to not fight with my younger brother, who wants to come with me everywhere I go. And please, help me to concentrate on my studies so I can go to the university and my parents will be proud of me." Then Sanjaya bows, kneels on the floor, laying his whole body down on the carpet, then begins to reverse the process, coming up on his knees, leaning back on his feet, ready to stand up. As he gets to his feet, out of the corner of his left eye, Sanjaya sees Ganesh smiling at him. In that glimmer, Sanjaya feels his heart light up.

Challenges and Progress on the Path

I've often taught Wisdom Walk as a ten-week class in a college or spiritual center, although sometimes I've taught a portion of the material as an afternoon workshop. In one Wisdom Walk series, we spent a couple of sessions on creating altars. One night I removed the usual seminar table, assembled an altar in the middle of the circle, and invited people to come in for our customary meditation. This particular altar was a low, round tabletop draped with crimson fabric and covered with different shells that I had gathered on my journeys to the islands of Hawaii and Tahiti. I lit some candles, then placed them around a statue of the goddess Sarasvati, goddess of voice and knowledge. This goddess is the protector of art and is credited with the invention of writing. She is also the goddess of speech, the power through which knowledge expresses itself in action. She is always pictured as an extremely beautiful woman with a milk-white complexion, often sitting on a water lily and playing a lute. We meditated in candlelight with music playing behind us.

As the meditation concluded, I invited people back into an open-eyed posture and asked them to gaze upon the altar and to give me some reactions. Judy, a woman in her sixties, with thin, gray hair cropped close to her scalp and large tortoise glasses, had her arms folded across her chest. She raised her thumb as a sign that she had something to say. "I feel a little irritated with all of this altar business. What am I supposed to get looking at a clay replica of somebody I don't even know? In my tradition, we don't think that God is outside of ourselves in a clay statue. We believe that God is within, so I feel that making me look at a statue on an altar is a violation of what I believe."

I told Judy that her comments were welcome and that I understood that this particular wisdom practice might not appeal to her at this time. I suggested to Judy that the icon on the table was not meant to violate anyone's beliefs; rather the experience of the altar was an invitation to open to the wisdom associated with Sarasvati. Could the altar induct us into the mystery she represented: inspiration for the sacred arts of writing, music, and other such expressions? The blessings of these qualities were available to us in this meditation. I then asked other people to comment.

Chris was the next to speak, his blond hair falling over one eye, his elbow leaning on a pair of jeans torn at the knee. "I don't know quite how to explain this," he said, "but when I walked into the room, I felt this change come upon me because this picture of Sarasvati was so beautiful that somehow it just spoke to a part of myself that was not in my control. I felt drawn into the beauty and this somehow changed and deepened my meditation. Something was coming through the arrangement of the statue and altar and candlelight. I can't explain it."

I responded that the atmosphere of the altar allows us to change our state of consciousness and attune to a vibration of the sacred. The altar allows us to come closer to divinity, however it is that we conceive of that. "Remember, in the Hindu tradition, you *are* that divinity; the transcendent is also immanent." By now, Judy seemed more relaxed. Her hands fell by her sides, and she seemed very focused on other people's comments.

Jane spoke next. In her midthirties, wearing a red tank top and jeans, she had penetrating dark eyes. "My altars at home don't look like this. I'm arranging some things on a tabletop, but somehow they don't have a quality of beauty or spiritual significance. I feel like I'm failing in creating altars."

"Jane, there's no prescribed way to arrange an altar," I explained. "An altar is meant to reflect what is meaningful to you. You don't have to compare your altar to another's. Each altar is unique and complete in itself. Also, what makes an altar special is the consciousness that you use to create it."

One suggestion that might help us create an altar is to spend a few moments in preparation. Just close your eyes for a few minutes in front of the altar and clear your mind of the events outside of the current moment. You can say to yourself, "I am open to creating an altar of beauty and significance to me." Then let yourself be guided to what this altar should reflect. You may really be surprised by how much your openness to creating something beautiful will manifest. There is no wrong way to create an altar. You may need to keep arranging different things in order to get the effect or meaning you're after.

Margie's hand waved above her head. Light complexioned, auburn-reddish haired, and slender, she looked younger than her fifty-eight years. "I'm really excited about the altars I've been creating at home. I have a special teacher, Gurumayi from the Siddha Yoga Center, and I have her picture on my altar. I also have a picture of my teacher's teacher, Swami Muktananda, along with several candles, a ceramic piece of praying hands, and a photo of my son. However, as a result of our class, Wisdom Walk, I've decided to redo my altar and add some items related to different religions." Margie was animated as she continued to speak, "I love the 'Om Namah Shivaya' chants. In Sanskrit this means, 'I honor the Self within me.' What I'm finding is that revitalizing an altar is helping me to remember more about the divinity within me and that this whole experience of my life is sacred."

Kristin interjected. Blond, blue-eyed, and eager to learn, she drank in the wisdom from different traditions as if she were enjoying lemonade at a summer picnic. "The altar that I spend the most time with is in my office. I've created one on the back wall of my office that spills over onto my desk. I have always filled my office with treasures from where I have traveled. But our assignment of creating a home altar encouraged me to look even deeper. First, I had to clean what already existed because the altar wanted to be in a place that was clean and well taken care of.

"I had been given a statue a while ago of the dancing Shiva. As we've talked about in class, Kali is the goddess of destruction; Shiva is male. The dance of Shiva is symbolic of the dynamic forces of creation and destruction, and the harmonious balance of opposites. Most images of the dancing Shiva depict him with four arms, which represent the four cardinal directions of space and are symbolic of Shiva's omnipresence. In each hand, the figure holds a different symbolic object or makes a meaningful gesture. A drum represents the sound of creation. A gesture (*abhaya*) means, 'Do not be afraid.' A gesture toward the lifted right foot is symbolic of release from the cycles of death and rebirth. Another hand holds a flame, which is the essence of creation and destruction. The small figure under Shiva's feet is the body of the dwarf Purusha (forgetfulness), who is symbolic of man's inertia, the ignorance that must be overcome. The circle of flames surrounding the figure denotes the universe in its entirety.

"I just felt like it was now time to bring out that statue and see how it could assist me in making a new venture in my business. I also added gorgeous red roses. I find that I feel inspired by keeping a supply of fresh flowers near the altar. Here's my question: Now that I have my office altar, I would like to create altars everywhere in my house. Is there anything wrong with creating altars everywhere?" The class laughed.

"I don't think so, Kristin," I said. "In some ways, we have many altars, perhaps created without conscious intention." We may think of a collection of photographs arranged on lace on the mantle of the fireplace as an altar. This contains objects of the family that you may consider beloved. Create as many altars in your home and office space as seem responsive to you. In her book, *Altars: Bringing Sacred Shrines into Your Everyday Life*, Denise Linn suggests that we create nine different altars in each designated area of our house, sanctifying each corner with the intention each sacred space represents.

❧

Altars connect us to the spiritual realms. They can add grace and beauty to our lives by infusing our home with a gateway to the mystery of the unseen. The home altar can open us to hallowed places within ourselves. A home shrine acquaints us to our link with the infinite and introduces us to our inner sanctuary that accompanies us wherever we go.

Wisdom Steps

FIND A PLACE IN YOUR HOME FOR YOUR ALTAR. Find an area in your home where you can have some peace and quiet. You can choose to have your altar in a designated room in your house or a favorite corner of a room. The location of your altar should contain a comfortable place to sit and an area such as a tabletop, a counter, or a corner of a floor in a room where you will be able to set down fabrics, candles, and other objects that evoke a sense of the sacred. When deciding on a place, keep in mind the activities in which you will be engaged at your altar, such as meditating, praying, journal writing, playing a musical instrument, or listening to meditative music.

CREATE YOUR OWN UNIQUE ALTAR. Now that you have a place for your altar, you can experiment with creating one that is unique to you. You want your altar to bring you a sense of peace and give you a sense of the sacred. There is no one way to create an altar, so relax and enjoy the process. Here are some ideas to begin with: It's helpful to have some surface space such as a small circular or rectangular table, a cardboard box, or the surface of a dresser. You can also use a designated area of the floor in a corner or under a window. Now more fun begins as you select cloth, candles, incense, fresh flowers, or replicas of spiritual objects that are meaningful to you. These can include statues of the Buddha or Quan Yin (Goddess of Compassion), for example. You may also choose to place treasures from nature on your altar such as beach shells, crimson autumn leaves, blue-jay feathers, or pinecones. Photographs of beloved teachers, family, and guides can also provide inspiration and meaning. As you create your special space, see how you feel with the presence of certain colors and objects. Your altar can be as simple as a candle on fabric that has your favorite colors. Or it can be complex and contain objects, mementos, and reminders of your spiritual journey.

LIGHT A CANDLE ON YOUR ALTAR. You may choose from many different types of candles: scented or unscented, tall and thin or short and wide, contained in glass or uncontained for an open flame. As a way of initiating a relationship between yourself and your altar, sit in front of this special place that you created and light a candle. Allow yourself ample time to savor the experience — listen to the way the match scrapes across the carbon strip to ignite, watch the wick catch the flame, see the radiance of the yellow and white hues light up the colors and objects of your sacred space. Sit for a moment in the candlelight. Feel the subtle presence, the illumination, the mystery. Your altar is an outward expression of your inner sanctuary. Become acquainted.

CHAPTER TWO

❧

BUDDHISM: *Meditate and Find Peace*

The main emphasis in Buddhism is to transform the mind,
and transformation depends on meditation.

— THE DALAI LAMA, *THE PATH TO TRANQUILITY*

From fall 1986 to summer 1987 I communed with other long-term hermits at the Christine Center for Meditation in Willard, Wisconsin. Distinguished from those who stayed for a weekend meditation retreat or intensive, long-term hermits lived on the premises anywhere from six months to several years. For almost a year, I lived in a small hermitage called Angel of Wisdom, sparsely decorated with a single bed, wood-burning stove, and compact desk. Mine was one of a dozen or so cabins — Angel of Peace, Angel of Love, Angel of Light, to name a few — that dotted the snow-covered, wooded property. We shared the acreage with roaming deer, black crows, and large black-and-white cows that grazed in an adjacent field.

It is not unusual for Wisconsin weather to be severe. Winter temperatures dip below zero and hover indefinitely around minus ten, twenty, and thirty degrees, sometimes with a windchill of fifty below zero. Yet despite harsh weather and a rigorous meditation schedule of four sittings a day — before breakfast, lunch, dinner, and bedtime, plus weekend and two-week-long intensives — I fell in love with meditation. But it was not love at first sight.

By early winter the enchantment of living in the woods with only a potbellied stove had worn off. The soot and splinters on my hands from carrying wood from outside to the stove, and getting up in the freezing 3:00 AM darkness to put another log on the fire were not as romantic in February as they'd been in October. Freezing, I'd walk across open fields to the meditation loft for our 5:00 AM sitting. As I climbed the stairs to the meditation loft in a converted barn with grainy, wood walls the color of honey, I'd spot my meditation bench in the middle of the room. Some mornings, staring at the black bench seemed like some kind of showdown. Though the environment looked peaceful, spotless — black futons and meditation benches lined up symmetrically in neat rows, sandlewood incense burning, warm, comfortable temperatures — meditating in this loft was not as easy as it looked.

The long sittings caused my thighs to go numb and my lower back to spasm in pain. I'd be thinking of sex instead of being still. My mind chattered endlessly, like a monkey swinging from limb to limb. Ron, the meditation teacher, whose reddish-blond hair tended to fall in his eyes when he turned his head, would interject certain words during long stretches of silence. "If you feel pain, concentrate on your breathing in and breathing out. Breathe into the pain." If my eyes hadn't been closed they would have rolled up to the ceiling in adolescent disgust. *Doesn't he know I've reached my limit?* I would rage in my inner misery. Sitting in silence sometimes seemed torturous. After what seemed like forever, I heard the meditation teacher say, in poised equanimity, "Don't become attached to your pain or your thoughts. Let go and return to your breathing in and breathing out, breathing in and breathing out."

Why are we sitting here day after day? Wouldn't it be a better use of time to accomplish something, contribute to the world in some way? This was a convincing inner voice that was hard to refute. Yet another part of me guided me into the meditative stillness — breathing in and breathing out.

Sometimes after a sitting Ron would ask if we had any questions. One morning I raised my hand. "Sometimes when I'm meditating I get these great ideas. Isn't it appropriate to stop meditating so I can write them down?" I was expecting Ron to recommend that I keep a pad and pencil near my meditation bench. Instead he said, "The ego does not like being unimportant. It's deflating to the ego to de-emphasize the thinking process, and sometimes it can be quite clever in tricking us out of the discipline of practice. Your great ideas will wait for you after meditation. I suggest turning your attention to the present moment and following your breath — breathing in and breathing out."

If I'd been a cat I would have hissed at him, swirled around, and strolled in the opposite direction. Part of me felt appalled as another part of me observed my ego having a tantrum. *Okay, that's it. It's gone too far. This does not make any sense, and I think —* In an instant I saw how my mind always created another reason, distraction, or scenario in which I could play a part. Yet I also saw that "I" was not only this actor. I was connected to something more, not "I" at all, but something deeper, more essential, my real self, which I'd experienced in meditation. The view of myself as an actor playing a starring role seemed wildly comical to me. I laughed at how seriously I had taken myself. I struggled much less after this.

Even in early March, snow clung to the ground. While the long winter had annoyed me, I now accepted the climate. In my hermitage, I'd write in the late mornings and afternoons. Looking up from time to time, my eyes would feast on the small drifts of snow outside my back window. Sometimes I'd see a doe walking silently in the white cover, other times only her tracks. Whenever I put a log in the wood-burning stove, I'd savor the smell of pine and cedar and the yellow-orange flames licking through the open door of the black stove. Sometimes I wondered, *How can I be so content with so little?* I no longer even minded that the bathrooms were in the main building five hundred feet from my cabin.

One morning I arrived early at the meditation loft. I took off my shoes and walked on the pea-green carpet, as I had done day after day for the past year. I knelt down on the black padded rectangle that served as a meditation mat. Then in one motion I placed the bench underneath me and sat back on it. My breathing was already taking on its familiar rhythm as I inhaled the sandalwood incense. I closed my eyes and sank into the peace, deeper and deeper with each breath, my mind like a serene lake at sunrise.

I smiled as I remembered my struggles over the past year. Now, sitting on my meditation bench, other hermits arriving in the meditation loft for the morning practice, I felt different. My mind was a lot less busy. I noticed the world more closely with my heart. I drank in the beauty of the cumulus clouds that inched across the expansive midwestern sky. I sighed at the kindness of retired men who trudged every day in the cold with their tractors and tools to help build and repair sheds, hermitages, and fences on our land.

Whenever Ron struck the meditation bowl that began every meditation in my year-long stay at the center, my soul attuned to the lingering tones that faded into silence. "Allowing ourselves to turn within and follow the breath..." Without thinking, I turned within to my inner sanctuary. Who could have predicted that following my breath day after day would lead me home to this priceless stillness and inner peace, this embrace of self-love and self-acceptance, this contentment to simply be a peaceful presence in the world?

Many who meditate confirm the transformative effects of this wisdom practice: more peace and clarity of mind, greater self-awareness, and stronger resiliency in response to life's ups and downs. If we take the time for stillness in our busy lives we will reap the benefits that meditation masters exemplify and praise.

Buddhism is a spiritual tradition based on the teachings of Siddhartha Gautama, who is known as the Buddha or Enlightened One. Founded in India around 500 BC, Buddhism has been a widespread cultural, religious, and social influence throughout most of Asia. Buddhism derived from Hinduism and developed in a distinctive direction.

Getting Our Bearings: Buddhism

NATURE OF THE DEITY. Buddhists do not believe in an external deity. Yet by discovering one's own Buddha nature, one can awaken to *nirvana*, a state of enlightenment. This awareness gives one access to qualities often associated with the divine in other religious systems — infinite blessings, goodness, serenity, all-knowingness.

RELATIONSHIP OF INDIVIDUAL TO THE DIVINE. The Buddha's instructions were to rely upon one's nature for the things that one needs in life: "Be lamps unto yourselves." He de-emphasized the reliance on a teacher and counseled people to find their way to the center of themselves through the teachings.

HOW TO WORSHIP. All Buddhists have faith in the Buddha; his teachings, the *dharma*; and the religious community he founded, the *sangha*. These are referred to as the Three Refuges or Three Jewels. Buddhists worship in temples and utilize meditation, prayer, prayer flags, and prayer wheels.

ETHICAL BELIEFS. Ethical conduct, which is intended as a way to enlightenment, is outlined in the Four Noble Truths and the Eightfold Path.

THE FOUR NOBLE TRUTHS

1. The basic characteristic of human existence is suffering.

2. The cause of suffering is clinging to a wrong point of view.

3. Suffering can be ended.

4. The way out of suffering is to follow the Eightfold Path.

THE EIGHTFOLD PATH

1. Right understanding concerning the nature of reality

2. Right thought, which is free of sensuous desire, ill will, and cruelty

3. Right speech, which does not contain harshness, falsehood, and meaningless chatter

4. Right action, which avoids killing, stealing, using intoxicants, and gambling

5. Right livelihood, which means earning one's living ethically, devoid of fraud in the transactions of one's trade

6. Right effort, which aims at wholesome states and purifying the mind

7. Right mindfulness, or meditative practice, which encourages awareness of self and seeing things as they are

8. Right concentration, which strives toward one-pointedness of mind, a state where all faculties of thought are directed toward a particular focus

THE SOUL AND BELIEFS ABOUT DEATH. Buddhists believe that the soul does not die and that it evolves through a series of incarnations. When the soul is enlightened it transcends the cycle of birth and death, and reaches a point of eternal bliss.

The Power of Awakening

Buddhism is a spiritual tradition that begins with the experiences of a man who awakened to his true self. His expanded awareness allowed him to see life from an enlightened perspective. Buddhists believe that each of us can also awaken and that one of the tools that can assist us is meditation. The story of the Buddha allows us to know the main ideas embraced by all branches of Buddhism. Followers of Buddhism take the story of the Buddha as inspiration for their own path of peace.

In *The Illustrated World's Religions*, Huston Smith gives an account of Buddha's awakening. At the time of his birth in India around the sixth century BC, fortune-tellers foresaw that Siddhartha Gautama (later named Buddha, meaning "the one who is awake") was no ordinary child. Either he would be a great ruler or a great redeemer. In an effort to guarantee the former, his father gave orders to have his son surrounded by the riches of the palace — voluptuous dancing girls, banquets of the finest foods — nothing was to be spared to make Siddhartha's world pleasant. In addition, his father gave orders to allow that nothing unpleasant enter his son's life of privilege and luxury.

One day runners, who were usually stationed outside the palace to clear away the old, ill, and dying, and those who sought help at the palace, did not carry out the king's orders. The once-shielded prince encountered old age, disease, and death. Over a few days, Siddhartha saw an old man with broken teeth leaning on a staff and

a woman lying on the road, her body ravaged by disease. He also encountered a shaven-headed monk who carried a begging bowl. Siddhartha's exposure to death, disease, and old age caused a great
upheaval within him. *What was the Truth? His life in the palace? Disease, death, and old age? What was illusion? The life he had lived or the
life outside the palace?* Siddhartha became impassioned with his
desire to know the Truth. Over a period of six years, he studied with
two Hindu masters and a band of ascetics who preached that fasting
and self-denial would lead the way to the Truth. He followed this
path by fasting, living in the woods, praying, and meditating, but
he did not find what he was looking for. He would have died of
starvation had it not been for a friend who gave him some warm
rice gruel. Buddha saw that the two extremes of his life experience
— luxury and renunciation — were not the way to the Truth. The
Middle Way must lie between these two extremes. His deep yearn-
ing to know the Truth led him to sit under the Bo tree (short for
Bodhi, or enlightenment) until he knew the Truth for himself.

That night Buddha had the awakening that opened his awareness to the Truth, which is known in Buddhism as the Four Noble
Truths. Like a spiritual physician, Buddha diagnosed, analyzed,
and prescribed the remedy for what ails the human condition.
First, he said that the basic characteristic of human existence is
suffering. Second, the cause of suffering is clinging to a wrong
point of view. Third, suffering can be ended. Fourth, the way out
of suffering is to follow the Eightfold Path, which includes,
among other things, meditation and a mindful awareness of one's
behavior and intentions.

What Is Meditation?

The wisdom teachings in Buddhism direct us to cultivate a meditation practice in order to live a healthy and effective life. Meditation

is an activity that directs us inward to practice the art of quieting our thoughts. Meditation helps us activate inner stillness, to detach from the myriad thoughts that incessantly occupy our attention and distract us from the present moment. The mind is constantly thinking, comparing, judging, recollecting the past, projecting into the future. Students in meditation classes struggle with their mental processes. *Am I doing this meditation exercise correctly? It seems like everyone in the class is meditating better than I am. Will this meditation time ever end?* Meditation helps us to still these thoughts and become more aware of the present moment, which gives us access to the only reality that exists — what is happening right now. Training the mind to be still leads us to a deep peace within us. The Dalai Lama, one of the leading contemporary voices of Tibetan Buddhism today, reminds us, "One of the things that meditation teaches us, when we slowly descend into ourselves, is that the sense of peace already exists in us: We all have a deep desire for it even if it's often hidden, masked, or thwarted."

BEGINNING TO MEDITATE. The two most common forms of meditation are done in a seated position or walking. With the former, it is best to have a quiet place to sit without being disturbed. Many people find that sitting near their altar creates a conducive environment for meditation.

To engage in sitting meditation, find a place where you can sit comfortably — cross-legged, in a chair, or kneeling. The head should be held upright but not rigid. One can meditate with eyes closed and attention focused inward, or with eyes open looking at the hands or at a place on the floor a few feet forward. Keeping the eyes open can keep one from falling asleep. Meditating while lying down is not a good idea because it allows one to fall asleep too easily.

There are several options for practicing meditation. The most basic form begins by watching the breath. You can inhale to the count of four: one, two, three, four; and exhale to the count of four: one, two, three, four. If you lose track, simply return to the beginning of your counting. Let your breath be slow and regular. Avoid forcing your breath or artificially controlling it. Let your breathing take on its natural rhythm, like the ebb and flow of the ocean. Another way of using your breath is to simply watch it as it enters and exits you. Be as aware as possible of the full process of breathing, the rising and falling of the diaphragm, the coolness of the breath entering the nostrils, the warmth of the breath coming through the nostrils.

Whether through the use of a specific technique, consistent meditation practice over a long time, or the wonderment of the mystery, meditation practice deepens over time. After considerable practice the mind becomes accustomed to stillness and can sink into deep quietude. You don't concentrate on anything; you simply practice quiet mindfulness. You let your mind be an observer reflecting back what comes before it as would a mirror. You remain unattached to the passing thoughts, feelings, sounds, aches, and smells. You let them pass like clouds drifting by on a summer's day. Attachment to the dazzle of mental constructs may be one way the mind might try to steal your attention from the discipline of meditation.

Don't build up expectations of having enlightenment or emptiness experiences. If you have great thoughts, fine. Write them down if you like, after you conclude your meditation time. It is best to get in the habit of making your meditation the priority. If you don't have great thoughts, fine. Whatever happens or doesn't happen, don't let yourself be too affected by it. Again and again, return to the breath. By doing this you will cultivate a meditative posture of your mind that will eventually become less and less attached to thoughts, outcomes, and feelings. You will learn to live more fully in each moment and cling less to the things that come to be and then pass away.

The Importance of Practice

One of the contemporary voices of Buddhism today comes from His Holiness the Dalai Lama. The translation of his name is "ocean of wisdom." He was awarded the Nobel Peace Prize in 1989. His directive is to integrate compassion into every area of our lives — the workplace, family, our relationships, anyone we meet. He says, "Kindness is my religion."

I had the privilege of attending a conference with the Dalai Lama in Dharamsala, India, his home in exile from Tibet, which is now under Chinese rule. The first day of the dialogues with His Holiness at the Norbulingka Palace, the Dalai Lama entered the room, humbly bowing to us and walking backwards so that his back was not to any of the hundred people in the audience. The peace and compassion he exuded lingered in the room like the perfume of a flower.

Talking to one of the monks who was a companion to the Dalai Lama, we learned that His Holiness rose at 3:30 AM to begin four hours of Buddhist meditation, exercises, and other spiritual disciplines, all of which had taken place before this 9:00 AM meeting. The countenance of peace we had just witnessed was not accidental but the result of practice — diligent, devoted, consistent practice. Inspired by the example of the Dalai Lama, a few of us at the conference agreed to meet the next morning to meditate with the Buddhist monks at the monastery in town.

Meditation Square in Dharamsala

When I awoke for meditation at 5:00 AM I remembered how
I had been inspired by the Dalai Lama's commitment to spiritual practice and how my own meditation practice seemed
too irregular and inconstant in comparison. *Today I begin a
new level of practice*, I thought to myself, as we left our hotel
for the twenty-minute walk to the site where the Buddhist
monks meditate each morning.

Cows, dogs, and monkeys roamed the narrow dirt
streets of Dharamsala, where people walked on their way
to work. Women scurried through the village in bright-
colored saris — pink, yellow, gold, orange. They looked
like wildflowers dotting the village landscape. I looked for
duplicate designs and colors in the women's dresses, but I
could not find them. The women laughed with each other
as they walked down the street, arms linked at the elbows.
Cab drivers honked their horns, trying to hurry the casual
swarm of people, cars, and animals. Lepers lined the
streets — some with missing limbs and teeth. Many smiled
as they outstretched their cups for rupees, one of which is
equal to ten cents, enough to feed a person for the day.
Shopkeepers, who thickly lined the streets, waved passersby
in to buy their fruit, fabric, and jewelry.

After walking through town we found a small road and
climbed the rugged hill to Meditation Square. The square
itself was an area of about five hundred feet. In the first
room we passed, hundreds of lit candles covered every table
and shelf. The monks had already completed their morning
prayers before we arrived. This seemed amazing to me. It
was still half-dark in the autumn morning chill. I stopped to

absorb the beauty of the rows of candlelight. The gesture of monks lighting this many candles so early in the morning touched me. What dedication to practice, love of stillness, and devotion to growth. I have recalled this candlelit room many times since then, especially when I have felt my own desire to stay in bed rather than get up to meditate.

Continuing the walk around the open doors on all four sides of the sanctuary revealed Buddhist men sitting cross-legged on the floor around the perimeter of the room, their eyes closed, hands folded in their laps. In the center of the front of the sanctuary a large golden Buddha also sat with his eyes closed, depicting composure and serenity. Pink and white flower petals surrounded the Buddha amid dozens of lit votives enclosed in glasses. To the right of the temple, other men were in varying phases of moving meditation — bowing, kneeling, and prostrating themselves on the cement floor.

At the farthest perimeter of the square several men and women ran their fingers across three large bronze prayer wheels with Buddhist prayers of peace inscribed across their surfaces. I joined this diverse group, some of whom were Buddhist, others from our conference of varying faiths, and ran my hands across the cold surface of the prayer wheels. The massive dome-shaped metal turned easily from the pressure of the palm of my hand. I felt the indented letters cool beneath my fingers. Breathing in and breathing out, I, as others before and after me, sent these prayers of peace out into the world. I said a prayer also for the grace of spiritual practice, hoping that prayer would implant in my own heart and inspire devotion to my own meditation practice.

Coming Home to the Present Moment

Another contemporary Buddhist voice is Thich Nhat Hanh, Zen Buddhist Vietnamese monk, who was nominated for the Nobel Peace Prize by Martin Luther King Jr. He reminds us that we can come home to the present moment and there find peace:

> Our true home is in the present moment. To live in the present moment is a miracle. The miracle is not to walk on water. The miracle is to walk on the green Earth in the present moment, to appreciate the peace and beauty that are available now. Peace is all around us — in the world and in nature — and within us — in our bodies and our spirits. Once we learn to touch this peace, we will be healed and transformed. It is not a matter of faith; it is a matter of practice.

Meditation teaches us mindfulness — how to focus our mind with one-pointed attention in the present moment. In sitting meditation we are cultivating this one-pointed attention as we count or watch the breath or observe our thoughts. Mindfulness can accompany every activity we engage in — walking, eating, listening. A Zen saying about mindfulness states, "When you sit, sit. When you stand, stand. Above all, don't wobble." The benefit of mastering this practice allows for our full resources to be engaged in any activity. We are not split with our bodies sitting, our minds projecting into the future with tasks that need to be done. When we split ourselves, we ring like a cracked bell.

The times when I have had minor accidents — tripping over the curb, missing exits on freeways — were times when I was not fully present. I was lost in thought, thinking about a project that was due or replaying in my mind a conversation with someone at work, only this time expressing what I really thought. Doing things with mindfulness is a kind of meditation. Like any skill we are developing, doing things mindfully takes practice. Such was the case when attendees of a Thich Nhat Hanh retreat practiced a walking meditation together.

Walking Meditation

Engaging in a walking meditation is a common Buddhist discipline that is different from taking a leisurely stroll or walking for aerobic exercise. When we are walking as a meditation, our intention is not focused on relaxation or getting our heartbeat up to a particular rate. Instead, the focus is practicing one-pointed attention at each moment, being fully present with our bodies as we walk. This can slow down our walk considerably. As in sitting meditation, when we walk mindfully we are aware of ourselves in the present moment. We notice how the heel lands on the ground and the foot touches the earth, as we spring forward from the ball of the toes gripping the surface. We observe that as we take another step we notice each breath, passing thoughts, the trees — things we miss when we're more involved in the past and future than the present moment.

Beach Walk

Several hundred people attended the five-day Thich Nhat Hanh retreat in Santa Barbara on the sprawling green University of California campus that sits right on the beach. The first night of the conference we were invited to participate in a morning walking meditation. At 7:00 AM the next day, eighty men and women of Caucasian, African, and Asian origin formed a single line from the dormitories to the beach. We walked slowly in the gray mist. The August humidity mixed with the cool morning air. With each step we practiced mindfulness. I noticed my breathing, the shape of the head in front of me, the silhouette of the campus dormitories.

As we reached the beach I inhaled smells of fish and seaweed mixed with the sweetness of the ocean air. Our single line dispersed into many paths as conference members followed wherever their walking meditation took them. I continued to walk mindfully, watching the slate-blue waves gently hit the taupe beach. The ebb and flow of the tides reminded me of breathing in and breathing out, as if the ocean were in a perpetual state of meditation. Walking farther, my eyes followed the contour of tall, green grasses of varying shades and heights that lined the curves of sand dunes and marshes leading from the beach back to campus.

I began to feel a melody of contentment within me. *Was this the feeling of home that Thich Nhat Hanh spoke of when he welcomed us back to the present moment? This feeling of unequivocal belonging and deep intimacy with myself?* The aid-to-mindfulness song that Thich Nhat Hanh had taught us the night before arose from my heart like a natural spring. I sang to myself as I walked up the hill back to my own room:

I have arrived.
I am home

in the here,
in the now.
I am solid.
I am free.
In the ultimate
I dwell.

Challenges and Progress on the Path

One Tuesday night when I was teaching Wisdom Walk, Kristin raised her hand with a warm smile. "I know the chapter we're reading this week says 'Meditate and Find Peace,' but my experience with meditation this week has been the opposite. I sit down and quiet myself only to find feelings of anger, frustration, or fear. I was unaware of these feelings until I started to meditate. It's not peace I find but emotional chaos! Am I doing this exercise wrong?"

A few others in class chimed in. Judy, who was usually irritated about something, blurted out, "I'm glad I'm not the only one who didn't find peace. All I could think about in my meditation was how angry I felt toward the neighbor upstairs for moving furniture around his apartment in the early morning. Before sitting down to meditate I wasn't even aware I was angry!"

I listened to these reports and smiled. "Maybe I should have named the chapter 'Meditate and Find Peace . . . *eventually*.'" The class laughed, which broke the tension.

Beginning meditators need to be reminded that everyone's experience is unique. As newcomers to the practice we need to relax and not be so afraid that we're failing at meditation. It's common for thoughts and feelings to run wild in our first several experiences. We may observe that our feelings seem unruly, like chattering monkeys or wild horses galloping through our minds. Meditation makes us aware, sometimes for the first time, of how our minds race incessantly from one thought to the next. As for feelings, meditation may heighten an awareness of our feelings, which we may ordinarily deny or push down into oblivion.

I shared with my students how Thich Nhat Hanh approached the topic of feelings. He said, "When you discover in meditation that you are afraid or angry, don't resist. Instead, invite these feelings to sit with you in meditation. Say 'Come here, my little friend, fear. Come here, my little friend, anger.'" When we do this we disarm these feelings instead of making them stronger. We embrace rather than disown these strong emotions and they, mixed with the energy of meditation, run their course and transform.

If we disown or deny our feelings, we lose the full force of our wholeness. It takes a lot of energy to keep dark parts of ourselves at bay. A fellow meditator I knew had firsthand knowledge of this. While sitting in meditation he came upon a deep loneliness he had tried to deny for most of his life. Sitting in meditation, he found nowhere to hide. Instead, he kept sitting, day after day, breathing in and breathing out. He remembered times of his suffering, from childhood to adulthood, until he developed such compassion for himself that he totally embraced his loneliness by just being present to it. His loving embrace transformed his loneliness.

When we sit or walk with whatever is, meditation teaches us to be aware of what is in front of us, reflect it back, without judgment or desire for revision, and just let it be in the moment, knowing the next moment will bring something new. This is called *witness consciousness* or *observer mind*.

One of my favorite stories about witness consciousness concerns a man who had begun a new relationship. One day while taking a bath, he found himself in the agony of jealousy and rage. From out of nowhere the witness consciousness within exclaimed, "Far out, jealous rage."

Evelyn raised her hand just barely over the seminar table. Although Evelyn was always deeply engaged in class and had wonderful things to share, she seemed shy. Wearing steel-framed glasses and usually dressed in business suits or slacks, she had a knack for blending into the background like a chameleon. I was always glad when she spoke. "I have to admit, I had a lot of resistance to sitting down to meditate this week." She then described what she called a perplexing contradiction. "On the one hand I feel better when I meditate. I am definitely more peaceful and calm. Why then don't I just run to my meditation chair? Instead I procrastinate and find a million chores to do instead of meditating! On Wednesday I set my alarm to meditate at six o'clock before work, then I hit the snooze alarm until seven. No time was left to meditate. On Thursday morning I reached for the phone like a Pavlovian dog and spoke to my sister long distance instead of meditating. Every morning this week something interfered with my morning meditation. The whole week slipped by."

What Evelyn was describing was familiar to the class, indicated by nodding heads and widened eyes now focused on me for an answer. "When we begin to meditate it is common to encounter the obstacle of resistance," I told the class.

The ego part of us — the part that likes to be in charge and receive applause — is often not that happy with the discipline of meditation. It will resist, rebel, and talk you out of the practice, sometimes in very cunning ways. It's best to deal with this part compassionately. Assure the ego it still has an important part to play in the whole show. Then gently but firmly take a seat in your meditation chair and return to your breathing. It's best not to resist the ego. Resistance can heighten the rebellion. Be patient with your meditation practice. It's part of the process to encounter obstacles. Over and over, return to the breath. Above all, be kind and gentle with yourself. It is not wise to beat yourself up for missing one or more meditation times. Simply love yourself and be compassionate about your process. You don't have to meditate perfectly. You just have to practice.

With Evelyn's permission I opened up a discussion with others in the class about what had worked for them in establishing a meditation practice.

Kristin was the first to speak. "I have two little ones at home, so it's best for me to wake before my family gets up. I bless that morning time from 5:00 AM to 6:30. It's often the only time I have to myself all day."

John, a large man in his forties with a naturally loud voice and a gentle heart, was the next to speak. "I find that I need some smaller time frames in the morning and throughout the day. On very busy days, or when I'm experiencing a lot of internal resistance, I give myself permission to sit for shorter amounts of time. Ten minutes in the morning still feels like it centers me, and I find the shorter time better than nothing. I also enjoy a five-minute meditation during my morning and afternoon breaks at work. These keep me alert yet calm throughout the day and act as a better pick-me-up than coffee."

Bobby, wearing cutoffs and a T-shirt, looked like the surfer he actually was. "Music does it for me. I find if I focus on a meditative melody like one of the selections from 'Shamanic Dream,' then I can reach a deeper stillness without too many thoughts. I like that the musical selections are about twenty to thirty minutes long, and when the cut is over so is my meditation."

Liticia, a pregnant African American woman in her thirties, was smiling. "I had a great experience with meditation this week. I went to my son's soccer game and I had about an hour's wait while the kids warmed up for the game. Instead of paying my bills or running more errands as I would have ordinarily done, I began a walking meditation around the soccer field. I loved it. Then I practiced being in the moment during the game. My son caught my eye several times during the game, especially when he made a good play. We exchanged smiles and hand waves. At the end of the game on the ride home we recounted the highlights of the game, which I was never able to do because my body used to be at the soccer game, but my mind was elsewhere. When I tucked Keith into bed he gave me an extra-long hug 'Thanks for coming to my game, Mom.'"

Liticia went on to describe how the practice of mindfulness increased the intimacy with her son. She realized how precious this time together was. We may realize, too, that the most precious thing we can give each other is our full, undivided attention.

We may also experience the opposite effects that occur when we fail to listen fully. I was once walking with a close friend through a park in northern California. My friend of several years began to disclose some personal information about herself and then turned to me for my response. Without even knowing it, I had drifted away and spaced out. I didn't fully hear what she was revealing about herself. When I asked her to repeat what she had said, she closed down like a door slamming tightly shut. "Never mind," she glared. I could not persuade her to tell me again. Instead we continued to walk with a wedge in our friendship that autumn afternoon. I felt guilty about missing this moment of closeness. My suffering during this walk in the park really brought home the importance of mindfulness in our personal relationships. I internally made a promise to practice mindfulness as best I could, especially when others were sharing from their hearts. I also had to forgive myself for being preoccupied that day. We all drift off from time to time. Mindfulness is a skill that gets better with practice.

Jim's Resistance

Jim was a quiet member of one Wisdom Walk class until I said that meditating every day and keeping a meditation journal was a requirement of the class. Usually I tell students that assignments are an invitation rather than a requirement. But if I sense that a particular class needs more structure, then I make the assignment a requirement. When I did, Jim's brown eyes, usually hidden behind gray-rimmed glasses, glared with resistance, red animating his normally pale coloring as he fidgeted in his chair. Sitting on the edge of his seat, his muscular torso reminded me of a cornered jungle cat.

"Yes, Jim?" I asked, even though he did not gesture with his hand to ask a question or express a comment.

"Look, I can barely get out of my house on time to get to work. When I sit down to meditate, my thoughts are racing like the cars on the freeway. Now you want me to write about it, too?" Jim's voice grew louder with each sentence.

I suggested an amended program for Jim as an experiment, which calmed down his inner rebellion. I suggested that he split his meditation into three-quarters movement meditation and one-quarter sitting meditation. I found out that because of the assignment to meditate Jim was skipping his morning jog, which he usually did for thirty minutes before getting into the shower. We agreed he would keep the jogging and use it as part of the meditation. We reviewed how he could do his jog mindfully, concentrating on his breathing, letting thoughts that arose go by like clouds on a summer day. Then after the mindful jog he would engage in five minutes of sitting meditation, adding increments of five minutes only if he wanted to, followed by five minutes of writing in his meditation journal, which he could also record on his mini-cassette recorder. Jim seemed satisfied. The volcano settled back down. We would take a look at the experiment the following week and make changes accordingly.

The next week Jim arrived early to class instead of his usual rushing to his seat a few minutes after class had begun. His shoulders seemed lower, his breathing seemed slower and deeper, and he smiled to other students as they greeted him before class began.

Jim raised his hand during our discussion of wisdom steps. "I loved jogging mindfully. I looked forward to it every morning. Instead of figuring out my day, I counted my breath as I inhaled and exhaled. When my thoughts crept in, I said out loud, 'Later.' But I didn't say this in a harsh voice. I sat for five minutes after I cooled down on a park bench near my house and continued to breathe in and breathe out. My wild-horse thoughts weren't racing as much. I seemed to sink into the green peace of the park. And then I said so into my recorder." Jim reached into his pocket and pulled out the mini-cassette recorder, and held it above his head in victory. The class cheered.

Evelyn said, "Jim, something definitely looks different about you this week. You feel calmer."

"Yes," Jim said. "My co-worker and my wife mentioned it, too, and my kids said they liked that I shot a few hoops with them before dinner instead of yelling at them to pick up their toys and finish their homework." The tone of his voice lowered and his face grew more ashen. "I guess I'm a stressed-out grouch like my father, whom I swore I'd never be."

"Don't be too hard on yourself, Jim," I responded. "You're learning a wisdom practice that will help you live with more peace in your life. You've just begun and you're doing great."

As we begin our meditation practice we will encounter obstacles, find ways to overcome these challenges, learn more about our thoughts and feelings, become more aware of the wonders of the present moment, gain access to our inner peace, and know the sacred. There are documented studies that link meditation to a decrease of stress and the promotion of better health and peace of mind.

Wisdom Steps

DEVELOP A REGULAR MEDITATION PRACTICE. To organize the many choices available to you, begin to develop your practice by choosing a time, place, and method of meditation. If you don't already know how to meditate, begin by reserving five to twenty minutes in the morning and/or in the evening "to sit quietly and do nothing," as the Zen masters advise. Many people find that meditating first thing in the morning is a wonderful way to create a centered and tranquil tone for the day. If you live in a house with others and it's noisy, consider getting up a half hour earlier to enjoy the silence. Your altar is a perfect place to meditate. In addition to your regular sittings, quick meditation breaks throughout the day in your office, car, or even the restroom can be extremely restorative. Wherever you are, at any time, choose a meditation method. Count or watch your breaths as you inhale and exhale. Choose a *mantra*, or word, to focus on, such as *peace*, *love*, or *Om*, the sound of universal harmony. Or meditate to music.

KEEP A MEDITATION JOURNAL. It can be helpful to your meditation practice to keep a journal about your experiences in the silence. Do your journaling after you spend your time in the silence. Remember, even if you think you have great insights to explore, it is still better to complete the meditation before journaling. The mind does not like discipline at first and may be tricking you out of your precious and invaluable time in the silence. You can record your restlessness, emotions, boredom, and impatience as well as insights and discoveries about yourself. Keeping a journal is a good way to reinforce the discipline of your practice. You can also include pictures, collages, and drawings in your journal that depict and inspire your meditation journey.

TAKE A MINDFULNESS WALK. You may find yourself sitting at a desk, computer, or in the driver's seat for much of the day. Take yourself outdoors and give yourself the treat of a meditation walk as one of your daily meditations. In a mindfulness walk, bring your attention to the present moment. If you're outside, notice the sparkle of sun on fresh-fallen snow, the shape of clouds, or the color of the ground where you are walking. Notice your breathing as you inhale and exhale, and the coolness of your breath in your nostrils. Remember to be aware of your mind's tendency to think of things to do, problems that need solving, or frets about the past. Gently but firmly bring your attention back to the present moment where peace can be found.

CHAPTER THREE

❧

ISLAM: *Surrender to Prayer*

There is a means of polishing all things
whereby rust may be removed.
That which polishes the heart
is the invocation of Allah.

THE KORAN

efore becoming a minister I didn't have much formal connection with prayer. My family attended synagogue during the high holy days. At these services we read responsively from prayer books, which could be thought of as praying. But for me it was more like reading than the spiritual experience I later came to associate with prayer.

The end of my marriage catapulted me into the experience of prayer. It was a challenging time. While teaching at the University of Wisconsin, I had received an eight-week summer grant to participate in a seminar at the University of California in Riverside. Since I had always wanted to live in California, I thought that spending the summer there held the extra bonus of exploring possibilities to live and teach in California. My husband and I decided that my stepdaughter, then twelve, should accompany me, since no one would be available to watch her while my husband worked.

Our marriage was strained, to say the least, as we struggled to untangle ourselves from the alcoholic and codependency patterns that held us captive. I had begun my own journey of recovery from over-control of other people's lives as well as alcohol and drug use, which was sometimes perplexing to me. *How can I be alcoholic and still have been functional enough to earn a PhD in philosophy? How could my attempts to help my loved ones turn into addiction?* In twelve-step meetings I heard that alcoholism and codependency were cunning and baffling; I could at least relate to that.

Three weeks into the grant I had still not heard from my husband. The last thing we had said to each other as we kissed good-bye at the airport was, "I love you. Speak to you soon." Now, almost five weeks later, I'd received no phone messages from him, no returned calls, only notices from the bank and overdraft fees from his bounced checks that were written against our joint account that had no money in it. *What the hell was going on?*

I looked around at the flimsy furniture of the student-housing apartment where my stepdaughter and I lived. My body felt numb except for the sharp throbbing in my gallbladder. I felt a shaking inside of me, as if the foundation of my life were crumbling. I was standing in the rubble of my dismantled life. I'd experienced abandonment in childhood, which suddenly returned to grip me in its vice; I felt like I was seven years old again, alone, lonely, and neglected.

The mounting stress went on for weeks: no calls, more bank notices, scattered thoughts, fragments of a life. I felt like I was falling into a deep well. I could not control my tears, my life, my husband, or even my thoughts. Nothing I could think, reason, or forge through could lift this nosedive my life was taking.

One night I had a dream in which a woman's voice whispered to me that my husband had moved in with another woman and the marriage was over. I saw myself in the dream free-falling off a cliff in slow motion; I woke up before I hit the ground, my heart racing. I felt afraid to breathe. If I could stay still, then maybe the truth of this dream wouldn't touch me. I'm amazed at this now, but at the time I woke up my stepdaughter and told her the dream. Half-asleep, she tried to comfort me, "Dad would never do something like that. Don't worry, Mom. Go back to sleep."

Still shaky, I slunk back into bed. My feet and hands were freezing. I wanted to put on socks, but the dresser on the other side of the room seemed too far. As my head touched the pillow I heard the same woman's voice from my dream. She was praying with me: "The Lord is my shepherd. I shall not want..." I hadn't heard this prayer since I was a child. I remembered my father reading me Bible passages before bedtime. "Yea, though I walk through the valley of the shadow of death, I will fear no evil, for thou art with me..." My heartbeat was finding a more regular rhythm. The words of the prayer felt like a lullaby. The voice and images of the psalm comforted me; I felt somehow supported. The prayer repeated itself in my mind over and over as if it were one of those loopless tapes. I found that if I could enter the prayer and surrender into its images, my fear dissipated. "He maketh me to lie down in green pastures..." I felt the cool, sticky grass on my arms and thighs as I lay down. "He leadeth me beside the still waters..." I transported myself to a deep, blue lake, hearing frogs, smelling fish, sensing stillness, and feeling peaceful. "He restoreth my soul..." Something was happening. The prayer was changing me. It was as if I were receiving a blood transfusion; vital blood with oxygen and nutrients was replacing the old, diseased blood. "Thou annointest my head with oil...." I began to feel better. As I kept going to the green pasture and still waters, a beloved poured oil through my hair. This was the last thing I remembered as I drifted off to sleep.

In the morning I wondered how I even remembered the

words to that psalm. It had been thirty years or more since I had last heard this prayer. A profound truth bathed my body in peace. *Oh my God. I am not alone.*

Prayer became the only solid ground upon which I could step. Again and again — when I thought I could not go on, when my strength waned, when I felt the pain of my broken heart — prayer lifted me, like a golden staircase, out of my dark night of the soul.

∾

How would our lives be different if we surrendered to prayer five times a day as the Muslims do? Islam reminds us to cultivate a life of prayer. Prayer is a way of remembering that we are connected to an infinite presence — call this God, Allah, compassion, or love. The quote that begins this chapter refers to prayer as polishing the heart. The invocation to God, prayer, allows us to return to a purity within ourselves as we remember our connection with God. We can renew ourselves throughout the day with fresh waters of the spirit; prayer washes away the rust and grit of daily life that can harden the heart.

Islam derives from *salam*, which primarily means "peace" and secondarily means "surrender." Combining these two meanings of Islam, the connotation is that peace comes from surrendering one's life to God, *Allah*. Those who practice Islam are called Muslims; their sacred text, the Koran, is the holy book of Islam revealed through God's prophet, Muhammad.

Getting Our Bearings: Islam

NATURE OF THE DEITY. Muslims believe that there is one God, Allah, and Muhammad is his messenger. God is beneficent, kind, wise, and compassionate. Surrender to God is central to the requirements of faith.

RELATIONSHIP OF INDIVIDUAL TO THE DIVINE. The individual is in close relationship with God through every part of life. The required five Muslim daily prayers keep the connection with Allah alive and vivid in believers' minds, hearts, and souls. The prayers take five to ten minutes.

HOW TO WORSHIP. Muslims worship in mosques. They have a Friday noon service, *jummah*, with a lay minister, *imam*, who speaks on a reading from the Koran.

ETHICAL BELIEFS. Ethical conduct is clearly delineated in the Five Pillars of Islam, which serve as the foundation for this spiritual tradition:

THE FIVE PILLARS OF ISLAM

1. The first pillar is the unity of God, *Shahadah*, expressed in the opening of the Koran, "There is no god but Allah, and Muhammad is His Prophet."

2. The second pillar, *Salat*, is canonical prayer. Muslims pray five times a day: on arising, when the sun is overhead, in the middle of the afternoon, when the sun sets, and at bedtime. Before making their prayers, Muslims engage in ritual bathing. The prayers take five to ten minutes. The physical movements of the Salat symbolize the believers' submission to God.

3. The third pillar is charity, *Zakat*. Muslims are required to help the poor and those in need. The almsgiving is to be 12.5 percent of one's income or more, and it is paid once a year in the form of a tax. Most Zakat goes to mosques, Islamic centers, or welfare organizations.

4. The fourth pillar is fasting during *Ramadan*, the holy month in the Islamic calendar. From the first rays of light at dawn to the last light of the day at sunset, no food, drink, or smoke passes the lips, nor are Muslims sexually active during this time.

5. Islam's fifth pillar is pilgrimage, *Hajj*. At least once during a lifetime, health and finances permitting, Muslims should visit Mecca, the birthplace of Muhammad. The pilgrimage helps to strengthen one's commitment to God.

THE SOUL AND BELIEFS ABOUT DEATH. Muslims believe in an afterlife; heaven is where you reside when you die according to your good deeds. If you have not led a good life, you are condemned to eternal damnation.

What Is Prayer?

The wisdom practice of surrendering to prayer adds a rich depth to our daily spiritual work. Prayer refers to reverent words and thoughts directed toward a deity, goddess, or object of worship; or an earnest request (also called a petition) to a higher authority. Prayer is also used as a vehicle of praise as we recognize the power and bounty of the invisible dimension with which we can connect. Often this posture of praise gives way to prayers of thanksgiving as we appreciate the many blessings of our lives. We are not alone; we have access to an infinite intelligence, love, and compassion. We can use prayer to obtain the support and guidance we need in our everyday lives. We access this dimension through prayer.

Meditation and prayer can be considered complementary aspects of a spiritual practice that links us to the infinite — whether it is God, Allah, or our own inherent strength, wisdom, and goodness. Some think of meditation as listening to God, whereas prayer can be viewed as talking to God. Meditation is the receptive aspect of contemplation and stillness; prayer is the active way of making a sacred request or creating reality through concentrating on affirmative thoughts.

The experience of prayer involves a shift in awareness, much like tuning in to a specific radio station. I sometimes joke with students that praying is like tuning in to the radio station KGOD, but it is not far from the truth. Prayer is an attunement to a particular frequency, a favorite station that plays beautiful music. We feel lifted by the melodies, changed by the arrangements. To pray is to experience a change in perspective from a problem to a solution, from an ordinary to an extraordinary feeling of awe or appreciation.

The Power of Surrender

It is not an easy thing to surrender. At least it wasn't for me. I was like the woman rock climber who, one day, lost her footing while climbing. Holding onto a tree limb, she dangled hundreds of feet over an abyss. She looked above her head and cried out, "God, if you're out there, I need your help. What should I do?" The voice answered her quickly, "Let go." The woman closed her eyes, considering this for a moment. She then asked, "Is anybody else there?"

The prospect of surrender conjures up images of defeat, giving up, relinquishing our power. The ego doesn't like this. Yet, in spiritual development, surrender opens us to a greater field. We surrender our personal sense of self to our infinite Self. Prayer helps us to remember this larger self as we focus our attention on the infinite presence of God. By doing this, we lift our attention from daily circumstances and the problems that engross our energy, to an awareness of God — the beneficent, compassionate, and merciful One.

The emphasis on surrender or submission in Islam comes from Muhammad's own life, as Huston Smith describes in *The Illustrated World's Religions*. Born in Mecca in approximately 570 AD, Muhammad's spiritual journey began in surrender. Both parents died when he was young. His uncle raised him and treated him affectionately. We are told that angels of God opened Muhammad's heart and filled it with light. Since he experienced loss early in life, he was sensitive to suffering and was always eager to help the poor or needy. As he reached maturity he met his wife, Khadja, a wealthy widow fifteen years his senior, to whom he stayed married for the rest of his life. Following his marriage, Muhammad spent fifteen years preparing for his ministry.

Muhammad would often go to a mountain cave outside Mecca to meditate and seek the wisdom of his own solitude. On one night, referred to as the Night of Power, Muhammad was lying on the floor of the cave when he heard an angel say, "Proclaim." Muhammad protested that he was not a proclaimer of truth, but the voice continued, "Proclaim your Lord is wondrous and kind, / Who teaches by the pen, / Things men knew not, being blind." This happened three times until finally Muhammad surrendered. When Muhammad arose from his trance, he felt that the words of the angel had spoken to his soul. He went home to Khadja and told her about his experience in the cave. "Am I a madman, a prophet?" Muhammad wondered. At first Khadja doubted him, but as Muhammad continued to unravel his whole story, she believed him and became his first follower.

Muhammad heard the voice of the angel Gabriel repeatedly, and the command was always the same: "Proclaim." Muhammad continued to surrender his life to the word of God. He proclaimed the truth by writing the words that God revealed to him for twenty-three years. Scholars have been baffled about the beauty of the lyrical Arabic prose depicted in the Koran. How could a barely educated man like Muhammad write such poetic and pithy language? Followers of Islam rest in the faith that Muhammad recorded the words of God. His students report that Muhammad was in a trancelike state whenever he wrote, as if he were taking dictation. These writings in the Koran and the words written about the example of Muhammad's life in the *Sunna* (a collection of Muhammad's words and acts) make up the foundation of Islamic life.

How to Pray

One of the first things to consider is, What does prayer mean to me? In Islam there are obligatory prescribed prayers. We may choose to recite prescribed prayers from a variety of traditions or leave room for spontaneous prayers. The important thing is to cultivate a relationship with God, Allah, or with the quality of love or wisdom if you do not resonate with a higher power from any spiritual tradition. In addition, you would be wise to consider when you will pray, how to quiet yourself before prayer, types and methods of prayer, and how to put these all together in a prayer practice.

CARVING OUT PRAYER TIME. Whether we take our inspiration from the Muslim dedication to prayer, five times a day, or find something that works for our lifestyles, we all need to set aside time for prayer. Whatever times we choose — in the morning when we arise, in the late afternoon when we're tired from working many hours, or before we drift off to sleep — it is wise to choose specific times for prayer. The structure can help us create a foundation of support and nurturance throughout the day. You may find it useful to build upon what you have established as a meditation practice. Remember also that your altar provides a sacred space for you to meditate and pray.

CHOOSING PRAYERS. We have many options when it comes to choosing prayers. We can select prescribed prayers from our own or another's tradition. We can use prayers of grace before meals, or blessings at special occasions such as birthdays, graduations, births, and transitions. We can also be spontaneous and choose our own words for prayers.

If you are new at speaking your own prayers, the first thing to do is to relax. There is no one way to pray and you cannot pray incorrectly. You can fill in the following blanks if you would like some support with your prayers:

> *God, the infinite, or love is* _____.
> *I believe it is possible to* _____.
> *I claim for myself or others* _____.
> *I give thanks for* _____.

Choose an ending that completes the prayer, such as "Amen," "Blessed be," or "So it is," which acts as a release of the prayer. One example of this completed prayer is:

> *God is an infinite presence of power and peace.*
> *I believe it is possible to have help in healing my sore throat and cold.*
> *I claim for myself divine, radiant health.*
> *I give thanks for this health.*
> *And so it is.*

EXPERIMENTING WITH PRAYER METHODS. We can experiment with many ways of saying prayers — out loud, quietly to ourselves, reading them, reciting the same prayer responsively with a group, taking turns to pray with a prayer partner, or saying different prayers aloud with a group, creating a chamber of prayer. We can also sing our prayers. I learned a beautiful Hindu chant that I sing as a prayer at different times throughout the day. Singing the prayer connects me with a bliss and harmony that is a welcome respite, not only when I find myself tired or depleted throughout the day but also as an inner background music to whatever I am doing. I have also found it very helpful to have one or two favorite prayers committed to memory. In this way, I can recite the Twenty-Third Psalm, for instance, whenever I need the calming effects this prayer has on me.

Prayer is a way to communicate with God. Not only can God answer prayers through a demonstration such as healing or a successful venture, but we can receive direct answers from the source of infinite intelligence that God is. In order to practice this form of prayer, we need to relax and enter into a state of consciousness that is receptive to wisdom. If you are experimenting with this form of prayer — receiving spiritual guidance from God — allow yourself to find some quiet time, and imagine a place in nature that is pleasing to you. Immersing yourself in such a scene can help you relax. With an inward gaze, allow yourself to focus on the heart center. In this relaxed state, ask a question and wait for an answer. Feel free to write down this spiritual guidance and keep it in a notebook so you can easily refer to it. It is wise to read over the answers we ascertain as spiritual guidance. The content should make sense to us and glisten like gems of truth.

MOVEMENT AND PRAYER. The specific movements of Salat encourage us to explore the integration of prayer with the body. In *How I Pray: People of Different Religions Share with Us That Most Sacred and Intimate Act of Faith*, edited by Jim Castelli, I was inspired by a man who wrote that he recited his morning prayers out loud while walking on the treadmill. Palmer, the husband of my prayer partner, Rev. Janet Garvey-Stangvik, takes the forty-five minutes of his morning run to pray for each member of his family, his friends, neighbors, and previous students from his teaching career.

When I experimented with learning the movements of Salat I was impressed with how powerful the prayer became when I involved my body as well. I had a similar experience when I lived at the Christine Center and participated in *zikr*, the Muslim dance with the Beloved.

Saturday Night Zikr

On Saturday nights at the Christine Center for Meditation, we gathered together in the meditation loft for a zikr, a Sufi dance of ecstasy. The first one I attended came toward the end of a two-week retreat. For fourteen days we had been pushed beyond our comfortable limits, meditating for long rounds, going to bed late, waking up early. The last thing I wanted to do on this particular Saturday night was be with the group. I would have been more than content to return to my hermitage and read any book that wasn't spiritual. I told Ron, the retreat leader, and he said, "Come to the zikr. You won't be sorry. Trust me." He walked away before I could answer.

I felt like I was carrying a hundred-pound boulder in the middle of my chest when I slogged into the meditation loft ten minutes late. The group was already gathered in a circle and Ron had begun talking about the Sufis. He explained that one or two centuries after Muhammad's death, a number of Muslims, who were attracted to the spiritual teachings of the Koran, began wearing coarse woolen garments to protest the silks and satins worn by sultans and caliphs. The name "Sufi" derives from the word *suf*, which means wool. The Sufi passion was to experience God in the present moment. Sufis have always been known to retire in off-hours to sing, dance, pray, and whirl in ecstasy for the love of God, the Beloved — all of which are forms of worship.

After his presentation, Ron stood up from his cross-legged position in the circle of twenty people. He glided barefoot to the center of the circle, his arms now outstretched like the wings of a great blue heron preparing for flight. His body began to twirl like the Turkish dervishes we'd seen in films. Quoting from *Rumi: Fragments, Ecstasies*, Ron invited us into the ecstasy of Rumi's encounter with the Beloved:

> we came whirling
> out of nothingness
> scattering stars
> like dust
> the stars made a circle
> and in the middle we danced.

Now Ron took the hand of Deborah, who was seated in the circle and wearing a white caftan trimmed in gold. He motioned to her to take the hand of the person next to her. When the hand next to me reached for mine, I saw red. *Who says I want to dance? What about what I want?* I flared inside like a wild stallion on hind legs. *No! to melting into Rumi. No! to sitting in meditation. No! to watching my breath. I refuse my bridle.*

I caught a crazed glimpse of myself, front legs stamping, ready to charge, daring anyone to oppose my willfulness. I'd hit a wall with the discipline required by the meditation retreat. It was so hard for me to completely surrender. I protested in defiance, acting out an infantile power drive. *What was I doing? I was depriving myself, not defying anyone else. My need to control was backfiring. Was my own defiance the real source of my feeling fenced in?* Exhausted, defeated, I resigned.

I then took hold of the offered hand. At first, the woman's hand I held seemed like a heavy stone. Any movement I made felt stiff, as if I'd been stuck in one position for a long time. But gradually the heaviness, along with my resistance, lifted as if I had been given a fresh blood and oxygen supply. As I stood up to join the others in the circle, I felt present, a gift of grace that allowed me to acclimate to the energy field of the zikr.

By now, we were all standing, circling the room with Ron like birds taking their place in formation. As if directed by instinct, our bodies moved as we chanted the Arabic names of God: "*A humdulila, a humdulila.* Praise to the blessed love of God." I watched my body move effortlessly, almost without my volition. I could recognize I was dancing, but where was the "I"? No longer weighed down by the burden of resistance, the movement of my body swayed with the chant, closer to the others, who were now entwined in a tight circle. We were dancing faster, savoring the names of God as if we were tasting honey. *Allah*, *Akbar*, God is most great, the barrier between me, others, I, the dance, freed through surrender, by invisible hands other than mine.

My eye caught Ron's as I got ready to leave the meditation loft to walk back to my hermitage. We smiled and somehow understood each other more than words could say. On my walk back through the woods to my hermitage my body felt light, carrying the Beloved like a melody playing in my heart.

Prayers Throughout the Day

The fullness of a day that spans from before sunrise to after sunset gives us many opportunities to touch the spiritual dimension of divine harmonies through prayer. I recognize that the times I stop to pray add melodies of grace to my experience. Prayer always connects me to a divine frequency that allows me to tune in to peace, love, and wisdom. Such attunement often softens the stress I associate with too many calls to return in too little time or the impossible stretch that seems to lie between me and my goals. Prayer gives me a respite as it connects me to the timeless and uplifts me to the solution that exists beyond the problem. Relaxed, restored, I am renewed by the sustenance of prayer to face my challenges. I remember that I am conjoined with the infinite. If we experience a challenge remembering to pray throughout the day, we can even more appreciate the Muslim dedication to pray five times a day.

THE CALL TO PRAYER. In the Islamic culture the call to prayer is something that is beautifully broadcast by a *muzzein*, a man who calls Muslims to prayer from the balcony of a tall, slender tower that is typically part of a mosque. People hear the call to prayer as not only an announcement that it is time to pray but as an invitation to connect with God. Such a call can be very supportive of one's prayer practice.

Many of us from different traditions do not have the daily support that reminds us five times a day to pray, nor do many of us have community support to interrupt our work schedules and pray. Nevertheless, we can cultivate an inner call to pray. When we notice some fatigue or a short temper, we can turn instead to prayer. We can also lean on practices from our own spiritual traditions that help us to remember to pray — grace at meal times or prayers at a Sunday service or Friday-night Shabbat meal.

EARLY MORNING PRAYER. In a beautiful book, *The Illuminated Prayer: The Five-Times Prayer of the Sufis*, authors Coleman Barks and Michael Green describe the five times of prayer as they synchronize with the rotations of the sun from morning to night. Muslims begin the day with early-morning prayer, *Fajar*, one hour before dawn, when the everyday world is still asleep. In such peace and quiet we can easily hear our own breath. Sufis say that God is close to us, closer even than our breath. At this dawn time of prayer it is easy to feel that presence.

Many who are not Muslims also find early morning a time to connect with their inner sanctuaries, to meditate and pray. My friend Sandy takes some time to walk to the ocean and pray along the way as she walks. She gives herself a range of time to do her morning devotional, anywhere from 6:00 to 10:00 AM. Rev. Janet does not pray at dawn but rather, later in the morning, after her morning walk and swim.

NOON PRAYER. Noon prayer, *Zuhr*, comes just after the sun has reached its zenith in the sky. The illumination of the sun fills the day. It is a time of full power, creativity, and perhaps forgetfulness about that connection we may have with God. The reminder to turn within and pray at this time presents an opportunity to remember our passion for God.

AFTERNOON PRAYER. Afternoon prayer, *Asr*, comes when the sun is halfway toward the horizon, around three o'clock in the afternoon. It is a time of winding down a bit, of being aware that objects cast shadows. There is a lessening of intensity in the emotional body. It is a good time to reconnect with the power and presence of God. I find late afternoon a great time to pray. Often I have used up a great deal of energy and I'm somewhat fatigued. Instead of reaching for my formerly usual coffee or diet coke late in the afternoon, I close my office door for a few minutes and sit quietly. Just a few minutes of being still releases some of the tension of the day. In my purse I carry a booklet of some favorite prayers. I turn the pages slowly and take time to absorb the beauty of each prayer. Even five to ten minutes of reading prayers can be extremely restorative.

EVENING PRAYER. Evening prayer, *Maghrib*, comes at a time when the sun falls beneath the horizon. The daylight colors fade to a quieter vibration. Turning to prayer at this time grounds us in a reality that is unchanging even though the thoughts and feelings of the day may leave us restless.

NIGHT PRAYER. Night prayer, *Isha*, comes about an hour after dark. The velvet sky displays the stars like jewels. The darkness is like death. Turning to prayer brings us to a realization that God alone is real.

Love Letters to God

Rev. Janet describes a time when she felt a dry spell in her spiritual life. Her meditation and prayer life felt stale, and her morning ritual of spiritual practice did not satisfy her soul. "I needed a more personal relationship with God, so I started writing God love letters." Janet filled notebooks with love letters to God. "Dear God, this is my lotus offering today. Guide me in all that I do, say, and be. You are the most fun and greatest playmate. I will be ready for our dance today. Love, Janet." Janet's prayer lotus looked like a flower, the center of which was God. The petals contained all of the things she was offering up to God for help: prayer for family, good health, the life of her church. She had a second prayer lotus for the things she was determined to work on: making good food choices, being sensitive to husband

and dog, telling the truth. At the end of the day she reviewed her list to see how well she kept her part of the prayer contract, making corrections where needed. As she explained it, "Prayer, for me, involves something for God and something for me. Together we have this affair of the heart."

At a difficult time during this past year, Janet's husband got sick. The diagnosis was something that she didn't want to hear. They found cancer in Palmer's kidney, and it had to be removed. The next morning in prayer, her love letter to God included turning over the health of her husband and their financial needs to meet this emergency. Then Janet continued, along with her prayer work, the responsibilities of daily life, including hospital visits and arrangements for her husband.

Two weeks later, she received a surprise phone call from a woman named Linda, who had a deep southern accent. "Is this Mrs. Stangvik?"

Janet replied, "Yes."

The stranger continued, "I am calling to let you know that the government has some money for you and to tell you how you can get it. This agency will send you the check if you call this number. Many people don't know about this and that's why I'm calling you." Janet was stunned. The total amount, two thousand dollars, would cover the co-pay on the medical costs for Palmer's surgery. She followed Linda's directions, but while waiting for the money to arrive, Janet began to doubt whether this was true. *Maybe my friends are playing a joke on me and collecting some money for this occasion.* Sure enough, the call was authentic and the check arrived. Grateful in her heart for answered prayer, Janet used the money to pay for hospital bills. She wrote

Linda a thank-you note and included a generous tithe check in the envelope.

A few weeks later Janet received a package in the mail. Inside, there was a note from Linda. "Dear Janet, thank you so much for your kind note and generous gift. In all the years that I have been doing this, no one has ever sent me a thank-you note or given me any money. So, thank you. I thought that this little gift would be perfect for you."

Janet cut open the box, sifted through the foam pellets, and pulled out something wrapped in white tissue paper. It looked like a nameplate that you sometimes see on the desk of an executive. On a solid black stand, elegant scripted letters carved into acrylic plastic read, "Prayer changes things."

The next morning, Janet's love letter to God was brief: "Dear God, thank you for all that you do in my life. I see clearly that answered prayer is your love letter back to me. I love you. Janet."

Challenges and Progress on the Path

Kristin was the first to raise her hand, her blue eyes sparkling in response to the past week's wisdom practice on surrendering to prayer. "I love praying so many times throughout the day. If I don't make the dawn meditation (which I must admit I have not been as successful at as I would like to be), I pray with my children in the car on the way to school. The other day when I was driving them to school, I had prayed at dawn and had forgotten to engage them in the prayer. They quickly told me that I had forgotten, so we prayed again, all together as a family. It has been truly wonderful. Even though I like to be in my own sanctuary with my prayer mats, even a quick prayer throughout the day gives me a sense of peace and connection with God, a kind of perspective about the busyness of the day. I don't lose myself as much in the day-to-day activities, which makes me feel more centered."

Margie interjected, "But how do you remember? My biggest problem is realizing it's four o'clock in the afternoon and I've missed the noon prayer and the afternoon prayer. The days whiz by and I just lose my sense of priorities. I'm afraid that I'll never be disciplined enough to pray with consistency, even though when I do, I feel much better. At least I'm doing one in the morning before work and at night before I go to sleep. That's good, isn't it?" I looked over at Margie and smiled, "You're not the only one who forgets and gets caught up in the activities of the day. Is that right, class? If so, raise your hands." Many in the group raised their hands.

Wearing a plaid button-down blouse and navy slacks, Paula picked up her pen — which always lay perpendicular to the large, three-hole black binder holding her notes and assignments — and waved it like an orchestra baton as she spoke. "One way that I've organized my prayer times is around my meals, since it's rare that I forget to eat." The class laughed, familiar with Paula's love of food, about which she had spoken throughout the term. She'd also gifted us with culinary delicacies from various traditions as the class had progressed. Paula continued, her blue eyes wide. "So, if I pray with breakfast, lunch, and dinner, add a prayer in the morning and a prayer before I go to sleep, then, presto — I've got the five prayers. Most days, it works just fine."

Walt leaned back in his chair slowly. His long legs, lanky body, and coloring reminded me of a lion stretching. "What if we don't use the prescribed prayers in Islam? Are we still honoring this tradition?" Walt looked at me in his serious way, his eyes intent on hearing the answer.

"It's a good question, Walt," I said. "Here's the way I see it.

The Islamic tradition of Salat is very specific within the context of Islam, and Muslims are required to pray in a prescribed way five times a day. However, we can be inspired by this wisdom practice and adapt it in our own lives with prayers from different traditions or our own, or with spontaneous prayers. The important thing we can use from Islam is that the inspiration to pray five times a day connects with our own spiritual source and allows us to find our connection to a greater infinite presence. That can be a tremendous balance in our lives. It's like an anchor that keeps us grounded in our spiritual selves. Prayers throughout the day remind us to not let our to-do lists or our busy lives run away with us and cause us to forget that we are both spiritual and physical."

"I like that answer, Rev. Sage. Pretty good."

Evelyn chimed in, "I've been doing really well with my portable prayers. Let me show you." Evelyn reached into her purse and pulled out a pocket-sized album of red fabric woven with designs that looked like the Islamic prayer mats I had seen in photographs. "Here I have all the prayers that I love: the prayer of Saint Francis, the Twenty-Third Psalm, the Shahadah from the Islamic tradition, a prayer of compassion from the Buddhist tradition, the Shema from Judaism. I have put them all together and when I feel like it, at my prayer times, I just open it and let my eyes gaze on a particular prayer, read it slowly, then close my eyes and let the prayer fill my body. Sometimes I use movements like the ones that we learned with the traditional Islamic prayer, and other times I just let myself make up my own movements. One day this week, I even walked along the beach and said the prayers out loud. It's a wonderful practice and I feel much better when I do it. It's just surprising that I haven't done it every day. I was able to fulfill the five-prayer requirement on only two days this week. It really makes me admire the discipline it takes to pray five times a day like the Muslims do."

Jane spoke with her usual intensity, "I looked on the Internet and found that there's a site where, no matter where you live, you can get the exact times to pray according to the Islamic tradition. Just imagine billions of Muslims praying around the world. I just had this vision of people praying at different latitudes and longitudes all over the globe, as if it were like one of those waves that you see at football games — except this was prayer. It's really powerful to think of people all over the world praying at all times of the day, around the clock, and around the movement of the sun. It's quite moving."

"Yes, what a powerful image. Thank you for bringing it to our attention," I said.

Susan surprised me when she raised her hand. A quiet woman in class, usually preferring not to share publicly, she wore a matching blouse and skirt set with tiny pink and purple flowers floating on white fabric. "My prayers have been simple. I found a way I can pray five times a day. I just share a prayer of gratitude. Like Paula, I've been using meal times to help me remember my prayers. I'm used to saying grace at meals. When I wake up in the morning, at meal time, and when I go to sleep I simply say, 'Thank you, God,' and then fill in the blanks. My prayers of gratitude are doable and they really uplift me. Prayers of gratitude are acceptable, aren't they?" Her question was answered by silent nods and smiles from the class.

Visiting a Mosque on Friday

I took six students from one Wisdom Walk class to a Friday noon-prayer service, which includes congregational prayers in a mosque. I wondered if we were ready for this field trip.

Only the night before, the class had engaged in heated discussions about the role of women in Islam. Were they oppressed? Was the required dress a sign of their subjugation? Since our intention was to let the class be a forum for all ideas, we let all members express themselves freely. We had agreed as a group to respect each other's ideas and not offer advice. We also agreed to heal our own hearts of any prejudice that might lead to anger, hatred, and resentments. Renee, a young woman in her twenties wearing no makeup and stylish black-framed glasses that complemented her dark hair and eyes, was skeptical about using Islam as an inspiration for prayer. "I can't respect a tradition that doesn't respect women."

I saw in Renee a younger part of myself, when I was struggling with Judaism around the same issue. "Renee, I can empathize with your position. I remember questioning my grandmother about how she felt sitting separately from and behind men in the synagogue. But it wasn't a problem for her even if I thought it should be. To her, sitting in *shul* to worship God was a deep, spiritual experience. She couldn't understand my frustration. The different values of our generations create unique lenses through which to view the world."

"It still doesn't make this treatment right," Renee asserted, her arms folded tightly across her chest. We ended the class with a candlelit prayer circle. Although prayer soothed the volcanic discharge of our class discussion, I was concerned about the timing of our class visit to the mosque the next day. My thoughts rumbled within me: *Is it too soon after our heated talks? Do we need more time to resolve our issues? I'm glad we'll be attending a prayer service. Can prayer assist the healing process we've begun?* I made an inner note to myself that if any student had an emotional charge in connection with the visit, I would recommend that they work on the suggested inventory questions we'd begun in class. If you as the reader have a charge while reading this story, I recommend that you turn to these same questions in Appendix 1, "Tool #2, Uncovering Your Beliefs about Other Spiritual Traditions."

As we entered the mosque, a large woman in white, flowing Muslim attire welcomed us. She reached out to hug each one of us. "Welcome, one and all. Christians, Jews, Hindus, we welcome everyone to our time of prayer." This greeting was quite different from the stereotypes we'd explored the night before. Even the most resistant women in the class seemed softened by this Muslim woman's warmth. She escorted the five women in our group to a separate room, while the two men walked to another prayer room.

"Don't you mind not being in there in the main room?" Renee asked, continuing with the inquiry we'd begun the night before about how men and women do not engage in the prostrations of prayer together.

"Not at all," the Muslim woman answered. "We women prefer our privacy. We do not want men looking at our behinds as we pray."

Leading us into a carpeted room, our guide gave us scarves to cover our heads and invited us to lay a prayer mat wherever we could find a space among the fifteen or so women already sprawled in different spots throughout the room. These women smiled at us warmly.

I watched and listened to our guide recite, "God is most great. Allahu Akbar," with such joy that it drew me deeper into such a great gratitude for this sanctuary of God that it began to fill the room with each gesture and movement. Together, my class members laced through the small group of Muslim women who proceeded to bow, prostrate, and utter the phrase, "Allahu Akbar, God is most great." Despite the different traditions we came from, the greatness of God brought us together.

As we completed Sulat, a joyous, peaceful energy filled the room. I watched as women took each other's hands and looked into each other's eyes. One of the pairs would say as they embraced, "*Asalaam uleikum*," May the peace of God be upon you. In return the other of the pair replied, "*Aleikum salaam*," May the peace of God be upon you as well.

Now, all the women in the room were hugging each other. I saw my students warmly greeted by fully-covered Muslim women dressed in varying shades of cloth, mostly earth tones of beige, gold, and brown. I know for myself that joining these women in Salat changed how I saw Muslim women in my own mind. Rence, who was seated next to me, did the motions of the prayer, but her brows seemed woven into a frown, and her body was rigid, not supple. Our guide, who sensed Renee's discomfort, approached her. "Do you have any questions you would like to ask? Something seems to be on your mind."

Renee's shoulders dropped. Her words rushed out like freed prisoners, "I have trouble with Islam because I think women are being controlled. For instance, why do you dress the way you do, every part of your body covered? Is that your choice?"

"Actually, I find our dress code freeing."

"Really! How so?"

"Well, first, modesty is a virtue praised in our sacred texts. A great advantage to dressing modestly is being known for who you really are, not judged by your beauty or lack of it."

Renee was startled. She had never considered that.

Now, it was the Muslim woman's turn to ask questions. "Aren't women in your culture bothered by being considered sex objects?"

Renee's face flushed. She hated the catcalls she'd receive walking through downtown Los Angeles at an earlier time in her life. She detested how business associates would sometimes stare at her breasts when she was expressing a point at a sales meeting.

"In our culture, our dress allows us to conduct business in an atmosphere of respect."

The women's eyes met. They smiled at each other. They had taken a baby step into each other's worlds.

The Muslim woman opened her arms to Renee and said, "*Asalaam aleikum*, may the peace of God be upon you." Renee accepted the hug. "May peace be with you, too."

I believe that praying together helped me and members of my class realize that you cannot understand another's culture if you only look through the lens of your own values. Communication is a bridge between worlds.

The wisdom practice of prayer helps us to connect with divine frequencies, which we can download into our lives in the form of healing answers to life's questions and dilemmas, and refreshed perspectives toward life that are in tune with the infinite. The discipline of carving out prayer time gives a personal relationship with the divine, a way to communicate our deepest realizations, needs, and visions. Surrendering to prayer opens our field of power as we cocreate with universal forces. Whether we choose prescribed, spontaneous, or affirmative prayers, or prayers of thanksgiving and praise, the important thing is that we practice. Whenever we pray, whether once, five times, or more, we give ourselves the many gifts that prayer is ready to offer us.

Wisdom Steps

CREATE A PORTABLE PRAYER COLLECTION. You probably have some favorite prayers from childhood or sacred times in your life. It is a delightful task to create a collection of prayers that are ready to inspire you throughout the day. In addition to your favorite prayers, you may select prayers from sacred texts of various spiritual traditions including the Old and New Testament, the Koran, the Tao Te Ching, the Bhagavad Gita, and others that attract you. You can use your personalized prayer collection at meal times, while waiting for appointments, and any time you would like to receive the elevating quality of prayer.

EXPERIMENT WITH PRAYING FIVE TIMES A DAY. Using the Islamic tradition for inspiration, set your intention of praying five times a day. It's not as hard as it may first appear. If you say a prayer when you wake up, at breakfast, lunch, dinner, and then before you go to sleep, you'll have one motif for praying five times a day. Feel free to use any prayers that you like — ones from your memory, portable prayer collection, or prayers spoken spontaneously from your appreciation of life. "Thank you, Spirit, for this day" can be a simple prayer for one of your designated prayer times.

ADD MOVEMENT TO YOUR PRAYERS. Many traditions combine prayer with movement. Let yourself experiment with prayer by dancing, whirling, or using hand movements. Involving the body can intensify the prayer, leading toward a greater embodiment of this spiritual practice.

Here are some simple hand gestures to try or to use as a springboard for your own prayers with movements. These can be done indoors or outdoors, facing the sun. Outstretch your hands and reach toward the sky. Say aloud, "I open myself to the radiance of Spirit all around and within me." Cross your hands, palms down, over your heart. "I am one with this radiance." Bring your hands together, fingers and palms touching each other, as if you were clapping, and bring your forefingers to your lips. "I trust that the radiance of Spirit lights my way with wisdom, peace, and love." Drop your hands to your sides, palms open, facing outwards. "I give thanks for the many gifts of Spirit in my life." Bend your elbows and make small circles with your wrists. "I release and I let go, believing these words are seeds falling on fertile earth. And so it is. Amen."

Try combining prayer with physical exercise such as walking, yoga, or movement classes. You may also visit mosques and partake in the Friday-noon prayers. Or you can join in Sufi dancing if it is provided in your area.

CHAPTER FOUR

CHRISTIANITY:
Forgive Yourself and Others

PRAYER OF SAINT FRANCIS
Lord, make me an instrument of Thy peace.
Where there is hatred, let me sow love,
Where there is offense, pardon . . .
For:
It is in giving that we receive,
It is in pardoning that we are pardoned.
It is in dying that we are born to eternal life.

s I approached the time of my divorce proceedings, I knew it would be better for my health, my heart, and my soul to forgive my soon-to-be ex-husband. But where to begin? At first I didn't even know that I was angry and resentful. In my family there hadn't been much room to express anger, so I had developed the automatic pattern of denying anger and covering it up with excess food or alcohol. At this time in my life I was recovering from substance abuse and was learning to apply the principles of Alcoholics Anonymous, which included making inventories of all persons I needed to forgive as well as those from whom I sought forgiveness. This helped me become aware of resentments I held from unfair treatment in my marriage and other life circumstances. I wanted to let them go, but I didn't know how. In my meditation and introspection I prayed for the willingness to let God help me.

When I first thought about forgiving Tony, a whole stream of events flashed across my mind that had seemed almost unforgivable when they had initially occurred — infidelity, abandonment, financial irresponsibility. I attended Al-Anon meetings almost daily to help me through this crisis. I was met with love, support, and counsel to release my judgments of him and put the focus back on myself. Easier said than done. *Didn't he remember that we were married when he moved in with another woman?* I was in a wrestling match with a venomous judge inside of me and whichever way I turned, I was losing. The more I steamed with righteous indignation, the more my gallbladder hurt.

I heard in these twelve-step rooms that I had to admit I was powerless to control the situation and that a higher power could and would restore me to sanity if I would let it. *What would it take for me to surrender?*

The rest of that summer was an emotional blur. I felt mostly shocked and numb while arranging to have my stepdaughter flown to her family in Kentucky as I consulted divorce lawyers. I informed the seminar leader in California, my philosophy department chair in Wisconsin, and my family in New York and Milwaukee about what had transpired.

My physical condition worsened. Even if I couldn't feel my pain, my body could. Doctors said I needed an operation to remove my gallbladder, which was filled with stones. *Had my resentments solidified in my body?* I knew I could not emotionally withstand the added trauma of surgery and the six-week recovery. This was it for me. I'd reached my limit. I was willing to do anything to heal — even if this meant forgiving someone who'd hurt me deeply.

The night before the divorce I meditated by candlelight. On opening my eyes after meditation, on my dresser I spotted a green page atop a pile of papers I'd resolved to sort. The handout, titled

"Forgiveness List," was part of a monthly mailing from New Thought author Catherine Ponder. I'd intended for a long time to answer the questions on that sheet. Now seemed like the perfect time. I followed the instructions: I listed the persons and events I needed to forgive and immersed myself in love and forgiveness by wishing each person on my list all the blessings of life.

In front of the candle that illuminated my darkened room, I envisioned Tony's face. I opened my heart and let the currents of universal love flow in and out of my heart to him and back to me, like the tides of the sea. I wished Tony well and hoped good things would happen in his life. I let the love wash away the debris of resentment that had felt like hardened particles in my body and in my attitude toward him. I wanted to be free and let love help me. After the meditation, I felt my body soften. My heart felt at peace.

When I saw Tony the next morning at the divorce proceedings, I felt released from my previous stance of righteous indignation and judgment. I went to hug him. He hesitated for a moment, as if anticipating daggers of rage flying toward him from my eyes; these had hit and hurt him many times before. Instead he was greeted by love that grace granted us as a divine gift.

In that split second — I can still see his blue eyes soften — we both remembered the love that had brought us together, that we had shared during our marriage, and that now permitted us to part peacefully. Tony returned the embrace.

Was there another way of looking at this? In my meditations I'd realized that Tony had done the best he could. He wasn't a vicious person. My leaving him to work on the grant had put him in a difficult situation. He hadn't been working steadily and we had given up our rented house to avoid paying rent while I was in California for the summer. This man had merely tried to survive, hence writing the checks and finding a place to live. My Al-Anon teachers had said I should stop enabling him. But it was a big leap for him to stand on his own. He had done the best he could, given the fact that he was in crisis as well. When I looked at him through the eyes of compassion, he looked different to me. Could it be that there was really nothing to forgive?

I also began to see my marriage with Tony as an important turning point in my life that helped me make that longest "twelve-inch journey" from the intellect to the heart. I had learned so much since this crisis. I found a direct path to my spiritual connection with God. Before this, I'd had an intellectual knowing, but now I had a direct experience with the spiritual presence in, around, and through me. It was also during this period that I found the Christine Center for Meditation, and that experience was one of the most meaningful ones of my life. Thankfully, I was also released from a relationship that was not working for either of us. Crisis had freed us. My perception of tragedy in my life became the stepping-stone to my liberation. I will always thank Tony for this. We settled our divorce arrangements amicably that day and said good-bye. I was ready to move on.

❧

The prayer attributed to Saint Francis that begins this chapter contains a blueprint for living wisely. By deliberately expressing ourselves as vehicles of love, peace, and forgiveness, we paradoxically receive even more than we give. We can learn the art of forgiveness.

One of the most central teachings of Christianity is the wisdom practice of forgiveness. Christianity is a religion founded by the followers of Jesus. While the three main groups of Christianity — Roman Catholics, Protestants, and Eastern Orthodox — have different beliefs, they all consider Jesus to be to the basis of their religion.

Getting Our Bearings: Christianity

NATURE OF THE DEITY. God is an omnipotent and transcendent deity. The Christian belief maintains that in one God there are three persons — the Father, the Son, and the Holy Spirit or Holy Ghost. Jesus is the second person of the Trinity.

RELATIONSHIP OF INDIVIDUAL TO THE DIVINE. Individuals connect with God through prayer and receive atonement for sins through the sacrifice of Jesus, the divine son of God. Jesus is an example of the embodiment of the divine on earth — God, in the flesh. Jesus represents the intersection between the human and the divine, depicted in the symbol of the cross.

HOW TO WORSHIP. Christians worship in churches with a leader called a priest, minister, or pastor. Special aspects of the service include the baptism, prayer, and reading from scripture.

ETHICAL BELIEFS. The teachings of Jesus are based in love. Above all, the message of Jesus directs one to be loving in one's life on earth. To accept Jesus into one's life is to commit oneself to being a loving presence in the world and to forgive the trespasses of others. The personal relationship with Christ is the road to redemption.

THE SOUL AND BELIEFS ABOUT DEATH. Christians believe that the soul does not die and that one experiences everlasting life in heaven or hell. Heaven is a place of blessings, hell is a punishment of eternal damnation. Entrance into heaven is guaranteed by believing in Jesus Christ.

What Is Forgiveness?

We harbor resentments against those we feel have harmed us or betrayed our trust. We form a judgment that a particular action toward us is wrong, hurtful, or unjustified. This causes us to react from anger or hurt. We may not be able to let go of the experience. Our initial anger hardens into resentment as we relive the event over and over in our minds. Now we are carrying a resentment toward another person. We may feel justified in maintaining this attitude until we realize that harboring this resentment is hurting us. It is easier to see in another what we can't always see in ourselves. We may know people in our lives who hold resentments toward another. As they repeatedly spew condemning remarks, we see how the dark cloud of their negativity makes them toxic to those around them as well as to themselves. Unresolved anger at the bottom of resentment can fester internally, leading to illness, depression, and addiction. Seeing the world through the eyes of anger taints our vision and contaminates our worldview so that we may miss what we might otherwise appreciate as good.

The teachings of Jesus on forgiveness include a practice of repeatedly pardoning others and ourselves in order to help clear the resentments and condemnation we may hold in our hearts. Harboring resentments blocks our purpose on earth, which is to love one another. To forgive an offense means to renounce anger or to give pardon. This process involves reflection, self-understanding, and maturity. Jesus's practice of exoneration of those who crucified him — "Forgive them, Father, for they know not what they do" — teaches the possibilities of forgiving the unforgivable.

The Power of Love

Jesus was very clear about the power of love, which is the essential teaching of his ministry. "I give you a new commandment, that you love one another. Just as I have loved you, you also should love one another." You cannot love others and harbor resentments toward them at the same time. The love we are speaking of is not romantic love, but a spiritual love that views another through the eyes of compassion. Love produces a quality of life that is more enjoyable and healthy than a life filled with resentment and anger.

To love is to not judge or condemn another. Jesus uses a parable in the Bible to answer the question, Who are we to judge another person? In the story, Jesus came upon a crowd that was gathered around a woman caught in the act of adultery, a crime that was punishable in ancient times by death through stoning. The crowd was angry and ready to smash this woman to death for her sexual indiscretions. Jesus was teaching a group nearby and was asked by the Pharisees (an ancient Jewish sect, distinguished by their strict observances of rites and ceremonies prescribed by traditional and written law) for his opinion concerning the convicted woman. Jesus put forth this challenge to the crowd: "Let the one who has not sinned pick up the first stone." One by one, the crowd dispersed; no one could claim to have not erred or fallen into sin. Only the woman and Jesus were left standing in the square. He asked, "Who is left to condemn you?" She answered, "No one." Jesus replied, "Then neither do I condemn you." He told her to go home and leave the path of sin.

Like the woman in the story, we may have the experience of being confronted by love and forgiveness instead of condemnation, even in the event of our own transgressions. As corroborated by Emmet Fox, "There is no difficulty that enough love will not conquer."

In writing this section, I remembered a time in my childhood when I received the gift of compassion.

Holiday Reprieve

When I was seven years old, I stole some change from my mother's purse to buy candy. This was in the fifties in Brooklyn near Christmastime. The five-and-dime that I passed walking home from school sold yummy chocolate Santas. After a week of my rifling through my mother's handbag when she was asleep in the early morning, she confronted me. She could tell by my silence and dropped jaw that I was guilty. "Wait until your father gets home," she threatened. "Now go to your room."

As I walked away I did not understand why her eyes were moist and her voice quivered. I had other things to think about as I stewed all day in my stress and fear. My stomach felt tangled up to my throat. I was in bad trouble, probably the worst in my young life.

When my father came home, my mother demanded his attention and called him into their bedroom. I overheard snippets of their conversation. "... I don't know why she would steal from me? ... she deserves to be punished."

I stood huddled in my bedroom, a condemned prisoner, suffering my punishment many times over: Would I get a spanking? "This is going to hurt me more than it's going to hurt you." Or be sent to bed after dinner? "No television for a week, young lady." By the time my father stepped through the doorway of my room, I was crying. He asked me why I was tearful and I spilled my remorse, relieved to confess. I didn't know why I had taken the money, but I realized it was wrong.

My father listened, his face slightly ashen and pale from

long hours at work. I looked into his brown eyes; they were warm like melted chocolate. He spoke more softly than my mother would have wanted. "What you did was wrong, and I want you to apologize to your mother. But I'm not going to punish you. It's the holidays — a time for love and forgiveness." My shame dissolved in his kindness.

I felt like I had been given a gift. This was better than my favorite vacation — swimming in Florida in December on a holiday break from the freezing cold of New York. I felt my father's love reach out to me like invisible arms I could rest in and feel safe. I was lovable, even though I had erred. I could make a mistake, be forgiven, and start again with a clean slate. I never took money from my mother's purse again.

Preparing to Forgive

Forgiveness does not mean that we condone unacceptable behavior. Nor does forgiving another mean that we have to befriend those with whom we have experienced conflict. Forgiveness involves a choice. We choose to engage constructively in activities of our current life rather than dwell destructively on the perceived injustices and difficulties of the past. In preparing to forgive, it is wise to consider the truth about how forgiveness affects us.

FORGIVENESS FREES US. The need to forgive arises from a judgment or criticism toward oneself or another. Without this condemnation there would be no reason to forgive. People and situations needing forgiveness appear daily. We might judge our sister as selfish for taking our sweater without asking. Or perhaps we told a friend we would meet them after work but then forgot and now condemn ourselves as worthless. We notice that we want people, ourselves, and circumstances to be different from the way they are. Our resentments, anger, and indignation harden within us. We are the ones stuck with the debris of condemnation, not the people we judge. We may think that forgiveness involves freeing another from their wrongdoing. But actually forgiveness frees us from the burden of hostility or resentment that we carry within our own heart.

FORGIVENESS IS A PROCESS. Listening to the wisdom teachings of Jesus, we glean that forgiveness involves a process that is to be done repeatedly. In a conversation with Jesus, Peter asks, "Lord, if another member of the church sins against me, how often should I forgive? As many as seven times?" Jesus replied, "Not seven times, but seventy times seven times."

It often takes several rounds of forgiving someone in order for the forgiveness to be complete. The layers of resentment peel away slowly, yielding insights along the way and, sometimes, new things to forgive. It is wise to give oneself time for the process.

The teaching of seventy times seven also indicates that in order to keep our hearts clear we need to continually forgive others and ourselves. Little things come up in day-to-day experiences of our lives that continually need our forgiveness — harsh words spoken in anger, grudges held, broken promises, little and big lies. At the end of the day, we can review the day's activities and interactions and cleanse our hearts by forgiving others and ourselves.

FORGIVENESS REQUIRES WILLINGNESS. Not everyone is ready to forgive, even if they feel inclined to do so. An unreadiness to forgive needs to be honored. Sometimes the hurt caused by certain events — the loss of a loved one through an accident or violence — may require a period of healing. It is not wise to force the process of forgiveness or to chastise oneself for being unready to forgive. At the same time it is wise to keep in mind that forgiving has tremendous potential to heal your pain and free you.

FORGIVENESS REQUIRES COURAGE. The journey of forgiveness involves us in a confrontation with our anger, shame, and feelings of betrayal. Such self-reflection is painful, although worth the price, because such self-honesty leads to emotional healing. All stages of the forgiveness process require the courage to heal.

How to Forgive

Even if we agree that it is a good idea to forgive someone, we may be clueless about how to actually accomplish this. We can look to the proven practices suggested by the twelve steps of Alcoholics Anonymous and other authorities on forgiveness to help us find our way.

CONFRONT YOUR ANGER. Being willing to face your anger and hurt is not an easy step. Realizing that you are angry can be painful. It is tempting to push anger under the conscious mind and pretend, minimize, or rationalize it away. Yet forgiveness does not happen without an acknowledgment that something has happened, that you have suffered, and that forgiveness will free you.

It is amazing to me that I had been unaware of how incredibly angry I was about my relationship with my ex-husband. I was angry that he had promised to work and share financial responsibilities and then didn't. I was angry that he had promised to be faithful and wasn't. I was angry to be in a failed marriage. I was angry that my anger ran deeper than this relationship, and I was angry that, after much reflection and therapy, I still needed to work more on my anger. I was angry that I had avoided dealing with my anger by overeating, overworking, and using drugs and alcohol. I was angry that my anger was negatively affecting my health by distressing my gallbladder. *Wasn't* gall *another word for "anger"?* I was angry that I was reluctant to enter into relationships again.

What is helpful to remember is that coming face-to-face with our anger, and other feelings, is a skill many people do not possess but can acquire. It took me many years to learn how to feel anger. Give yourself time to discover this process, and by all means, allow yourself to learn from others who are ahead of you on this path of confronting anger.

GET SUPPORT. Confronting feelings and beginning the forgiveness process is difficult work that you don't have to do alone. It is wise to get support from someone experienced and trained in the forgiveness process: a professional therapist, a member of the clergy, or a twelve-step sponsor. It is helpful to write inventories of your feelings, share them with your trusted companion on the forgiveness journey, and let the truth of your feelings and experiences be witnessed by a higher power that you believe in. Having a companion that is your witness and guide is a great gift to give yourself. By telling the truth to yourself and another, you will experience the meaning of the statement in the Bible: "The truth shall set you free."

DECIDE WHOM TO FORGIVE. An exercise that I facilitate in classes helps students identify persons they still need to forgive. In a guided meditation I invite students to turn within and imagine that their heart is a corridor through which people in their lives could walk safely, because they would feel surrounded by love. This is an adaptation of a meditation exercise inspired by Dr. Michael Bernard Beckwith, which we used at a Revelations Conference where I was part of a team that cocreated the conference. I ask students, "Notice which persons stand at the threshold of your heart, afraid to enter out of fear of becoming drive-by shooting victims of your condemnation and criticism." Those who are afraid to step down the corridors of our hearts are the ones to put on our list to forgive. In guided meditation, when we envision people afraid to enter the corridors of our hearts, it can be startling. We may realize, for the first time, that we actually do condemn others in our minds. We may further uncover that these resentments hold us in bondage as well.

FORGIVE YOURSELF. Sometimes in the corridors of the heart meditation, members of Wisdom Walk classes see *themselves* standing at the entrances of their own hearts, afraid to step in. It is always interesting, although not always easy, to see that the finger pointed toward others also points back to ourselves. Often what we condemn in others is also what we cannot tolerate in ourselves. We may find it too painful to take responsibility for our misdeeds, so we disown them and project them onto others.

Jesus saw this tendency of projection when he challenged the clan who wanted to stone a woman for adultery. No one threw a stone, because they realized their own transgressions. Looking at ourselves and admitting our shortcomings is not our first inclination. It is much easier to condemn another. Yet, in the long run it is most freeing to look honestly at our own actions, embrace our transgressions, and forgive ourselves as well.

ASK FOR FORGIVENESS. As the twelve steps of Alcoholics Anonymous suggest, our moral inventories may reveal regrets. Part of the process of forgiveness includes admitting that we were wrong and humbly asking for forgiveness. While we cannot control other people's reactions, we can attend to what is within our power: taking responsibility for our own actions, admitting our shortcomings, and asking for forgiveness from others and ourselves.

The Gift of Forgiveness

Abagail, a lean, attractive, dark-haired woman in her early forties, realized that she had falsely accused a neighbor, who had been a dear friend of her family, of molesting her when she was a teenager. In her early twenties she was in therapy. In one of her sessions she underwent hypnotherapy and recalled some scenes of what she thought were retrieved memories of sexual abuse involving her neighbor. At the urgings of her therapist, she confronted her family with the news that Mr. Shuttle had inappropriately touched her when she was babysitting his children. Fifteen years later she realized, through other developments on her transformational journey, that what she had thought were retrieved memories, actually were metaphorical images of her own emerging adolescent sexuality. Now in her forties she was convinced that her accusation had been a lie.

Abagail felt tremendous remorse because, as a result of her accusation, the Shuttle family had been ostracized in the community, had experienced a broken relationship with her family, and had felt forced to move. It was painful for Abagail to admit her mistake, but she knew she had to tell the truth and ask for forgiveness.

She found the address of the Shuttle family, who were still living in a nearby town. Abagail arranged a meeting and humbly asked for forgiveness. She explained how she had realized she had made a mistake and was so sorry that her lie had caused the family pain.

To her amazement, Mr. and Mrs. Shuttle listened to her with great tenderness. They said it had happened a long time ago, that she was very young at the time, and it must have been a painful time for her.

Abagail's eyes filled with tears. "Their compassion helped me forgive myself. I will never forget how precious the gift of their forgiveness was to me. I believe that what opened the door of their heart was my complete humility and my willingness to admit my wrongdoing. Their love changed me."

ACT AS IF. There is sometimes a leap that takes place in the forgiveness process. We want to forgive, but it's an intellectual, not an emotional, process. I knew it was a good idea to forgive my soon-to-be ex-husband, but I didn't know how. I felt guided to jump into the process and trust that something would happen.

Lyra, an educator, counselor, and nurse practitioner, assisted hospital patients in their healing processes by helping them practice the art of forgiveness. "I tell clients to begin the forgiveness process even if they don't feel it is genuine at first. Jump in and act as if; saying, 'I forgive _____ for _____' often jumpstarts the process that eventually leads to authentic forgiveness."

Lyra described how she engaged in a forgiveness meditation before a business meeting that was potentially difficult due to her conflict with two male administrators. By clearing her own mental, emotional, and spiritual fields regarding the conflict, forgiving the administrators for past conflicts, and wishing them peace of mind and the best that life has to offer, the potentially volatile meeting was neutralized even though nothing formally had been spoken about forgiveness. "When I walked into the boardroom, I was different without saying a word. I believe others felt my forgiveness, which altered them. We were able to communicate with more ease and respect than we had in the past. I believe my forgiveness work paved the way for this change."

IMAGINE BEING CLEANSED BY A RIVER OF LOVE. A powerful conclusion to the corridors-of-the-heart meditation involves the image of the abiding river of love. I tell students and clients to imagine that their heart is connected to a universal source of love. I have them imagine that a river of love is flowing from a universal source through their heart to the heart of the person they want to forgive. In the process, I encourage clients to imagine the river of love washing away the debris of anger, resentments, and criticism, leaving only love in its wake.

SEE THROUGH THE EYES OF COMPASSION. Eventually in the process of forgiveness, the spell of our own self-centeredness dissolves and we can see the story through the eyes of another character with whom we have played out the drama. Our own suffering cracks the heart open to compassion. I witnessed the flowering of compassion in my client, Joan, whose heart had been tangled with self-condemnation and regret.

Pain of Regret

After Joan retired, she had more time to reflect on her life. In our work together, she was developing her inventory and forgiveness list. One morning she admitted she was ashamed about something she felt she'd handled insensitively. Her repeated self-criticism and replaying of her regret over and over in her mind left her, understandably, feeling distraught. She said, "I almost didn't have the courage to tell you this. I felt so ashamed." Joan felt she'd made mistakes with her husband Frank's estate. Although she followed his instructions regarding investing money from the estate into property, Joan felt guilty for not giving some money from the estate to her mother-in-law. Joan felt terrible remorse for treating her late mother-in-law insensitively.

As Joan and I continued to talk, I pointed out that her criticism toward herself was a form of punishment. "Joan, instead of beating yourself up, you could forgive yourself."

"But how?" she cried. I asked Joan to relax and turn within. "Imagine that you are connected to the very heart of God. And imagine that a river of love is flowing from God's heart to your heart. Just allow yourself to feel this love washing over you and washing away your regrets, criticism, and condemnation. Let the river of love purify you with its power." After several minutes of bathing in unconditional love, Joan felt relieved, the burden of her regrets lessened.

One of the things that Joan was most upset about was how she could be forgiven by someone who was already deceased. Could she be forgiven without her mother-in-law's conscious absolution?

"The forgiveness process can occur even if that person is not present," I told Joan. "Continue with your forgiveness work this week. Let your forgiveness exercise be that you see yourself in front of your mother-in-law. Let the river of love pass over both of you as you repeat the words, 'I am fully and freely forgiven by Martha. She wishes for me all the blessings of life.' Allow yourself to feel forgiven. Let the love that you are both bathed in wash away your guilt." Joan reported the following week that she noticed how different her life seemed without the constant barrage of self-condemnation.

Anyone can try this simple guided imagery with great results. After identifying the hurt, regret, or shame, admit them to another trusted person and to God. Be willing to make amends. Close your eyes. Allow the universal river of love to wash away the debris of your resentments and condemnation.

Challenges and Progress on the Path

In a Tuesday evening Wisdom Walk class, Sylvia, a woman in her late forties, was the first to speak about the wisdom practice of forgiveness. As she sat at the far corner of the seminar table, her pale-blue sweater brought out the blue in her eyes. "I did not make a list of all the people and institutions I wanted to forgive. I thought that making such a list would be so overwhelming that I would avoid the forgiveness work altogether." Instead, Sylvia revealed that she had approached a person whom she needed to forgive: her estranged husband.

"I started with my estranged husband by calculating the seventy-times-seven prescription that Jesus gave us. If there are twenty-four hours in a day and I can be somewhat cognitive for fourteen of those hours, then I would have to say 'I forgive' five times per hour for fourteen hours a day for seven days! I have not been successful in carrying out this formula. Yet I have turned inward in meditation: 'I forgive Harold for leaving me. I now release him to his good.' I often stayed with, 'I forgive Harold for leaving me. I forgive Harold for leaving me.' Sometimes this turned into, 'I forgive Harold for leaving me. We are both moving to our higher good.'"

When Sylvia saw Harold later in the week, she noticed that her work on forgiveness made her feel less reactive and more at ease. "Even though he asked for a divorce, I was able to listen, express my feelings, and also say what I wanted. In the past I was defensive and would fly off the handle."

Later that evening Sylvia awakened to tears rolling down her cheeks. She realized that Harold had left her emotionally long before he'd actually declared it. "A light went on in my head. That's why divorce was easier for him." Sylvia then deepened her forgiveness work: "'I forgive Harold for leaving me emotionally. May he move toward his highest good.' This is giving me the space to let go on an emotional level as well."

I told Sylvia that she was right on target with her forgiveness work. The process of forgiveness leads to insights and shifts in perspective. "Good for you for sticking with the process," I told her.

Margie spoke next. Her curly, red hair accentuated the way her face flushed when she revealed intimate details of her experiences. "I feel similar to the way Sylvia felt. Of all the assignments for the class, this one seemed the most daunting. Why? I've known that forgiveness work has been the missing link to my truly enjoying life, free from limiting thoughts. I comforted myself with the affirmation for self-forgiveness that you gave us in class. Whenever I caught myself in a self-deprecating thought, I would stop and say, 'I forgive myself for judging myself as not good enough. I accept for myself all the blessings life has to offer.' These words were like a healing balm on my self-inflicted wounds. The more I realized how I was hurting myself, the more I needed to forgive myself."

Kristin's usual exuberance was subdued. Her eyes reflected a gray cast, the way the ocean looks when the sun is hidden behind clouds. "Forgiving myself is the hardest. When we did the corridor-of-the-heart meditation, I was shocked to see *myself* standing at the entrance. For the first time, I saw how it feels to receive what is sometimes constant self-criticism. My heart opened to myself as that woman standing at my own heart, afraid to enter. I watched her cower, trying to avoid the many lashes that cut deep into her heart and soul. I never before realized the effect I was having on my own self-esteem." Throughout the week, Kristin said that she'd thought deeply about why she had been so hard on herself and, although this exercise was difficult, it also opened to her a realization that she felt a new commitment to reverse.

I looked into Kristin's eyes, which were cast downward until I spoke. "Kristin, you do not have to be hard on yourself." She nodded in appreciation.

"The deeper realization for me," she said, "is that without even knowing it, I've internalized my mother's harsh, critical voice always telling me what I am doing wrong. I further realized that this was also the way my mother treated herself."

"The pattern can stop with you, Kristin. As you model this differently through treating yourself with love and forgiveness, you will not be passing on the same message to your children." Kristin's eyes began to brighten as if some internal fog were lifting.

"Yes, I'm grateful, not only for being able to treat myself with more love, but also modeling this to my children."

Margie interjected, "Oh my god, Kristin. I do the same thing. And even though I know we are trying to change this, it feels good knowing that I'm not alone. I think the most shame I have about this tendency to judge and condemn is when I do it to myself."

Liticia bubbled up, her dark eyes and black dreadlocks framing her beauty. "I am still having some battles with forgiveness regarding the father of the child that is growing inside of me. Just when I think I've arrived at forgiveness, I backslide into judgment, doubt, fear, and anger. Aren't these the opposite of forgiveness? I want so much to clear my mind of negative thoughts."

My heart opened. "I really understand what you're saying, Liticia. Let's remember together that the forgiveness process takes us through a journey of many insights and feelings. Be assured that you are not doing anything wrong with the exercise. You are simply experiencing some of the transformation and clearing initiated by the forgiveness process. There's nothing wrong with having feelings. You just don't want to pitch a tent in any one of them. Let them arise, feel them, and then let them go." Our eyes met in understanding.

The forgiveness process brings out many things, such as releasing judgment, accepting people where they are, noticing the tendency to hold onto seemingly justified anger, and being willing to let go. We can focus on pain and resentment, which separates us, or on love and compassion, which connects us all. We can now understand why Jesus said seventy times seven. The process of forgiveness requires willingness, patience, and lots of practice.

Kristin was the last to speak. "The freedom and lightness that comes with forgiveness are such gifts. My thoughts are clear and more relaxed. I have tons more energy. I realize that oftentimes there's nothing to forgive. People are just who they are, mistakes and all."

Janet's Story

It was past seven o'clock and Rev. Janet was still working at her desk in the little church in Napa. Her mind was absorbed in planning Sunday service and arrangements for the coming week. A door in her pale-mauve office, which opened to the street and was usually locked, startled her when it flung open to a large man standing in the doorway, panting heavily.

"I need to speak to someone right away."

Rev. Janet rose to her feet, and before she realized what

she was doing, blurted to the stranger, "Come around to the front, and I'll open the door."

"I didn't mean to scare you," the stranger uttered and receded in the dark night air on his way to the front door.

Rev. Janet fumbled to find the key; her hands were shaking as adrenaline pumped through her system. The man's words, "I didn't mean to scare you," ran through Janet's mind. The words made her feel safe enough to open the door.

"I have to tell someone, to relieve my guilt. A few months ago I robbed a purse from someone in this church."

Janet's mind flew to the nuisance of calling credit card companies to cancel and replace the stolen cards. "That purse was mine, and you're lucky it was mine because I've been praying for you every day since I found that it was missing. I've been praying for you to know and love yourself as God loves you. I've been praying that you would have enough dignity to not take something that was not yours."

As Rev. Janet continued to talk to the stranger, the spiritual counsel flowing from her like a mighty river, she witnessed the healing presence of forgiveness wash over both of them. The stranger's eyes softened. His body became more relaxed. The tough exterior of his countenance became more porous, like a loosely knit curtain that lets in morning sunlight.

And then Janet realized a remarkable thing. This whole experience was not about forgiving the man who stole her purse. She was the one experiencing forgiveness for all the things in her life that she'd ever done and held against herself. She experienced a river of God's love washing over her and cleansing her of self-judgments.

What was more, hearing this stranger knock on the door had initially frightened her. But now her faith had deepened. She knew the hand of God was protecting her and keeping her safe. She says about the experience, "By forgiving him, I was forgiven."

Accepting the invitation to engage in the practice of forgiveness will open the door to insights, feelings, and changes in attitudes toward those you've held hostage in your own mind. You, too, have been a prisoner. Remember that, most of all, forgiveness frees you. As Catherine Ponder writes, "Forgiveness is a pleasant inner act that helps you 'give up' negative emotions and clears away the blocks to your good."

Wisdom Steps

VISUALIZE PEOPLE WALKING DOWN THE CORRIDORS OF YOUR HEART. A simple and effective way to discover who needs to be on your forgiveness list is to simply turn within and let your inner wisdom guide you. Feel free to audio-record these instructions to listen to, or read them silently to yourself.

- Close your eyes, turn within, and take a few deep breaths.

- Allow yourself to imagine that your heart has corridors that people in your life can walk through.

- Let appear at the entrance of your heart those people who want to be in your heart. Trust the process. Those who appear are the ones your inner wisdom wants you to see.

- Invite the people who are standing at the threshold of your heart to now enter into the interior. Notice the ones who enter your heart out of a sense of safety and feeling surrounded by love and acceptance.

- Notice also the acquaintances who are afraid to enter because they fear becoming drive-by-shooting victims of your condemnation and criticism.

- When you are ready, return to the present moment and gently open your eyes.

- This visualization shows you the places within your own heart where you hold resentments, judgments, and condemnation toward others. Forgiveness frees you to have a heart space of love.

MAKE A LIST OF THOSE YOU WANT TO FORGIVE AND CHOOSE ONE PERSON TO JOURNAL ABOUT. To begin your forgiveness work, write down the people in your life that you want to forgive and the circumstances that surround your lack of forgiveness. The people you've discovered are afraid to enter the corridors of your heart are good candidates for your forgiveness list. Give yourself some journal time to confront your feelings connected to the person you want to forgive and the circumstances involved.

SPEND FIFTEEN TO THIRTY MINUTES A DAY IN FORGIVENESS. Designate a week or two to concentrate on forgiving others and yourself. Take one person from your forgiveness list and imagine the person is in front of you. In your mind's eye, imagine that a river of love is flowing from your heart to his or her heart. Say to that person, "I fully and freely forgive you for _____. I wish you all the blessings of life. I release you and set you free. I release myself from criticism, condemnation, and blame. I fully and freely forgive you." Continue until you can feel no contradiction in your words. Proceed to the next person when you are ready.

CHAPTER FIVE

JUDAISM: *Make Time for the Sabbath*

*If you call the Sabbath a delight
you shall take delight in the Lord,
And it will make you ride upon the heights of the earth.*

— ISAIAH 58:13–14

he aftermath of the divorce led me to ruminate about family. The warmth and love of my grandmother's house was a sharp contrast to the home I'd just left. After many years of feeling little about the spiritual tradition of my birth, Judaism came alive for me through the memory of my grandmother, Esther, and the lighting of Sabbath candles.

She'd been a stout woman, less than five feet tall, with silver hair and dark, hazel eyes. During the summers I'd visited my grandmother in Long Beach, New York. Fridays meant cleaning — scrubbing the bathroom, vacuuming, and wiping the chandeliers with a solution of vinegar and water until the glass sparkled on the freshly polished wooden table beneath it. I was unenthusiastic about this cleaning ritual, while my grandmother was passionate about it.

After cleaning and cooking for a good part of the day, with the sunlight fading into the half-light shadows of dusk, my grandmother would call me to light the Sabbath candles. This was her way to worship while others attended the Friday synagogue service. I was only eight years old, but I knew this gesture was a sacred honor. As I reached to the last unlit candle, she guided my hand with hers, and we lit it together. The yellow flames flickered in her eyes. Wearing a lace head-covering shaped like a doily, my grandmother would say a few words in Hebrew during these twilight moments of the Sabbath. What I remember most is the silence, the sweet hush of the presence of God during this sacred time around the Sabbath candles.

Soon after lighting the candles I would hear the lock turn on the front door. My grandfather returned from temple with aunts, uncles, and cousins. We hugged one another in the tiny foyer of the ocean-side apartment. Echoes of "*Shabbat shalom*," "*Shabbat shalom*" ("Peace to you on the Sabbath") could be heard above the sound of kisses on cheeks. Then my grandmother would call us to the dinner table. On the way I inhaled the mixed aroma of chicken, rice, and beans, and underneath, the faint smell of ammonia from the day's cleaning.

At the dinner table my grandfather stood tall next to my grandmother. She held a basin of warm water with a white cloth over her arm. My grandfather washed his hands before blessing the wine and the traditional golden *challah* bread that, only hours before, I'd watched my grandmother braid before putting into the oven. My grandfather's dark-brown eyes were smiling. His bald head shone beneath the sparkling chandelier. He raised his glass, as did the rest of the family, as we viewed a Sephardic banquet of delectable food — stuffed zucchini, tomatoes, peppers, rice, beans, salad, chicken, and deep-purple beets pickled in oil, vinegar, and garlic.

"I have one prayer on this Shabbat," my grandfather would say as he raised his glass of wine in a toast. "May the family always stay together." Everyone waited for my grandmother's toast as well, which she said in Ladino, the dialect spoken by Spanish Jews. "*Salud, amor, dinero, y tiempo para gozarlos.*" This was her favorite saying on this occasion, "May we have health, love, money, and the time to enjoy them." My grandfather clinked glasses with my grandmother, "*L'Chaim.*" We all clinked glasses, too, echoing, "*L'Chaim,*" "*L'Chaim*" ("To life").

As an adult, I hadn't practiced Shabbat before remembering how my grandmother taught me to light Sabbath candles. Now, weekly, this practice leads me warmly home.

⟡

Even when we love our work, it is wise to take time to rest, rejuvenate, be with friends and family, and appreciate the blessings of our lives and our connection with God. This is the wisdom of the Sabbath. The Sabbath involves us in delight, bringing us greater enjoyment of our lives and a closer connection with God, which yield not only the fulfillment of the soul but success in our chosen endeavors. If we can learn to be content with not being busy, finding ways to honor our relationships, and contemplating our spiritual lives, we will rejoice. What we find in taking regular time off to connect with God is so valuable that it enhances our living to the highest degree — as if we are riding "the heights of the earth."

Judaism originated in Jerusalem (also known as Palestine) in the Middle East (circa 1800 BC). Although the terms *Jew* and *Judaism* were not used until three hundred years after their time, Abraham, Isaac, and Jacob are credited with founding what is now known as Judaism. They are considered the physical and spiritual ancestors of Judaism, and their descendants are known as the Jewish people. Judaism is the oldest major religion to believe in one God. Christianity and Islam developed from Judaism.

Getting Our Bearings: Judaism

NATURE OF THE DEITY. Jews believe in one eternal God, creator of heaven and earth — omnipotent, omniscient, and omnipresent. Although the Bible speaks about God in the masculine gender, the nature of the deity is beyond determination of male and female. In fact it is understood that any name limits the infinite, since it is beyond finite descriptors.

RELATIONSHIP OF INDIVIDUAL TO THE DIVINE. Each individual can have an intimate, personal relationship with God. Jews believe they have a special covenant, or sacred agreement, with God that originates from the agreement that God made with Abraham. According to the Bible, God promised to bless and protect the descendants of Abraham, the Jewish people, if they worshipped and remained faithful only to God. God renewed this covenant with Abraham's son, Isaac, and his son, Jacob, who was also called Israel. Thus, the descendants of Jacob were called Israelites. God has designated them as the "chosen people." This means they have taken on special responsibilities, for instance, to build a just and fair society and to serve only God. Jews also believe that God will send them a Messiah, "the anointed one," to save them. Many people believe that the Messiah will come as a just ruler who will unite them and lead them in God's ways. Others speak of a Messianic age, which refers to a time when all people will be guided by God to live together cooperatively in peace and justice.

HOW TO WORSHIP. Jews attend services in synagogues, which are also called temples. The religious leader and teacher is called *rabbi*. A *cantor* chants or sings the songs at a service and also may lead a choir. Prayers are made directly to God without any intermediary; congregational prayer is a foundation of Jewish practice. Living a good life with family, friends, and neighbors is another way in which one practices religion.

ETHICAL BELIEFS. Judaism teaches that one serves God by studying scripture and living according to the ritual practices and ethical laws that are taught in the Bible. God gave the Israelites the Ten Commandments and other laws through Moses, who is considered to be the greatest of prophets. These were intended to show the Jews how to live a good life and build community.

THE TEN COMMANDMENTS

1. I am the Lord thy God. Thou shalt have no other gods before me.

2. Thou shalt not make unto thee any graven image, or any likeness of any thing that is in heaven above, or that is in the earth beneath, or that is in the water under the earth. . . .

3. Thou shalt not take the name of the Lord thy God in vain.

4. Remember the Sabbath day, to keep it holy.

5. Honor thy father and thy mother.

6. Thou shalt not kill.

7. Thou shalt not commit adultery.

8. Thou shalt not steal.

9. Thou shalt not bear false witness against thy neighbor.

10. Thou shalt not covet thy neighbor's house, thou shalt not covet thy neighbor's wife, nor his manservant, nor his maidservant, nor his ox, nor his ass, nor any thing that is thy neighbor's.

THE SOUL AND BELIEFS ABOUT DEATH. The four movements
of Judaism — Orthodox, Conservative, Reform, and Recon-
structionist — view this topic slightly differently. All believe in
the immortality of the soul, which returns to God, or the universe, after death. Immortality also occurs when the memories
of the deceased are kept alive in the hearts of those who loved
them. Some accept, others reject, the belief in a physical life after
death.

What Is the Sabbath?

The Sabbath is a weekly, twenty-four-hour period in which one
rests, reflects, and connects with God. It is one of the best known
of all Jewish observances. Keeping the Sabbath helps us to remember the importance of taking time to restore, rejuvenate, and
refrain from the daily routine of work. The *Sabbath*, called Shabbat in Hebrew, means "to cease" or "to rest." The strong spiritual
aspect of the Sabbath satisfies the individual's longing for God. As
the psalmists beautifully write, "As a doe longs for running
streams, so longs my soul for you, my God." The Sabbath becomes a time for spiritual reflection and connection with the divine. Much space opens within us when we stop working. Freed
from busyness and endless to-do lists, our awareness shifts to
simple, precious moments that we overlook when we're living
too fast. When we stop working, we are graced with another level
of awareness that notices, for instance, the drawings of hearts and
rainbows on the refrigerator from our five-year-old, or how our
partner surprised us by picking up our clothes from the cleaners
during a busy work week.

In Judaism it is believed that on the Sabbath we are given an
extra soul, *neshemah yeterah*. This Sabbath soul allows us to have

a wider perspective on our lives. The Jewish Sabbath mirrors the story of Genesis. God created heaven and earth, and on the seventh day God rested and appreciated his creation. The Sabbath soul gives us the opportunity for the spiritual practice of gratitude and appreciation of the wonders we already have in our lives. Such an activity can fill us with a deep satisfaction of the goodness of God's creation in our lives.

The practice of the Sabbath and the gift of the Sabbath soul allow us to become aware of the miraculous bounty of life itself. When we take the time to pause, we appreciate this divine gift in everyday activities — candlelight, the company of loved ones around the Sabbath meal, the beauty of white cirrus clouds in cornflower-blue skies noticed on our Sabbath walk, a lover's embrace. The Sabbath allows us to see the gift of life everywhere. Rabbi Abraham Heschel said it well: "Just to be is a blessing. Just to live is holy."

The Sabbath is also a time of delight. The traditional Friday night dinner with friends and family encourages observers to enjoy the pleasures of relationships and delicious food. The Sabbath also allows for delight during favorite Saturday activities: walks in nature, lovemaking, enjoying meals, or lighting candles.

Beginning the Sabbath

The Sabbath sweeps into Jewish homes like an honored guest, a bride, a revered queen. The medieval mystics said, "Come, my beloved, to meet the bride. Let us welcome the face of the Sabbath." These are the first lines of the original poem, *Lekhah Dodi*, which the kabbalists of Safed sang as they gathered in a field before sunset to meet the Sabbath bride. The song is still sung weekly in Jewish homes throughout the world. Continuing in the twentieth century, Rabbi Abraham Heschel exclaimed, "The Sabbath is a bride and its celebration is like a wedding."

The traditional Jewish Sabbath begins at sundown on Friday night and ends at the same time Saturday evening. Those who are working outside of the home begin to gather the loose ends of the day by three or four o'clock in order to be home, bathed, and ready to begin the Friday-night ritual. In Judaism, the home is as important as the synagogue; it is the place where spirituality is lived and passed on to future generations. At home, family members or designated others clean the house and set the table with the family's best linen and china. Everyone in the family dresses up for the festive Sabbath dinner with family and friends. At sundown or shortly after, the Sabbath begins with a blessing and the lighting of Sabbath candles. The candles literally bring light to the household and create a tangible demarcation between the weekday and the Sabbath. This ritual officially starts Shabbat. The family may then attend a brief evening service and come home to a leisurely meal.

Before dinner, one prayer (*kiddush*) is said over wine, sanctifying the Sabbath. Another prayer (*motzi*), along with a ritual of cleansing the hands, is recited upon eating bread especially prepared for the Sabbath — two loaves of challah, a sweet, eggy bread shaped like a braid. Many families have a special Sabbath cup for wine, which is filled to the brim to represent joy and abundant blessings. The prayer spoken over the wine refers to the story of creation and freedom from slavery, both of which are prominent themes of the Sabbath. The two loaves of special challah bread present a reminder about the manna sent by God from heaven during the forty years that the Jews wandered in the wilderness. A special blessing of children also takes place before family and guests enjoy the scrumptious Sabbath meal.

After dinner, the family and invited guests spend the rest of the evening in prayer, conversation, studying the Torah, or other relaxing activities, which for many families excludes watching television or using the computer.

A SANCTUARY IN TIME. The Jewish Sabbath became a lifeline to exiled Jews when the temple was destroyed in 70 CE. While the Jews were in exile, the Sabbath served as their temple, even while they wandered the desert. On the Sabbath the Jews would stop and worship in the context of this holy day. The sanctuary was not a physical temple but a sanctuary in time, as Rabbi Abraham Heschel describes it. The ritual of the Sabbath accompanied the Jews through adversities and became an oasis in the drought of exile and unpredictable life challenges.

For those of us who apply the wisdom of the Sabbath in our modern lives, this observance creates a sanctuary in time, as it did for the Jews in antiquity. Spending our days in endless work can create an exile from ourselves, friends, family, and the divine. We may keep hoping that one day we'll find balance, but that time eludes us as we find ourselves under a deluge of things to do. Such was the case with my cousin Fran, until she and her family began to practice the Sabbath.

Sabbath Comfort

For many years my cousin Fran lived in exile from Judaism, but she reclaimed her Jewish heritage by immersing herself in the formal teachings. She transformed her dissatisfaction about not having received a Jewish education in her youth into an active pursuit of her Jewish heritage as an adult. She joined a temple in Minneapolis, where she lived, and enrolled in Hebrew school with other adult women who were preparing for the *bat mitzvah*, a rite of passage for girls that usually takes place at age thirteen. Through her studies she learned the meaning behind the Jewish traditions, like the Sabbath, which she now practiced consistently with her family.

When I asked her about her motivation for doing this, she replied, "The main reason was so that I could be more knowledgeable and participate in my children's journey in Judaism. I also remember how Grandma did not participate in religious ceremonies but had more of a background role. I wanted to forge a new direction as a woman, having a voice and being more visible in the temple."

Like many suburban couples, Fran and Bernie worked outside the home and chauffeured their children to extracurricular activities such as soccer, rehearsals for school plays, and tennis lessons. Fran is a dark-haired, slim woman in her forties, and Bernie is a physically fit, tall man with salt-and-pepper hair and blue eyes. As therapists, their lives had been full and busy as they engaged in the balancing act of raising children, developing private practices, and growing spiritually.

Despite their best intentions to have time to meditate, relax, and enjoy the fruits of their labor, these pursuits seemed to evade their grasp year after year. Hour-long commutes to work, forty-hour workweeks, and running two private practices and a household had left little time for slowing down and being still.

When Fran started formal training in Judaism, she committed to the practice of the Sabbath with her family. Each Friday evening, they cleared their schedules for Shabbat dinner, and the Sabbath became a lighthouse in a sea of activity.

Friday nights became a time to check in with each other as a family, slow down, and reflect together about the week. With busy schedules and dietary concerns, Shabbat dinners did not have to look like the extravagant spreads of previous generations. Wheat-free crackers could replace challah; grape juice could substitute for wine. During one of our conversations, Fran recalled the past year: "Bernie grieved the death of his mother. I had a long bout of respiratory infection. Jeremiah had his tenth birthday, and Jessica started bat mitzvah lessons. Yet through it all, we have gathered around the Sabbath dinner table on Friday nights. Unlike other nights of the week, we use a tablecloth on Shabbat. Sometimes we feel close, other times we are crabby. Every week, we continue to show up. The regularity of the Sabbath is comforting."

Sabbath Day

Traditional Jewish Sabbath activities on Saturdays can include Shabbat services in temple, which begin around 9:00 AM and conclude at noon. After the service the family says the kiddush again, blessing over wine, and has another leisurely, festive meal. Afternoons may include taking a walk, talking to one another, playing checkers, singing songs, being in nature, meditating, praying, or engaging in other leisurely activities. Naps are a common Sabbath activity. It is traditional to have a third meal before Shabbat is over. It is usually a light meal in the late afternoon.

FREEDOM THROUGH RESTRICTIONS. The list of traditional items of work to avoid on Shabbat served as guidelines for people who observed the ritual. One cannot carry money, use a telephone, knit, sew, write, drive a car, cook, clean, or do any work at all. An important point is that what seems like restriction is really meant to assert freedom. The rules are meant to create space so that we can savor life. Refraining from work becomes a spiritual discipline. Approached from the perspective of prohibition, the Sabbath may seem confining; yet the opposite is true. The Sabbath unleashes us from habitual work, and this frees us to experience an inner freedom that we do not always attend to. The Sabbath is a reminder that we are at liberty to engage in activities other than work. For Jews this remembrance includes the history of their enslavement in Egypt, with the Sabbath a symbol of freedom. Yet in a broader sense the Sabbath frees us from our daily responsibilities, deadlines, commitments, creditors, and our own to-do lists, reminding us that we are not slaves to any of these or even our own drives for success.

Not Answering the Call

In a film I show to students from the BBC series, *The Long Search*, narrator Ronald Eyres interviews a rabbi who is simulating a Sabbath meal on a Tuesday for the film. The rabbi, of course, would not be interviewed on Shabbat, because to do so would be a form of work as a rabbi, which is not permitted on the Sabbath. The narrator asked the rabbi whether he minded not answering the telephone on Shabbat. The rabbi answered, "No. On the Sabbath I am reminded that I am free. We sometimes become enslaved to the phone and answer it like a conditioned dog. The phone rings, we answer. Even in the middle of a conversation with a family member, we may answer the phone only to find it's some *nudnik* (a pesty or annoying person) we don't even know trying to sell us something we don't need. I'm glad to turn the phone off on Shabbat and break the hypnotism of the worldly pull. The Sabbath reminds us we are free and do not have to respond to every request from the outside world."

BALANCING WORK AND REST. Most poignant for me and many of my students, the Sabbath helps us to balance work and rest. The rhythm in nature presents us with a model of balance. The tides of the ocean flow and ebb. The sun rises and sets. The phases of the moon wax and wane. The seasons revolve around the cycles of rebirth and flowering with spring and summer, as well as the releasing and dormancy of fall and winter. With the Sabbath we enter a natural balance between work and rest that can be lost in our culture. Unlike the natural rhythm of rest found in the cycles of nature, contemporary culture reflects a world that values productivity at full tide. We are a culture that promotes endless work — from twenty-four-hour copy stores and all-night markets to overnight mail, as well as fax and email messages that we can send any hour of the day or night. We may ask the question, Why do we need to balance such activities? If work is productive and profitable five days a week, wouldn't two additional days of work simply extend the productivity and profits?

Similar to the way planting the same crops year after year depletes the soil, so, too, are our own resources depleted when we overwork. I conduct an exercise with students in class about how they know when they are out of balance. The answers come quickly: "I am irritable with my spouse." "I feel pessimistic about my life." "I stop exercising." "I feel overwhelmed." In contrast, when I ask, "What are signs that indicate that you are in balance?" I notice a repetition of more positive experiences: "I feel like my whole body is singing." " I love my life." "I feel full of energy." "I know my purpose." Like the soil, when we give ourselves a chance to lie fallow and take our Sabbath time, we give the mind, body, and soul a chance to restore. In balance, the soul sings.

Permission to Stop

At a retreat I facilitated at Casa de Maria in Santa Barbara, I introduced the Sabbath as an essential spiritual practice. I spoke to fifty African American, Caucasian, and Asian men and women, mostly in their forties and fifties, who were advancing in a ministerial graduate program. Like other professionals who are in service to others, ministers also get out of balance; they can spend so much time helping others that they forget about themselves. This happens to people in all walks of life. It even happens in the lives of people who don't work, yet deplete themselves by overscheduling activities.

On Friday night at the retreat, I introduced the Sabbath by displaying my grandmother's silver candleholder and sharing my childhood memories of the Sabbath. I told them that by practicing a weekly Sabbath, I enjoyed more balance and inner fulfillment. Everyone was sitting in a circle that surrounded an altar draped in white lace and illuminated by thirty or more votive candles. The altar cradled an abundant arrangement of magenta orchids and white star lilies, all of which circled my grandmother's silver candleholder.

I asked a member from each of four groups to come up, light a candle, and name a quality they would like to experience during the Sabbath. One by one, students approached the altar, lit their candles, and spoke aloud their qualities — beauty, peace, love, radiance. I told the groups that we would practice the Sabbath this weekend, and I encouraged each person to rest, relax, commune with God, and refrain from the work of their jobs and school. One student raised his hand. "Are you asking me to do nothing?" The class laughed. "Exactly," I said, "and for extra credit, enjoy yourself as well."

The next morning at breakfast I noticed Jamal, an African American student with white hair mixed into a graying mustache and goatee. With one front tooth outlined in gold among his otherwise white teeth, he grinned broadly as I walked by. "How are things going, Jamal?" "Great," he beamed, lacing his fingers behind his head. "I have permission to do nothing." He was not alone. The clusters of students at breakfast chatted loudly, laughed, and enjoyed time to just talk with one another. An air of relaxation filled the room. Many students remarked that they hadn't felt this free in many years. The Sabbath was allowing them to take a long exhale from very busy lives and just let themselves be.

When we came back together after an afternoon of Sabbath time, everyone returned to their small groups to share the highlights of the Sabbath. Then a representative from each group came to the center of the room near the altar of tea lights and fresh flowers to express what the group enjoyed best about the Sabbath. Marianne, a petite Asian

American beauty, walked briskly to the altar. "Our group summed it up in one word — napping." Everyone laughed as Marianne returned to her seat.

Cheryl, a lithe African American woman who moved like a dancer, with honey-red hair braided in dreadlocks, talked about enjoying the luxury of time to do whatever moved her in the moment. "It's amazing that I live with every minute accounted for and structured. It feels so different to have free time."

Leonard, who had hiked in the Santa Barbara mountains, said, "I loved moving my body. The landscape of fir trees and pines, and sweeping vistas of the ocean delighted my senses, and I was surprised that worries about overdue schoolwork still haunted me. I had to be really stern with myself and not let these thoughts dominate my mind."

At the end our time together, I gave the retreatants one more homework assignment: to do one activity that expressed the delight of the Sabbath. Karina, a woman always stylishly dressed in glittery clothing and makeup, sent me an email Sunday night after the retreat.

"I left the retreat and went straight to a spa. Soaking in the hot jacuzzi brought me deep relaxation. I felt close to myself, close to God. Enveloped by the warm water, I felt reminded about being supported by friends, family, God. By practicing the Sabbath I could support myself. Then after a long, hot shower followed by some time wrapped up in towels, I was ready to dress. On the way home all I kept thinking was that this was the most wonderful homework assignment I'd ever been given."

ENDING THE SABBATH. The ritual that marks the end of Shabbat is called *havdalah* (literally "division"). It is performed no earlier than nightfall on Saturday evening, when three stars can be seen in the sky. This is usually forty-five minutes to an hour after sundown; this timing deliberately transforms the Sabbath into a twenty-five-hour day, so sweet that no one wants to let it go. It is a time when the family comes together to share the blessings of the week to come.

At havdalah we relinquish the Sabbath soul and hope that the sweetness and holiness of the day will remain with us during the week. We take a cup of wine, a box of spices, and a braided havdalah candle, and sing or recite the blessings. These blessings talk about the polarities of the holy and the everyday, the light and the dark, the seventh day of rest and the six days of work. The braided havdalah candle symbolizes these divisions. We then make a blessing over the wine, a symbol of joy, to sanctify the moment, and we sniff the spices to carry the sweet scent of Shabbat into the week and to take us gently to our responsibilities. Then, with palms facing up and fingers closed into loose fists, we look at our fingernails. The light from the candle creates shadows of our fingers, which distinguish the light from the darkness.

Many Jewish communities delay the ending of the Sabbath until later in the evening with a special celebration, *Melaveh Malkah*, which literally means "accompanying the Sabbath queen." Envisioned symbolically as a queen (and bride), the ending of Shabbat is escorted away with blessings, songs, and delicacies.

Extinguishing the Flame

Joshua, a handsome man in his early fifties, extremely fit and health conscious, spoke to me about his remembrance of havdalah. An attorney in Chicago, he said his life was too busy to practice Judaism the way he did when he was a boy. He seldom practiced the Sabbath anymore. But he remembered the Shabbat of his youth, and havdalah was his favorite part. As he shared memories of when he was seven years old, growing up in the Chicago suburbs, his dark-brown eyes took on an added sheen. The corners of his mouth turned upward as he spoke at a quickened pace, "At dark, a little past our bedtime, probably eight o'clock, my younger sister and I would be called into the study. Already, my mother and father had gathered around a table with a deep-red cloth. The silver wine cups, matching havdalah spice box, and braided yellow-and-red candle danced in the room as we began to sing Hebrew songs. Then my father blessed the wine and passed the spice box to each of us so we could smell the sweetness of cinnamon, nutmeg, and cloves. Sometimes I wondered how they could get baked apples in such a small box because that's what these spices smelled like. But before I could figure it out, my father lit the havdalah candle and said another blessing over the torch, which signaled the extinguishing of the light of the Sabbath so that we could start the week of school and work. Then the best happened. My father would take a small bottle of clear liquid from his pocket, which looked like water but was really vodka, and he would pour it over the havdalah candle. Whoosh — the candle would flame like fireworks and, every time, my sister and I would laugh at the sparkling light. I can still feel my mother's arms around my shoulders as she continued to sing with my father. We would look at our fingernails and see if we could see shadows and light in the flame of the candle. Sometimes even when I didn't see them I said I did anyway. Then each of us would make a wish for the coming week. Sometimes I could hear my mother whisper to herself, 'Good-bye to the queen.' I always went to bed smiling on Saturday night."

Joshua grew quiet after the story. I waited with him in the silence. "It's odd that I don't practice the Sabbath when I loved it so much as a child. Maybe I've made work more important than I should."

Challenges and Progress on the Path

I tell my students that the Sabbath is a helpful practice to integrate into their busy lives; I encourage them to try this activity and see how they like and benefit from it. When I ask students to create Sabbath time, I am almost always met with anxious faces and questions. "Do I have to carve out an entire twenty-four-hour period?" "What if I already made a commitment to study with a friend on Saturday?" "But I promised my kids we'd go to the movies." "What if my boss asks me to work overtime on Friday night?" "I'm completely booked this weekend."

I encourage my students, and anyone reading this book, to relax into the Sabbath time. If twenty-four hours seems too long, then start with an evening, morning, or afternoon. A few hours of Sabbath time is better than none, and it's quite common to begin making time for the Sabbath with a few hours at first, then building up to a twenty-four-hour period.

Although favorite activities for the Sabbath include napping, taking a walk, praying, meditating, and spending time with family and friends, in adapting the Sabbath into our lives, we are free to experiment with activities that nourish our souls and give us a rest from usual work tasks.

When first beginning to take Sabbath time, it may be unclear what actually qualifies as Sabbath activities. As a general rule I discourage students from tasks like balancing checkbooks, answering emails, or talking on the telephone. But there are exceptions. Evelyn reported to our class that talking to her daughters who live in another city was a great Sabbath activity since her busy work schedule leaves her little time to leisurely converse with them. The lengthy phone conversations provided family time since they couldn't share a traditional dinner on Friday night.

Margie was a woman in her fifties who was passionate about returning to school to finish her bachelor's degree and develop herself as a writer. She came to class with a sheepish look and then confessed that she took time to leisurely read a book on her Sabbath evening. But she agonized over this because she was afraid that reading would count as work and that she was performing the Sabbath incorrectly. It is important to be gentle with ourselves when we begin to practice the Sabbath. Although many people report that they feel guilty when first beginning to do things other than work, they find that Sabbath time becomes easier with practice.

In creating Sabbath time in our lives, we need to give ourselves permission to experiment. If you find that an activity provides rest and relaxation and is different from the activities of your usual work, then by all means give yourself the gift that these activities bring you during your Sabbath time. There is no wrong way to enjoy Sabbath time. The beneficial results will be undeniable.

A Night of Candlelight

Tuesday evening Liticia walked into class smiling, her white teeth shining against her dark-brown skin. Her petite frame accentuated her protruding belly; she was in her seventh month. We felt inducted into the Sabbath space as she described her experience. Liticia said that on Friday night she had come home and, instead of automatically turning on the television, lit several candles around the house — in the living room, bedroom, and kitchen — and finished her take out dinner in candlelight. Since her son was staying with his father in another residence for the evening, a regular occurrence since she and her husband had separated, Liticia gave herself the gift of silence as she meditated in candlelight and just sat quietly in the stillness.

As she recalled her meditative posture, her voice slowed down and her eyes closed for a moment. "I *loved* this time in the silence. Ordinarily I would just be doing little chores around the house against the backdrop of the mindless television chatter. I so preferred my night in candlelight. It was amazing how it nourished my soul."

The Sabbath continued for Liticia the next day when her nine-year-old son, Keith, came back home. Instead of having him watch movies or play computer games, she suggested an alternative. On the Sabbath, families could spend time together talking and playing games. Although he was reluctant at first to break the routine they had become accustomed to, he perked up when Liticia suggested they play a game of Scrabble. Before long, they laughed and talked through the afternoon. Liticia said it was one of the closest times she and her son had enjoyed together in a long time. Keith concluded, after winning at Scrabble, "This was fun, Mom. Can we play like this again next Saturday?"

Taking a rest even from activities that we love allows us to return with renewed passion and fresh perspectives. Integrating Sabbath time into our lives yields many more dividends than the original investment of time off from work and stress. We return to ourselves, friends, and family, and have time to appreciate the blessings of our lives.

Wisdom Steps

DESIGNATE A SABBATH TIME THAT YOU CAN KEEP EVERY WEEK. You can choose the traditional Jewish Sabbath time of sundown Friday night to sundown Saturday night. If the Sabbath time works better for you in another twenty-four-hour period, then feel free to switch to that time. You may find that a twenty-four-hour period is too long to begin with. Experiment with a shorter period of a morning, afternoon, or evening. It may be helpful to start small and build up to twenty-four hours. You don't have to do the Sabbath perfectly. By making time for the Sabbath you are honoring yourself through giving yourself the gift of rest, rejuvenation, and time for soul-nourishing relaxation. If you find yourself feeling guilty because you are not being productive, or feeling restless without your usual pace or to-do list, be gentle with yourself. You are learning a new practice that I believe you will come to cherish and love.

EXPERIMENT WITH FAVORITE SABBATH ACTIVITIES. Reserving Sabbath time each week gives you an opportunity to explore new and favorite ventures. Try napping. Take an extra-long candlelit bath. Meditate. Pray. Invite friends over for a Sabbath meal. Soak up the beauty of a walk along the river, a mountain hike, or a bike ride through the countryside. Give yourself a break from checking emails and balancing your checkbook. Your errands will wait for you. You may also enjoy Sabbath time without the sound of ringing telephones and without driving your car. These are suggestions for possible Sabbath activities. Choose your own Sabbath guidelines. Keep in mind that the Sabbath is more about being than doing.

COUNT YOUR BLESSINGS. As you slow down during the Sabbath, you have time to appreciate the good things of your life. Take note of the gifts or blessings in your life, such as friends and family who love you and whom you love, health, or the insights that come from illness. Notice the beauty of sunsets and the pleasures derived from the five senses that allow you to experience the precious gift of your life. The Sabbath gives us an opportunity to acknowledge the lives we have created.

CHAPTER SIX

NATIVE AMERICAN SPIRITUALITY:
Let Nature Be Your Teacher

*O Great Spirit, let me walk in beauty, and make my
eyes ever behold the red and purple sunset. Make
my hands respect the things you have made and my ears
sharp to hear your voice. Let me learn the lessons you
have hidden in every leaf and rock.*

—— FROM A SIOUX INDIAN PRAYER

Native American cultures teach us that Spirit is alive in nature and that we are intimately a part of this grand matrix of life. As I learned on a sailing trip, it is one thing to be familiar with this teaching and another thing to experience it.

One of the dilemmas I face when sailing is that, while I love the ocean, I invariably get seasick. I tend to shy away from too much moving about; I'm afraid I'll feel the discomfort of nausea and the dread of what could come next. In all my times sailing, I'd been content to stay on the sidelines. I'd never realized that my apprehension on the boat had kept me from fully experiencing my connection with nature.

One September morning my companion, Sandy, a licensed captain, and I started over to Catalina, an island thirty miles south of Marina del Rey, California. It was a gray and overcast day, conveying a unique charm as we motored out of the marina. But only forty-five minutes past the breakwater, we were rolling with unusual and unanticipated vigor.

"Damn, we've got a *confused sea*," Sandy suddenly declared.

"What's a confused sea?" I asked.

"Typically the wind and the swells come from the northwest. But when there's a storm at sea, swells come from the south as well. Then these swells from opposing directions crash into each other."

I adjusted my footing while the boat moved slowly and deeply left, then right, in a kind of seesaw motion.

"If I'd known this was going to happen I would have put on a patch. Too late now," Sandy said, as she checked various functions on the boat while I temporarily steered.

The boat was undulating from side to side, but because I had a medicinal patch behind my ear, I was protected from seasickness. Sandy, however, was turning green.

"Sage, take the wheel, would ya? Keep the compass at 180 degrees, and head for the island. I've got to lie down." Sandy didn't wait for an answer and disappeared below.

At first I felt shocked, as if suddenly shaken awake from a cozy slumber. But there was no chance to go back to sleep. I didn't even have time to protest, be annoyed, or feel scared. I was at the helm on a confused sea, and to my surprise, some part within me was rising up, taking charge, and sensing exactly what to do.

The moisture of saltwater gathered on my face. I felt as though Mother Ocean and I were cheek to cheek. In this intimacy, she lifted her veil and I saw her as never before.

The tame waters of the marina had unfurled into the open sea with formidable strength. Steering wheel tight between my hands, I fell into the rhythm of turning left, then right, to keep the boat steady as the sea turned into itself from both sides.

I watched Mother Ocean stretch, her soft and pliable body expanding from the confines of the breakwater as if she were taking off a girdle and relaxing in her living room. The wind caused swells on the ocean's surface that seemed like ripples on her giant belly. These swells, which rocked our ten-ton boat as if it were a bathtub toy, were nothing against her vastness. For the three-and-a-half hours to Catalina, I looked out on the expanse of grays and blues. The rhythm of the overcast clouds inching across the sky reminded me of the sound of slow-jazz saxophones. The dim morning light stretched unbroken across the horizon except for an occasional lone blackbird flying overhead.

Out of the choppy waters, twenty feet to my right, three dolphins jumped over the waves, their arched gray bodies diving into the water and then out again several times. I imagined all of the ocean's children safe underneath Mother Ocean's expansive skirt. Wet seals, arching gray dolphins, translucent jellyfish, sharks, whales, and sea horses all have her color, the way offspring resemble their parent.

"Why do I feel so happy surrounded by this gray mystery of rolling waves, cool sea mist on my face, and hours folding into eternity?" I was close to something — some delight, some primordial remembrance of the mother, Mother Ocean, God in form. She wrapped her arms around my shoulders and supported me as I drove the boat, like a mother assisting a first ride on a two-wheeler. I heard her voice within me: "You belong to me. Sky, sun, moon, the children who swim, and those that fly overhead — all of these are your family."

Mother Ocean taught me that I was a part of the clan of nature. I also learned that if I pushed past the fears that had kept me on the sidelines, not only could I participate more fully in my life, I could also experience something within me that was more powerful than I'd dreamed. Seeing Mother Ocean enabled me to see myself.

❧

The Native American (also referred to as First Nations and Native People) wisdom practice, "Let Nature Be Your Teacher," allows us to reclaim a connection with the natural world while still living in a technological, modern world. Opening our eyes to the beauty of nature's many wonders, awakening to the wisdom of her vast life systems, reminds us not only that we are an integral part of this matrix, but that we also have access to her haunting beauty and mystery. Such a homecoming, a return to our own spiritual rootedness, awaits us as we learn the lessons embedded in nature. A deeper connection with nature also inspires our responsibility to care for what is precious to us.

Native American spirituality is a philosophy and, even more, a way of life. According to Matlins and Magida in *How to Be a Perfect Stranger*, indigenous Americans (whom the U.S. law recognizes as Native Indians or Alaska Native) and First Nations people in Canada comprise approximately 2.4 million people. A large majority of First Nations people do not consider themselves to be Americans; they identify more with First Nation communities, for example, Peepeckisis First Nations, Shawanaga First Nations, or Whata First Nations. There are five large tribal groups in the United States: the Sioux, which include the Lakota, Dakota, and Nakota (throughout the northern plains); the Cherokee (in North Carolina and Oklahoma); the Chippewa (northern and Great Lakes region); the Navajo (Arizona, New Mexico, and Utah); and the Choctaw (Mississippi and Oklahoma). This diversity shows itself in the languages spoken by these tribes. For instance, nine major languages are spoken, comprising almost two hundred dialects. In addition, each tribe varies according to cultural practices and spiritual ceremonies. Therefore, applying general statements to all tribes can be misleading.

Getting Our Bearings: Native American Spirituality

NATURE OF THE DEITY. The entire natural world is sacred and one whole. The whole of life — a sacred circle or web of life — is inextricably imbued with the sacred power of the Creator, the Great Spirit. The Great Spirit is an expression of physical forces of nature.

RELATIONSHIP OF INDIVIDUAL TO THE DIVINE. Native spirituality emphasizes lived experience through ritual, customs, and traditions; each person has a direct relationship to the Great Spirit. Relationship to the Great Spirit also results from a connection to aspects of the natural world; plants, animals, rocks, and trees — alive with the Great Spirit — are considered teachers that provide a means to communicate directly with the Great Spirit.

HOW TO WORSHIP. Many ceremonies and rituals take place outdoors at locations sacred to the specific tribe. Native People value geographic locations as part of their context for worship, which creates a connection to a particular natural environment that is sacred. Native American spiritual expression consists of personal and communal experiences. Ceremonies may last more than a few hours, sometimes extending for days. Worship can include prayer, sweat lodges, dancing, the sun-dance ceremony, seasonal ceremonies, and most church services. The inherent respect for every living thing in nature is an act of worship.

ETHICAL BELIEFS. Native People's spirituality ascribes person-hood to living creatures other than human beings. Treating the two-legged, the four-legged, the winged ones, those that swim or crawl on the earth, Mother Earth, and Father Sky with respect leads to balance. Living one's own life in balance, as well as living in harmony with the world, is central to Native thought. Great care needs to be taken to nurture Mother Earth and all aspects of the environment, which are considered sacred.

THE SOUL AND BELIEFS ABOUT DEATH. Many Native People understand that life continues after the physical form dies, that death initiates a journey into the next world. Family members can assist their loved ones in making this journey, and they often make sacrifices to assure an easy passage. Toward this aim, living relatives often follow strict guidelines regarding their food, drink, and activities.

How Can Nature Be Our Teacher?

All of nature is our teacher, from the ant that crawls on dirt roads to the eagle that soars through cloudless skies. Our connection with the earth — her running streams, cherry blossoms, the way she dies back in winter or bursts forth in spring blooms — teaches us about life and the changes of our inner and outer worlds. She is like the mother who passes on her wisdom to those of us who are less experienced in the ways of the world.

This poem expresses how the earth can be our teacher:

Earth, teach me stillness
    as the grasses are stilled with light.
Earth, teach me suffering
    as old stones suffer with memory.

Earth, teach me humility
   as blossoms are humble with beginning.
Earth, teach me caring
   as the mother who secures her young.
Earth, teach me courage
   as the tree which stands all alone.
Earth, teach me limitation
   as the ant which crawls on the ground.
Earth, teach me freedom
   as the eagle which soars in the sky.
Earth, teach me resignation
   as the leaves which die in the fall.
Earth, teach me regeneration
   as the seed which rises in the spring.
Earth, teach me to forget myself
   as melted snow forgets its life.
Earth, teach me to remember kindness
   as dry fields weep with rain.

(UTE, NORTH AMERICA)

As we observe each aspect of nature — a tree standing alone, a seed that rises in spring — we access the inherent harmony and wisdom contained in its cycles. By being keenly present, we become like the dog in the park that hears a sound and focuses all of its attention on what is taking place. This attentiveness awakens our innate intuition, which allows us to know what nature is communicating to us. Intuition is our faculty that allows us to know with the heart, body, and spirit, not only the mind. Through our intuition we can access spiritual realms of knowledge. For Native People all communication with nature is a conversation with the Great Spirit.

When Miranda had purchased her new house, situated on two acres, she had not been fully conscious that the land held thirty-seven trees, but something had felt right about buying the property. Now, months after the purchase, she walked the land, and an important realization flashed across her mind. "Buying this home was part of a larger synchronicity." In Miranda's words, "Not only are the trees here to help me be grounded in myself, as they so aptly demonstrate with their natural rooted-ness, but I am also here to care for them. I have loved trees since I was a girl and I know they need me to care for them. I'm grate-ful for the chance to have this responsibility and continue to learn from their wisdom."

Sandy had always loved the ocean. As a young girl growing up in the desert, she knew she wanted to live near the water. "The sea reminds me of the need to be fluid and flexible. It's never the same. Each day reflects a new mood. Yet there's a constancy you can count on, a cyclical way that the tides come in and out around the cycles of the moon. This helps me honor the cycles of change in my own life and reminds me to expect change."

In the 1950s Ann Morrow Lindbergh took a break from her hectic schedule as a mother of five and freelance writer. She went to Martha's Vineyard for a short restorative retreat by the sea. In her book, *Gift from the Sea*, she wrote about being empty in the way that the sandy beach waits for a gift of the sea to reveal itself in its own time:

> The sea does not reward those who are too anxious or too greedy, or too impatient. To dig for treasures shows not only impatience and greed, but lack of faith. Pa-tience, patience, patience is what the sea teaches. Patience and faith. One should lie empty, open, choiceless as a beach — waiting for a gift from the sea.

The Native wisdom to let nature be our teacher touches our hearts and opens us to a connection with the living world around us that the soul knows. Inhabiting the world today — intertwined with cell phones, cyberspace, radio, television, and compelling work that demands our attention for hours on end — we may get further and further removed from the simple wonders of snow sparkling under moonlight or flowers blooming on desert cacti, and thus the Great Spirit that flows through all things. Each time I remember to return to nature in any way, my soul feels restored at my homecoming. Loving, respecting, and caring for the earth is our sacred legacy from the Native People.

Cultivating a Relationship with Nature

We can balance our busy lives with nature's gifts once we allow ourselves to have a relationship with the natural world. In another era we would have already had a connection with nature — we'd need to walk through the woods to fetch water, gather nuts and fruits, or hunt. Living in an industrialized world, we have to deliberately seek out that relationship. We can learn to cultivate a relationship with nature, just as we would devote time and energy to develop any association.

EXPLORING SOLITUDE IN NATURE. We give ourselves a tremendous gift when we take time to join the harmony of the natural world. Whether we stroll along a beach and hear the waves clapping, or feel the still dryness of the desert and marvel at the hints of pinks and purples in what first appeared as washed-out sand, we need to take ourselves out into nature to experience her. We can schedule a lunch hour, devote a Sunday afternoon, or plan a weekend or week away in a natural setting that attracts us. We can benefit from the adventure of being open and receptive and just seeing what unfolds.

Marcy works in the marketing department for a large financial planning conglomerate. Her workweek is long, sometimes over fifty hours. But she lives five minutes from her office and her house is near a park. "I think what keeps me sane is taking time to go home for lunch and walk in the park. It's not always easy to leave the hectic pace of deadlines and ringing phones, but I'm so glad when I do. As soon as I enter the park, my eyes feast on the shades of green. I relax as the grass invites me into another landscape. Like a nurturing hostess, she says to me, 'Come in and relax. You're welcome here.' As I step onto the soft body of the earth, I feel my breathing deepen as if I had been holding my breath without realizing it. Spending even twenty to thirty minutes in this peace shifts something inside of me. Being in nature breaks the illusion that the details of my work environment are the only things that matter. My walk in the park reminds me that there's a whole other world outside the stress of the office. It puts things in perspective, and I can go back to the office and do my work but not get so caught up in it."

RETREATING IN NATURE. An extended time in nature, three or four days to a week in solitude, can be likened to the vision quest in the Native traditions. For thousands of years humans have retreated into nature in solitude to learn about who they are, assisted by the lessons that nature has to offer. In Native cultures this quest often has been used as a rite of passage into adulthood. The guidance they receive from their quests helps determine their roles in their tribes. Later they can return to the quest experience whenever they seek guidance from the spirit powers.

For tribal people the vision quest has been a way to practice their spirituality intimately tied to the earth they walk on, the sky above, and the whole family of things alive and around them. Life is seen as a continuous dialogue with the Great Spirit who speaks through every sunrise and sunset, every gentle evening breeze.

Traditional Native vision quests entailed going out into nature with very little. In some traditions the young men went out naked and barefoot even in winter. In other traditions, taking a blanket and the clothes on your back was permissible.

Denise Linn, author of *Quest: A Guide for Creating Your Own Vision Quest*, directs people on three- to four-day quests to bring a notebook in which to journal. She also provides people with different options for writing, including:

- Examining your life
- Facing old fears and releasing attachments
- Tapping into the spirit power within
- Giving thanks for the blessings in one's life
- Requesting guidance about life purpose

On my own vision quest of three days and three nights, I was not allowed to bring notebook, pen, food, water, or anything else except the blanket I wore around my shoulders, a rattle, and the clothes on the back. Yet despite the seeming scarcity, it was the most plentiful experience of my life: I finally found my way home.

Welcome Home

I studied Native ways with a female shaman named Dancing Cloud. Her hair was white-blond and curled out of control, a sharp contrast to her kind face. She was a special-education teacher who was appointed to teach Mescalero Apache ways. I met her through a connection I had with the Rainbow Heart Lodge in Riverside, California. I had previously done a short vision quest when I lived in the meditation center in Wisconsin, and I loved the shamanic teachings that connected me intimately to nature.

My inner guidance compelled me to do a vision quest under the direction of Dancing Cloud, even though it required a six-month preparation of intermittent fasting each week and rigorous inner work. I chose the date of the full moon in August, when I would have time off from work.

I was at a point in my life where I sought inner guidance about my soul's purpose. The vision quest was my opportunity to receive a vision and gather all the fragments of my soul toward the direction of completing my life's purpose.

I talked to Dancing Cloud at a weekend retreat in the San Bernardino Mountains. Tall pines and dense woods surrounded us as we talked. Dancing Cloud's white-blond hair was wild on her head. "Again," she counseled me, "it is a rigorous journey." Her sweet and loving voice made me feel safe. I saw gentleness in her blue eyes and, where the blue faded into gray, unbending steel strength.

"Yes," I answered, "I am aware of the rigor." I was surprised at how calm I felt.

After six months of prescribed fasting on juice, water, or nothing at all, for one or two days a week, I was led into the two-week fast with only liquids before actually going up on the mountain. This would be for three days and three nights — no food, no water.

During this time of preparation I sometimes questioned my sanity — especially on the days when fasting left me tired and hungry at the end of a full day of work. Falling down on my bed to rest, my mind would drift to thoughts of going up on the mountain. My worst fear was of snakes. I imagined them crawling into my circle and biting me as I dozed, their venom coursing through my veins until I succumbed to the poison through death. Other people had shared their fears of freezing at night or being mauled by a bear. Dancing Cloud would let us sit with our fears, sometimes chuckling as we conjured up gruesome stories.

I was led to my spot through inner guidance. As I walked up the mountain I saw a cleared space surrounded by a few trees. The earth seemed to welcome me; I felt my heart open like a door swung wide to a summer's day. I heard a calm and confident inner whisper, "This is the place." My feet stopped moving, and my attention focused sharply as my eyes followed the contours of branches and surveyed the dusty ground. I found my spot and gathered rocks to form my sacred circle, where I would spend the next three days and nights. If I left my circle of power while on the mountain, the ceremony would be over. If I wanted to proceed with the vision quest after that, I would have to start over with six-months' preparation of fasting.

For the first day I watched the mountainside's population of ants, birds, crickets, and flies. I was aware that they were letting me coexist and blend into the natural rhythm, which I thought was extremely generous. The ants continued their fastidious work of building, carrying, and marching on their way. I watched them for hours, learning from their patience and perseverance. I thanked them for being my teachers.

The hummingbirds came by and shared their joy with

me. I felt happy to see them as they hovered before me on their short visits. Their fluttering and delicate beauty opened my heart and reminded me about joy every time they came to visit — usually after sunrise and before sunset, but sometimes at random throughout the day.

As night fell I appreciated the respite from the heat. "Thank you, night. Thank you, clouds, for giving me rest from the heat of the sun." I was lucky to experience rather mild weather for the August summer in the San Bernardino Mountains. It felt like the eighties and nineties instead of the hundred-degree temperatures I'd feared. Yet as hot as it was during the day, the night air chilled me and inspired gratitude as I wrapped my blanket around me, savoring the warmth.

I loved watching the revolution of day and night. I enjoyed how the light dimmed in the sky as the animal world grew progressively still and quiet, preparing me for sleep. It was as if daylight played touch tag with the night. The sound of birdsong gave way to the chirping of crickets.

On the first night, as darkness enveloped the mountaintop, I was shaken out of my meditative musings when I heard the sound of an animal approaching the perimeter of my sacred circle. My inner circle, enclosed with sacred rocks, was about ten feet in diameter. But the outer circle of my energy field extended fifty yards beyond the inner circle.

I heard only footsteps and felt the presence of I knew not what. My heart began to race as I imagined a bear or coyote. It seemed smaller than a bear but I wasn't sure. I knew that if I allowed my fear to expand I would broadcast my vulnerability to the impending presence.

I reached for my rattle and began to shake it loudly. I spoke out loud, "I am one with the Great Spirit of life. No one may enter my sacred circle of power. I am here in peace. Now go." I continued to shake my rattle, and sang songs of power that spontaneously rose to my lips. I was speaking in an ancient, Native tongue, which I did not consciously know. I continued to pray.

As I felt my power rise, my fear dissipated, and I heard footsteps recede in the darkness. I gave thanks to the Great Spirit. I recognized that I lived in a safe and loving universe. "Welcome home, my daughter," were the words I heard as I dozed off to sleep in the arms of Mother Earth.

VALUING NATURE AS SACRED. Native People view every part of nature as alive, as animated by the Great Spirit. This makes the tiniest ant and the largest wolf sacred gifts of life and interconnected like a family in which every part is invaluable. The four-leggeds, the winged ones, those that swim — as well as rocks, earth, trees, and flowers — comprise the sacred family of which humans, the two-leggeds, are only a part.

Having a less dominant role may challenge our personal and cultural beliefs that lay claim to a dominating worldview. From this perspective, nature is an inanimate resource to be used, conquered, or owned without question. With such an attitude toward nature, we are divorced, separate, and unrelated to the world around us. Alienation results, since all of nature is seen as an inferior commodity to use for our own benefit. Opening ourselves to a sacred view of nature may make us aware of our own beliefs as well as those of the culture.

Entering the sacred worldview requires a reversal. We see

ourselves connected to the earth, the sky, and the moon as if we were parts of the same family. We refer to our Mother Earth and walk upon her with loving care. We feel sorrow if she is hurt, and we are moved to help her in times of need. Love and respect of the natural world come from this sacred worldview, leading to changes in our actions.

We may gently remove a spider from our kitchen to the backyard, as did the character May in Sue Monk Kidd's *The Secret Lives of Bees*, who made a trail of marshmallows and graham crackers to lure a cockroach out of the house rather than kill it.

Native People have traditionally thanked the earth for her crops and the buffalo for sacrificing its life that the tribe may live. Donald, a massage therapist in Louisville, Kentucky, is a vegetarian who feels that slaughtering animals for food doesn't honor them. Therefore, he chooses not to eat fowl, meat, or fish, which is his way of valuing nature as sacred. Betty, mother of three in Wisconsin, instituted a prayer ritual before meals in which each person says a blessing of gratitude for a different part of the meal, including the garden for producing vegetables, rain for nourishing the harvest, and the cows for fertilizing the crops. Her children delight in discovering new ways to acknowledge their gratitude for things in nature, which strengthens their bonds to the earth.

Sandy educates celebrants of memorials and weddings to not use balloons to commemorate their events. "When the balloons deflate and drop into the oceans or onto nearby beaches, the birds mistake the balloon pieces for food and die."

BECOMING A STUDENT. To open to a teacher means that you want to learn and that you believe that your teacher has something valuable to impart to you. You take the posture of receptivity; you are open to learning something you didn't know before. Most important, you don't think you know everything, but, rather, you are humble before someone or something that knows more than you. Being a receptive student doesn't mean you are passive. Instead, you are dynamically attentive to absorbing new lessons and perspectives, and are ready to make connections and weave them into new ways of understanding.

Irene became a student of rain. Recently relocated to the Northwest, she initially hated the constant mists and downpours. She knew that if she were going to enjoy her life in Seattle, she needed to make peace with the rain. One day, while walking in the rain, she screamed, "Why am I so angry with you?"

Her mind flashed to a time when she was six years old and her father was packing the trunk of his car to leave for a business trip. It was raining that day and she remembered getting wet as she hugged her dad good-bye. On the way to the airport her father's vehicle crashed into oncoming traffic and he was killed. As Irene remembered this trauma, a lot of stored-up tears began to pour down her face. There was something comforting about standing in the rain and crying. As she turned her face toward the sky, it was as if the rain were speaking to her: "It's okay to cry, little one. Let your tears fall freely." Irene realized that she'd held back her tears for many years. The rainy winter helped Irene grieve unfelt losses. "Rain showed me how."

EMBRACING THE MYSTERY. Learning from nature is like entering a mystery, which speaks in a language that is not your native tongue. You become a visitor in another land, required to develop keen observational skills to fill in the blanks of what is not spoken directly. The more time you spend in nature, the more awestruck you become at how brilliantly everything fits together. You begin to trust that if something exists, or is in process, there's a reason for it, a place that it holds in the grand matrix. Even if you can't comprehend the reason, you begin to treat it more reverently, because all events are an expression of the Great Spirit.

CONNECTING WITH YOUR ANIMAL-SPIRIT TEACHERS. We can all receive wisdom from animals if we enter into the Native People's understanding that every part of nature is here to offer a lesson if we are willing to receive one. If you have a pet dog or cat, you may already be familiar with what these animals convey. Our dog can teach us unconditional love and loyalty as it daily greets us with a wagging tail or snuggles closely at night as one of the pack. Your cat may teach you independence as it becomes clear that she has a will all her own.

As you become open to animals and what they offer, you can begin to notice them around you. You may notice that in your daily experience you repeatedly encounter a hawk flying overhead or see a deer cross your path. Pay attention to this repetition. This may signal a connection with your animal-spirit teacher. You can also find your animal totem through a shamanic journey, a dream, designated time alone, or in a meditation you design for that purpose.

To discover your animal-spirit guide, center yourself and invite it to reveal itself to you in your meditation. After encountering your animal-spirit teacher, allow yourself to enter its world — the world of Wolf, Dragonfly, Spider, or Eagle. Make a collage containing photos or drawings of your animal teacher. Look up information on the Internet. Take out books from the library. Many anthologies of Native American stories contain specific examples of how animals are viewed in that culture and what "medicine," or healing properties they bring to you.

Wolf

At the Christine Center in Wisconsin we once had visitors who shared with us some of the Native ways. A small group of us gathered to experience a shamanic journey. Our leader, Brent, was a friendly, unassuming man, who spoke very little. He was accompanied by his wife, Mart, who, in contrast, spoke as sweetly and steadily as a mockingbird in the early morning.

To begin, Brent lit an abalone shell piled high with sage to purify each of us, as well as the large drum used for the ceremony. After they'd smudged each other, Mart took the lit sage from him and continued to fan us with sweeps of a large feather that scooped the smoke around the front and back of our torsos. Brent waited silently until Mart had finished smudging everyone.

Brent's silence was a speech in itself. You could feel the power emanating from the center of his body like a panther's attention to night sounds. We were drawn into the vortex of his presence even before he spoke.

"First, I give thanks to Creator for this ceremony that allows us to communicate with the Great Spirit." Brent closed his eyes as he prayed and raised the shell of burning sage above his head.

He continued, "The shamanic journey is one of the oldest ceremonies known to humankind. A shaman was the person in the tribe who played the role of leader and spiritual guide. The shaman was adept at spiritual 'seeing' in the spirit world and was conversant with animal spirits that teach those in the physical world. Each of us has at least one animal-spirit guide or totem. This ceremony helps you find your animal-spirit teacher."

Brent instructed us to sit or lie down in a comfortable position and listen carefully to the drumbeats, which, like the beating heart of Mother Earth, would start slowly and then gain momentum as the journey progressed. The drumbeats hypnotically carried us to another realm as we followed Brent's directions.

"Allow yourself, with your inner sight, to find a place where you can enter the earth, like a rabbit hole or a hollow space in a tree trunk where you can find your way to the roots underneath the earth. On your way, allow yourself to meet your animal-spirit guide and let this teacher lead you underground to a place and experience that serves as the medicine or healing that you need."

The drumbeats continued, sometimes wildly, transporting us beyond time and space. Hearing a signal that we agreed upon, the drum changed rhythm to guide us back up through the earth to the cozy cabin called Angel of Peace.

When we'd finished the journey, we sat in a circle and had a chance to share our experiences. Amy, who had thin, brown hair, pale skin, and no makeup, and was wearing a faded blue-denim long-sleeve shirt and faded jeans, was the first to share.

"I was not in a great place when we started this journey. I've been kind of bummed out lately because Ralph and I were trying to have a baby and we haven't been able to conceive. Frankly, I wanted to mope about in my room, but Ralph convinced me to join him tonight for the circle. I must confess, I was neither enthusiastic nor thrilled to be here, but I mumbled to myself, 'Okay, it's probably better than feeling sorry for myself.' I found my way inside the tree trunk and journeyed through the roots down into what felt like the fertile earth. I was met by Wolf. His piercing gray eyes looked down into my soul for what seemed like a long time. Then Wolf turned away and walked slowly through the dense, tall forest of pines and cedars into a small clearing. Tucked in the soft hills I saw what looked like a cave. Wolf walked into the cave and turned around as if to summon me. I followed. To my delight, I discovered that this cave was a den where two small wolf pups were nursing with their mother. Wolf came up close to me again and looked into my eyes. Through his eyes I heard a message in my heart. 'You must keep the vision of your unborn children alive in your heart. Otherwise, your doubt and fear close the door to their coming.'

"My eyes, still locked into Wolf's, filled with tears. Every night, I'd cried because I wasn't pregnant. How could Wolf know my heart? Yes, I was afraid that I might never conceive and that my own womb and home would be barren.

"'Change the picture inside of your heart. See little ones fill your home and heart. Rejoice in their homecoming,' Wolf seemed to say.

"I caught the message: Of, course, my empty womb is matching my fearful picture. But am I really ready for what I am saying that I want?

"At this point I heard the drumbeat signal that it was time to go back to the tree roots. Wolf led me safely back to our starting point. I'm not sure how all of this happened, or what I'll do with this information, but I do know that something shifted inside of me as I became more acquainted with my fears and more clear about my responsibility to keep the vision of my heart's desire alive. I also feel I can go back and talk to Wolf, and I will."

Challenges and Progress on the Path

I had given students in my current Wisdom Walk class the assignment of spending time alone in nature. Jane greeted me with a pinecone that she'd brought back from her visit to the forest. "This is for you," she said, holding her pinecone out toward me as if it were a great treasure. I smiled back at her gleaming eyes as I accepted the gift. "Following in the tradition of Native People's respect for nature, which we discussed in class, when I took the pinecone from the forest, I asked its permission. I also left some tobacco on the ground in gratitude for the offering."

"How was your trip?" I asked Jane.

"It was amazing," she added quickly. "Being in the woods felt like coming home in some way I couldn't quite understand. Surrounded by the redwoods, I placed my hand on the trees and received great assurance that I was proceeding in the right direction with a project I'm working on. Among the towering trees I felt like I was in a cathedral of trees, which were simultaneously wise beings revealing to me what I needed to know. My only problem is understanding why I don't spend more time in forests when they are so fulfilling to my soul."

Jill's hand shot up. "I know why, I know why. It's because you get busy like I do. I get so wrapped up in my job and the routine of my life, that I feel like I can't get away. My problem with the assignment this week was feeling like I was too busy. Last night I was stretched out on my couch fretting over not completing the assignment, and then my eyes fell upon the droopy, green leaves of my philodendrons. They looked thirsty. I walked across the living room and sprinkled water over the leaves and into the pots. As I watered my little green friends, they immediately perked up; the flat surfaces of green lifted as if they were grateful for the water and my attention. Their responsiveness drove home the point: these plants are living beings. Gently wiping the dust from the thin, strong leaves, I traced the network of veins with my finger. It was as if we were holding hands. I whispered, 'I'm sorry I've neglected you. I'll try to do better.' In the silence, as if these plants were speaking to me, I heard, 'Slow down, so you don't miss what's important.' I appreciated the wisdom message they gave me."

"Sounds like you did the assignment, Jill," I said, looking into her face. "It's a good reminder to all of us. I know for myself that if I overwork without touching into nature, after a while I start to feel disconnected from myself and my environment."

Margie chimed in, "Yeah, I definitely felt that as I did the assignment. I was having a stressful and busy week at my job. Because I have to be a perfect student —" The class laughed, then Margie continued, "I made a point to take a morning walk around the lake, which is near my home. What amazed me is that, although I pass the location every day, I hadn't noticed that the leaves were turning and that the reds and golds were exquisitely vibrant. I remembered my childhood when I used to love to walk in autumn leaves and hear them rustle underneath my feet. It gave me great pleasure, and I wondered, too, 'Why don't I take more time to be in nature when I love it?' I'd forgotten it was autumn until I walked around the lake. I sat under a tree and wrote some ideas about what fall meant to me. I remembered that fall was a time of harvest and dying. The wisdom of autumn helped me accept that my parents were aging, yet, as difficult as that is, their aging is a natural part of the life cycle."

"Good for you for listening and receiving nature's wisdom," I told her.

I looked at the corner of the room and saw Walt, a familiar face since he'd taken many classes with me, sometimes repeating the same class. A tall, blond man in his late sixties, he attentively followed the discussion. I decided to investigate the smoldering fire of restraint that I felt coming from him.

"What's going on, Walt?" This question was enough of a draft to let the fire catch.

"Well, I hate to be the one to crash the party, but this assignment to ask a tree a question didn't work for me. I feel silly talking to trees, birds, or the moon. I'm from the city, and too much peace and quiet gets on my nerves."

I could hear friendly giggles from other members of the class.

"The best I could do was take my dog, Skip, for a long walk in the park on Sunday after reading the paper. I can say we had a relaxing time walking on the path, seeing hints of crimson and gold in the fall colors. Skip had a great time spotting squirrels and lunging on the leash as he tried to run after them."

"How did you know Skip had a good time?"

"He told me so." In a split second Walt realized he'd caught himself in the trap of his own mental resistance. He smiled at the irony of his last statement.

"Thanks for sharing, Walt. Would anyone else like to share?"

Riane's voice quivered as she spoke. A second-generation Japanese American woman, she was often detained at work in downtown Los Angeles and would arrive at class thirty minutes late. "I'm embarrassed to say this, but I'm scared to be alone in nature. What if someone sees me, tries to hurt me, and there's no one around to help? I didn't feel safe enough to do this assignment."

I looked into Riane's face. Although in her midforties, she looked as young as a child of seven at this moment. "Riane, it's good that you took care of yourself by not doing the assignment. It's certainly wise to make sure that if we are alone in nature, we feel safe. I've had other students in classes who also felt uncomfortable being alone, so you're not the only one with this problem.

In one class some students decided to join together and visit a park as a group. They agreed on a time for their solitude experiment and decided to meet back at the appointed place in a half hour. It comforted them to know that if they needed help, someone was around whom they could count on. They also carried whistles with them in case of an emergency."

"That sounds much better," Riane said, breathing easier.

"Would anyone be interested in participating in a group trip? Maybe we could all go and have a field trip?" Many hands went up. "Riane, I'm sorry I didn't mention this possibility before."

"It's okay," Riane smiled. "Thanks for understanding."

"I also know from experience that sometimes our fears come up when we're alone. Being in nature can be a place of healing. I once facilitated a small group in a day of silence in the woods. One woman, Francine, took me aside and said she was afraid to be alone for such a long time. I told her I would visit her periodically, and in between those times, she might connect with one of her totems and seek protection. On my first check-in, she informed me that I needn't come back. She had done a meditation and connected with Hawk flying overhead. She intuitively felt a presence watching over her. She knew on another level of her being that she was safe and protected. She told me, 'Every time I see Hawk flying over, I connect with that sense of peace from my meditation, and I'm reminded of a sense of protection that I have never experienced before now.' Being in nature can give us unexpected gifts if we are open to receive these."

Native American spirituality invites us to come home to ourselves by connecting to nature and receiving the wisdom of her teachings. As we do this, we remember that we are a part of a larger whole in which we, and every other living being, hold an essential place, worthy of respect. We do not have to feel alone or alienated from the world around us. Paradoxically, we can connect with the whole by spending time alone in nature. It is through our solitude that we remember our interrelatedness to all living things in nature.

Wisdom Steps

SPEND SOME TIME ALONE IN NATURE. Choose a time — a morning or afternoon, a whole day, a weekend — where you will have some uninterrupted time alone in nature. Take as little as possible to this place so that you will not be distracted from placing your attention on the natural environment around you. Go to the places in nature that you love — a wooded area, the mountains, the seashore, or the high desert. Allow yourself to be receptive to the natural world. Notice the animals or insects that come your way, the position of the sun or moon, the sound of birds flying overhead. Notice how you feel in nature. Explore how you fit into the natural scheme. See your relatedness to all life, and be open to the teachings. You may choose to write down your insights or just let them add a dimension to your solitude.

OPEN YOURSELF TO THE WORLD OF ANIMALS AS YOUR TEACHERS. Through the course of your day, notice your interactions with animals and open to their wisdom. You may already have an affinity to your pet as teacher. Your cat, which never comes when called, may teach you independence and autonomy. Your dog, which follows you from room to room, may teach you community or the loyalty of staying close to members of your pack. Let yourself notice the hawk that flies over your head. Pause for a moment. Inwardly ask, What does Hawk teach? Be open to receive an answer. "By flying high, you see things from a different perspective." "Rise above the circumstances." "You are free to soar."

If you're walking in the woods and you see a deer, be open to the wisdom of this four-legged creature. You may be struck by Deer's beauty or gentleness. This may translate into a wisdom message for you: "Honor the gentleness of your own nature." "Remember, there is a place for exquisite beauty."

TOUCH THE EARTH THROUGH GARDENING. A practical way to expose yourself to the wondrous cycles of nature is through gardening. Find a patch of ground in your own backyard. Or spend some time in a friend's garden. Feel free to have your hands dig in the earth as you plant seeds or weed. Notice the cycle of growth as the bulb takes root in the dark soil, as it lies seemingly dormant until the first seedling breaks through the earth into the light. Receive the lessons that the garden can teach you about the cycles of your own life. Be aware of how you feel in the space of the garden, connected to the plants, flowers, seasons, and cycles of nature. Grow herbs, lettuce, or tomatoes. Witness the miracle of life and how nature nourishes us every day.

CHAPTER SEVEN

TAOISM: *Go with the Flow*

How can a man's life keep its course
If he will not let it flow?
Those who flow as life flows know
They need no other force:
They feel no wear, they feel no tear,
They need no mending, no repair.

— LAO-TZU, *TAO TE CHING*

I'd had a challenging year as the dean of a ministerial program with three campuses — Los Angeles, Oakland, and Seattle. The student base was growing but the staff had not. In addition to administering the programs at three campuses, teaching classes, counseling with clients, making occasional hospital visits, attending Sunday services, and guest-speaking at various pulpits, my internal rhythm was completely off. I felt tired, but I kept pushing my body to show up to teach or answer students' questions.

My internal cues told me to rest, but I didn't find the time. I promised myself I would rest later, but that time never came. Eventually I didn't hear the cues anymore; I was just going fast, from one meeting to the next, one class to another, one phone call to the next. I lost contact with myself, even though I didn't know it at the time. I drank coffee, ate sugary doughnuts, and indulged in large meals out — all on the run. Eventually I lost track of the different speeds of my life; I was just "on," and eventually the buzz turned into numb.

I gained weight, had challenges at home, and couldn't sleep well. I always had just one more thing to attend to before going home for the night. My mind had so much to do that I was never *not* at work. I had turned into a "human doing," and like a hamster running circles on her ring, the faster I ran, the more I went in circles.

Every morning in meditation I couldn't stop the hamster wheel of my mind, and I realized something was absolutely out of balance. This was not why I chose to be a minister or have a spiritual life. Where was my connection to Spirit?

Tired, even depleted, I finally conceded to the flow. Respecting my need to turn inward, I gave myself some retreat time alone over a long weekend. The first thing I did was sleep, which led to long hours of undisturbed rest. I remember how my acupuncturist, Luciana, would say that sleep was powerful medicine for healing and restoration, helping to restore the full flow of *chi*, or vital energy, in the body. She would often counsel me that my outer activity, or *yang*, was overactive, needing more *yin*, rest and receptivity, to balance me out. In my retreat time I gave myself permission to only move or engage in activities that compelled me from an inner urge. As I slept and rested I felt more vitalized. I became aware of the river of energy running through my body that, at first, wanted to recede deeper and deeper into rest, as if it knew its way to source. I watched how, in its own time, it felt replenished, as if touching into source and then flowing gradually back in the other direction.

After three days of sleep and rest, I looked out on the water from the deck of my boat and began to feel a glimmer of energy to do something. The fog in my mind and awareness was lifting, and some sparkle of light was energizing from some part of me that had been asleep. I was waking up, thawing from my numbness. I was beginning to feel like myself again.

I wrote in my journal about the delight of going with the flow through listening to my internal rhythm: *I've been noticing some of this in my life in a way that helps me cherish the balance between inward and outward activities. Yesterday I spent time at home on my boat, Sophia, giving myself the luxury of an inward focus. On the deck, enjoying the summer warmth and refreshing breeze, I gazed on the blue ripples going in the direction of the wind. Although I am weaving my attention in and out of writing, I have spent a good part of the day in silence. Creativity flows easily from the center of me. I watch how, when I feel satiated with the inward focus of writing, my energy naturally moves to an outward focus.*

The river took me outward. I felt like doing the dishes, dusting, and taking the dog for a walk. I welcomed the relief of balance from yin to yang. I was supposed to have dinner with my brother, but I felt like I needed some more time in this nourishing solitude. When he called, I told him I'd meet him later on, around six o'clock. When that time came, I felt my body, mind, and spirit delighted to move into activity outside of myself. We had a lovely visit.

The next morning I told the members of a class I was teaching that I loved the cosmic dance that I experienced between the inner and the outer, the flowing from an inner focus to the readiness to be with people again. It was a gift to allow myself the freedom to go with the flow throughout the day, attuning to the mysterious rhythm of the Tao *— the nameless, formless power of the universe.*

Spontaneous flow seemed so different from my way of trying to force situations in my life, which had resulted in door after door shutting. Now looking through the lens of effortless action, I wondered if I was squandering precious energy that wanted to go in a different direction than the way I was trying to push it?

Going with the flow seemed so much easier and more enjoyable. What if I let go of the folly of trying to control the course
of my life? What if, when doors closed I accepted this, and when
they were open I walked through? Where did the river of my life
want to go? Could I trust this flow? Could I really let go? Would
I still be able to get everything done? Something shifted for me
that weekend. But it would take many years to fully extricate myself from the pattern of shaping the flow instead of letting it transform me.

❧

Taoism is one of the main religions of China. Founded on the
philosophy of Lao-tzu, it teaches that natural simplicity and
humility lead to harmony and balance in life. Taoism and Con-
fucianism are complementary aspects of Chinese thought. Confu-
cianism, which began around 500 BC, maintains that people can
live a good life by following societal parameters of ceremony,
duty, and modesty. In contrast, the Taoist ideal has an individual
avoid social convention and lead a simple, spontaneous, and meditative life close to nature.

Taoism, based on the writings of Lao-tzu and Chang Tzu,
emphasizes living according to the Tao, meaning "the Way" or
"Path," which refers to the nameless, formless, all-pervasive
power that permeates all things.

As Huston Smith in *The Illustrated World's Religions* tells the
story, Lao-tzu, the old master who founded Taoism (pronounced
"Dowism"), was born in China around 604 BC. We only know
about him through a tapestry of legends. A commonly accepted
story reports that Lao-tzu was disillusioned with the way his con-
temporaries failed to cultivate the way of life in harmony with
nature. Seeking greater solitude for the last years of his life, he

mounted a water buffalo and rode to the west toward what is now
known as Tibet. A gatekeeper who learned of his intention to
leave society behind him tried to persuade him to turn back and
not give up on the people. Failing this, he convinced Lao-tzu to
at least record the essence of his teachings so that others might
profit from his wisdom. Lao-tzu consented to do this and, three
days later, returned with a pithy volume of eighty-one aphorisms
titled *Tao Te Ching*, meaning "The Way and Its Power." One of
the main insights of the book is that if we observe nature, which
expresses the unnamable mystery of the Tao, we will be led to
the intuitive wisdom inside of ourselves that will guide us in every
situation.

Many people in the West know the principles of Taoism
through the practices of *tai chi chuan*, a meditation of slow movements practiced for the purposes of health, balance, and longevity;
chi gong, an ancient Chinese system of breathing and movements
designed to improve health and well-being and prevent disease;
feng shui, the Chinese art of creating environments based on patterns of yin and yang and the flow of energy; and *acupuncture*,
a form of complementary medicine that balances the polarity
of bodily energies using needles along specific meridian lines of
the body to release the flow of chi necessary for good health.

Getting Our Bearings: Taoism

NATURE OF THE DEITY. The divine manifests in a variety of
ways in Taoism. In one sense, all things come from the Tao and
eventually return to it. Tao is not a supreme being, but rather a
cosmic principle that infuses all aspects of creation with vitality.
Cosmologically, first there is the Tao, or undifferentiated potential, which moves and becomes the two polarities that flow

between each other, known as the yin and the yang, and then springs the material world referred to as the "ten-thousand things," in seeming contradiction to this unity.

RELATIONSHIP OF INDIVIDUAL TO THE DIVINE. The Tao is available to each individual without an intermediary. The individual is called to a state of receptivity, to be aware of the natural flow of life.

HOW TO WORSHIP. The way to practice Taoism is to follow the Tao and learn to live in harmony with its wisdom. The Tao Te Ching advises quiescence and *wu wei*, or taking no action that is contrary to nature. Water is a common symbol in Taoist texts, reminding individuals that pliability is also a sign of strength. Nothing seems more flexible than water, yet it can also wear away stone.

ETHICAL BELIEFS. The ethics of the earliest Taoist texts honor the Tao, which creates, nurtures, destroys, and embraces all things. Human conventions, which divide things into opposites such as good and bad, are not to be trusted. At the core of Taoism is wu wei, or "noninterference," which instructs one to move with, rather than against, natural processes and change. To practice wu wei is also to value flexibility and humility, and to embrace the feminine side.

BELIEFS ABOUT DEATH AND THE AFTERLIFE. Especially through the writings of Chang Tzu, death and life are alternating parts of a cycle that are to be neither sought nor feared. One's fate is to participate in the coagulation and dissipation of chi. There is also an emphasis on preserving chi for longevity, and even immortality, through practices of inner and outer alchemy — meditation, visualization exercises, and physical practices such as tai chi chuan and chi gong.

What Is the Flow?

We may all be familiar with the yin and yang symbol. A circle is divided in the center by a line that looks like a winding river running from the top to the bottom of the circle. Half of the circle is black, and the other is white. Contained in each side of black and white is a small circle of its opposite — a white circle in the black, and a black circle in the white. The symbolism is that energy flows from one polarity to the other in the continual dance of the Tao between these polarities. Day turns to night, and night turns to day. The ocean tides ebb and flow. Temperature turns from warm to cool. We have health and sickness, happiness and sadness. We experience in our everyday lives the dance of the Tao through this flow between polarities.

In the same way that winter turns to spring and new buds replace the bare branches of winter, so, too, our lives have an intelligence and mystery guiding them like an invisible river that knows its way back to its source. This intelligence that weaves through seasonal changes runs through our lives.

We may see evidence of this river in our lives bringing to us the people we need to meet, the opportunities that allow us to prosper, and the challenges that cultivate our inner resources. What if an intelligence greater than ours is running our lives? Wouldn't it be wise to bring ourselves in accord with this flow, be humble in front of its mystery, and be willing to yield to this intelligence?

To do this, the ancient Taoists invite us to be receptive to the Tao by observing the Tao in the simplicity of nature and cultivating an inner, intuitive sense that allows us to yield (the feminine principle, yin) or act (the masculine principle, yang) when it is appropriate. Neither is considered good or bad. Both are necessary for balance. In Taoism, balance exists in the flow of energy between opposites. Yin and yang represent the polarities between which the Tao flows. Yin is dark, wet, and feminine like the earth. Yang is light, dry, and masculine like the sky.

Underwater Dance

While snorkeling in Tahiti I experienced the dance of the Tao as I observed how the sea anemone interacts with the clown fish. When the sea anemone opens in the receptive posture of yin, the clown fish moves close to the sides of the sea anemone to get its food, representing the active posture of yang — which is also a cleaning process for the sea anemone. I watched them perform this dance, back and forth, like the cha-cha — one step forward and your partner steps back. Your partner steps forward and you step back. All of this happens in the rhythm of underwater melodies of silence, the music moving you nevertheless.

Resisting the Flow

Whether we are talking about the unfoldment of our spiritual path, the blossoming of an intimate relationship, a job search, or finding our right livelihood, we realize the way is fluid. We're involved in a process.

We may also know that at times we resist this flow. We don't want our children to pierce their body parts. We put our hands over our ears to block our partner's declaration of leaving the relationship. We hold on to a dying parent. Yet despite our resistance, the body piercing happens, the relationship ends, and our parents die. Kicking and screaming, we go down the river of our lives anyway. In hindsight we may see the folly of our opposition, not only because it is futile but also because the outcome that we feared brought unexpected gifts. Our teenager soon grew up to be a creative, independent thinker, exhibiting traits we admired. The divorce opened up a new spiritual depth that only independence could awaken. The death of a loved one put us in touch with the inevitability of life's passages and brought forth a new passion for living each moment of our lives. Even in the in-between stages of feeling powerless, bereft, and grief stricken, we notice that allowing ourselves to feel, rather than avoid, such emotions brings us a deep and strange peace. We realize that it is wiser to be in accord with the river of our lives. How can we do this? How can we go with the flow?

The Power of Water

To go with the flow involves being relaxed with the process, accepting situations rather than trying to alter or control them. Taoism offers us a way to navigate through the elusive waters of following the Tao. The ancient Taoists loved the imagery of the water. We are to learn from water how to be. Water is unobtrusive and adapts to its container; it seeks out the lowest places. Water subdues what is hard and brittle. Water carves out canyons from granite and melts the hills. Water is infinitely supple and flexible, yet infinitely strong.

It seems ridiculous to try to push the river, doesn't it? The water running through our fingers, we cannot hold back or push forward these elusive currents. Yet in other contexts we try to push the river all of the time. I saw this more than once when I was the dean of a ministerial program in which men and women answered a call to ministry; it was an inner torrent that often stayed inside a person until it would no longer be contained, like the thawing of a frozen rivulet in early spring.

Pushing the River

Occasionally, I witnessed a student answering the call too early. The individual is not quite ready but doesn't know it. Such was the case with Charles, a young man with a frail build, who looked younger than his fifty years. He was in another spiritual program when he applied to enter our program. This was my first hesitation. "Don't you think your workload will be too heavy attending both programs simultaneously?" I asked him.

"No, I believe I'm ready now. I'm already fifty years old and I want to get out and be a minister before I'm an old man."

"Sounds reasonable," I answered. "Yet it may be wiser to give yourself a chance to deepen first, before you begin our ministerial program."

"I'm ready," he assured me.

I told him when the entrance panels were scheduled, but he said he'd be out of town. Could I set up a special panel for him? Since I had done so for other students, I said I would arrange for three ministers to panel him.

Charles's panel was unusually long, an hour and a half. At that time, the ministers called me into the room while Charles waited outside.

"We don't think he's ready," Rev. Mary Louise told me. "He needs a little more simmering."

"That's why we have these panels."

I thanked them and called Charles into the room. I left them alone to discuss their evaluation.

After the panel Charles came into my office. His face was flushed. His tie seemed too tight around his neck. He looked understandably dejected. I remembered my reflections about the river from my weekend retreat.

"You know, Charles, maybe the recent events — your missing the first panels and then the determination by the ministers today — are trying to tell you something. What do you think that is?"

He answered quickly, "If you really want to be a minister, don't let obstacles stop you." Charles then brought to my attention that in certain cases he'd heard that ministers could be repaneled.

"Charles, do you think it's wise to push the river? Maybe this is not the best time to begin this training."

Charles was fiercely determined to do what he described as answering the call of his ministry. Amazingly, he won the right for a second panel. The newly selected ministers passed him, and Charles entered his first year of ministerial training despite all odds. Throughout the years, more red flags appeared in the form of concerns from his teachers and mentors, but Charles charged on. At the end of four years of classes, internships, study intensives, and exams, Charles approached the final hurdle that would qualify him as a minister. In front of seventy-five student peers and ministers standing in a nearby grove of trees ready to congratulate the new ministers, we waited for the candidates to leave their panels and walk down the hill to the reception of the support circle.

Charles was the only student who failed to pass his final panels. The committee unanimously agreed that it was

necessary for Charles to wait another year and panel again
the following year.

It is a hard walk down the hill when you've not passed.
Some students cry. Others muddle through their disappointment as best they can. Even sincere hugs and prayers
cannot console. I would have wanted to spare Charles this
despair and humiliation if I could. But no one could. As I
watched this defeated man walk down the hill, the coloring
in his face seemed washed out, pallid, even though he
squared his shoulders, walked firmly, and managed a half
smile. I realized it was too soon for him to receive the gifts
of insight that I hoped he'd someday receive.

I remembered a time in my own graduate training when
I was determined to proceed despite the signs to desist. I
failed an oral comprehensive exam because I refused to listen to my mentors' advice that I take another approach.
Headstrong and defiant, I pushed ahead. I called it integrity.
Life called it defiance. It almost crushed me. I missed the
gentle tap, the stronger shake, the abrasive tackle, until
the final two-by-four stopped me. Sometimes it is nearly
drowning in the river that teaches us to respect the wisdom
of its ways.

Harmonizing with the Flow

The inner posture, or approach, that allows us to go with the flow
is deftly described in this poetic paraphrase of Lao Tzu's philosophy, a favorite of mine:

We must let ripen
And then fall.

Force is not
The way at all.

Biting into a sweet, juicy orange or marveling at the radiant daffodils on the dinner table reminds us of the exquisite perfection of the Tao. It's humbling that creative acts in nature come to fruition by a mysterious process, independent of our action. Why interfere with, or try to control, what already is magnificent in its own natural flow? Still, it is challenging to keep our hands off. We want to control, alter, and sometimes force things to go our way. What can we do to cultivate a way of life that does not resist the river?

BEING PRESENT. Perhaps you've observed a tai chi class in which people make slow and deliberate movements, breathing responsively. This meditative process gives us a clue to being present. We need to slow down our habitual ways of thinking and acting in order to be aware of what is happening in the present moment. If we observe the Tao, we can then know how to respond appropriately.

Dancing Down the River

My friend Sandra, tall and slender with square shoulders and brown hair that fell a little wildly around her angular chin, shared her insights about harmonizing with the flow. She was having a difficult time. Having been audited by the IRS, she found that she owed fifteen thousand dollars in back taxes. Her health practitioner business was slow and she had heavy expenses that were pending. In quiet desperation, she had a talk with God. She realized she'd been waltzing with God but the tempo had changed to a tango.

She knew she needed to switch her dance steps. Instead of lamenting about her situation, she shifted to accepting her new financial responsibilities. She thought of some new ways to attract clients, shifted her attitude about the IRS to being grateful that the IRS was only asking her to pay $150 a month. In the interim she received a partial scholarship for a conference she had wanted to attend but had feared she could not afford.

Instead of being stuck, she now seemed to be in the flow.

"So, what changed it for you?" I asked. "Being receptive to the flow?"

"I'd say it was more about being present to the rhythm of my life right now. I was responding in an old way and it wasn't working. Life was stepping on my toes because I was still waltzing. Once I became aware of the change, I could adjust my dance steps to go along with the current music that was playing."

"So, how's your tango with life going?"

Green eyes smiling, Sandra said, "We're now doing the salsa."

LETTING GO OF CONTROL. Probably one of the hardest challenges that westerners face is to *let* things happen instead of *make* them happen. We have strong ego drives that convince us that being in control, or in the driver's seat, is being responsible, self-determined, and in charge. This posture is not always the best approach.

Let's unravel some of these implications. Many of us may feel that meaningful work requires us to push boulders up hills.

We may also find that our meaningful accomplishments are difficult and feel like fighting the flow. Letting go of control does not preclude exerting appropriate effort. Putting forth extra effort when needed does not have to be contrary to going with the flow. In fact, it may be exactly what is appropriate. Just as a river flows in full force when going downhill, so there are times when it is appropriate to expend more effort. Completing a book, coordinating a weekend conference, cooking for a large family during the holidays — all require a great expenditure of effort. This needn't be seen as pushing the river but rather, as appropriately responding to what is needed at the time.

We need to be aware of the signs along the way. Life tells us when we're out of balance. We may be finishing our book or other project, and our families may complain that we're never home, or perhaps our health begins to fail from overworking. Or we experience roadblocks that may cause us to reconsider whether it is wise to go forward. Insufficient registrations for a conference or stormy weather during the holidays may suggest that we reconsider our positions. Haven't we all had times when the signs were there to stop or let go but we insisted on doing it our way? Acting contrary to where the river of life seems to be going indicates whether we are trying to *make* something happen rather than *let* it happen. If we are sensitive to the flow, we can adjust our effort and see whether yielding or acting is most appropriate. Ignoring the signs and either pushing forward or declining at any cost usually implies we're controlling rather than yielding to the wisdom that the flow of life offers us in each moment.

Can we trust enough to let go? This is not a reckless relinquishing of control. Yielding to the direction of a higher intelligence, the Tao, is a sagacious choice. Although it sometimes feels effortless, it is not always easy.

Lorraine's Story

A client of mine named Lorraine had been working on balance in her life. Her natural strengths shone through: taking responsibility, getting things done, and taking charge. But she realized her life could be more if she could loosen this posture of control. She had been working on developing her feminine side, the posture of yin. Over the months we worked together, she began to value a softer approach. I encouraged her to rest more, take some time off in between projects, and let others step in and take more responsibility. After a bout with pneumonia and meeting a new friend, she was enthusiastic about trying a new approach.

In a phone session between Lorraine in Vancouver and me in Los Angeles, we began with a centering prayer. After a few minutes sharing the silence, I intuited where she was on her spiritual journey through some images that came into my mind: I saw Lorraine at the helm of a motorboat that was coasting along the water toward the location of her new consulting position. I saw her give up the driver's seat of a boat that she was driving and place it on automatic pilot. In the vision she said, "Oh, well, the Universe is in charge." She then resumed a conversation with a man who was aboard the boat. What struck me was how interested and intent she seemed on her conversation. I sensed this marked a shift in Lorraine's letting go of control.

"That's exactly what's happening in my life," she responded in her usual zealous demeanor. "I realize that I cannot control the people I'm managing in my new consulting job. In the early part of my business career I thought that if

I kept my hands on every operation of the company I'd be a responsible leader. But it's impossible to control people's participation, their contribution, and the future. I can let go more because I trust the divine flow of events. I'm watching how things will unfold. In the meantime, I'm finding myself enjoying just being in the moment and watching this new relationship develop in my life. Letting go of control allows me to actually be present to what is occurring now, instead of trying to assuage my fear of what is going to happen later."

As we continued to talk, Lorraine expressed the joy she was feeling from releasing control. Having time for simple activities like kicking back to watch a movie with her new friend or taking long walks after dinner, instead of pouring over strategic goals or financial plans, gave Lorraine the balance she was seeking.

I enjoyed the expression of her delight, remembering how that same balance of work, rest, and time for relationships added an indescribable satisfaction to my life as well. Listening to Lorraine's story and witnessing the balance of yin and yang in her life seemed like a melody orchestrated by the Tao.

TRUSTING THE PROCESS. We cannot always see where the river of our lives is leading us. If we trust the Tao, then we will feel more secure as we venture forward into the unknown. I tell my students in classes that they can learn to be more comfortable in the moment if they remember, "More will be revealed."

Sometimes when we're feeling fearful we reach for certainty. We want to be sure we'll get where we're going. We may create a life that is small and predictable to avoid the discomfort of facing the unknown. Nevertheless, life shakes us into surrender. We may unexpectedly lose our job, become ill, or face natural disasters like hurricanes or tornadoes.

Yet from these unexpected events, new ways arise with which to approach our lives. New resources within us come to fruition. If we haven't learned the graceful approach of wu wei, we get a chance to do so.

Elizabeth's Story

On the last day of a ten-week Wisdom Walk class, Elizabeth sat down in her chair with a heaviness weighing much more than her petite frame indicated. A thick cloud surrounded her. Her eyelids looked half-closed, the ends of her mouth drooped, and her face was drained of its usual vitality. After a brief meditation, Walt blurted out his concern, "What's happened to you, Elizabeth?"

"I look that bad, huh?"

"Uh-huh," Walt nodded.

"I lost my job today. My new boss said it wasn't going to work out. She said, 'Take your time leaving but consider that your job will be over by the end of the month.'"

Various members of the class expressed their concern, shared similar experiences, and offered support. Still, Elizabeth looked disoriented and shocked.

She decided to come in for counseling. In our first session we talked about the wisdom of the river of her life.

"Elizabeth, what if the river of your life were taking you where you needed to go? What then?"

She took a deep sigh, "What do I need to do?"

"What if you're to do nothing, and instead of *doing*, you practice being receptive. Let yourself be open to your innate, intuitive knowing that is connected to this river of your life.

"If you had to take a guess about where your inner wisdom is directing you at this time, what would that be?"

"I feel like resting. I'm exhausted. But I think I should be looking for a job, so I push away my tiredness and make a list of people to call, and squeeze out energy to update my résumé and send it out. I've got to get a job before the holidays; otherwise I may not get one until the next year."

I sat with Elizabeth every week for several months. I suggested to her that she could take this time to experiment with taking another approach, one that seemed like going with the river of her life instead of against it. She agreed to it.

First she let herself rest. I challenged her to take no action unless it came from the center of her being instead of her head. She learned to distinguish the two and agreed to follow this advice even if it felt uncomfortable. I told her napping could be part of her day. If she felt tired, she should rest. I also suggested she get to bed by ten and let herself sleep.

After a couple of weeks of resting, napping, walking along the ocean, journaling, and keeping a low profile, she reported feeling a shift inside. Like an ocean tide that had ebbed, she was feeling an inner movement for some activity. That week, Elizabeth received a call from a potential mentor whom she had asked for some guidance in finding the right job. The mentor also invited her to be his guest at a business-lunch networking event that cost five hundred dollars a plate.

Feeling rested and ready to meet people, Elizabeth met some contacts that led to several job interviews. She was learning to ask herself whether yin or yang was needed in situations, and eventually shifted to an inner knowing about it.

"It's as if things are happening without my doing anything. Opportunities are happening to me."

"Maybe the river is taking you where you need to go — now that you stopped trying to control everything," I suggested.

Then the flurry of job interviews, which did not lead to any positions, stopped. Elizabeth was puzzled.

"What am I doing wrong?"

"Nothing," I told her. "The job currents are not flowing right now. Is there another area of your life where you feel the river may be taking you?"

"Now that you mention it, I've been wanting to move from my West Hollywood apartment. I've been wanting to invest in a condo on the Westside. But then I think, shouldn't I put all of my energy into finding a job?"

I waited for Elizabeth to answer her own question.

"If I trust the river, I should go with the flow rather than against it. Finding my true home has been part of my larger intuition. Maybe this is the right time to house-shop while nothing is happening on the job scene."

"You'll know if it's right if the doors open instead of close."

In the next week, Elizabeth looked at two condos in her

price range and loved the second one she viewed; it met all of her criteria.

"But I've only looked at two. I thought it was going to take months of drudgery."

"Does it feel like it's your true home?" I asked.

"Yes," Elizabeth replied without hesitation. "But another buyer has made an offer and I don't know if mine will be accepted."

"Why not? See what opens. If it's right for you, you'll know."

Elizabeth continued to report the details. Both buyers were asked to make a higher bid, which they did. The sale was still deadlocked. When her broker told her the seller needed a still-higher asking price, Elizabeth said, "No." She'd reached her limit. She released the condo and was willing to start from scratch, even though she viewed it as an exhausting option. Two days later, the other buyer pulled out and the seller accepted her offer.

After a couple of months of working with contractors, designers, and shopkeepers, Elizabeth exclaimed that this whole venture was a full-time job and that she couldn't imagine how she would have accomplished this had she been working or, even worse, starting a new job. Elizabeth was seeing the benefits of harmonizing with the river even though the ride was rocky at times.

"And in the midst of it all, I have a secret admirer," Elizabeth's eyes twinkled. I knew this was another of her heartfelt desires.

Richard pursued Elizabeth graciously. He chose lovely restaurants, surprised her with flowers, and listened attentively to what she had to say. Elizabeth felt respected and cherished, two things that were important to her. The relationship blossomed over a couple of months despite Richard's heavy travel schedule. Though he was often in a different time zone and sometimes on a different continent, Richard managed to call Elizabeth every night.

After Richard's two-week trip in South America, Elizabeth was eager to see him. She had missed him, wanted to hear about his trip, and was looking forward to finalizing plans of a trip they were planning to the East Coast to attend the wedding of a close friend of hers.

When Richard arrived at her door, she immediately sensed impending doom. His body seemed rigid, forgetful of how they once embraced in tenderness.

"Elizabeth, I'm sorry but this relationship is not going anywhere for me. It doesn't have enough passion."

Shocked and disappointed, she watched him turn around and walk out the door.

"He came back from Brazil and broke up with me," she said, letting herself feel the mixture of sentiments that go along with such a scene.

We talked about trusting the river. "Sometimes, Elizabeth, we can't quite see where the river is taking us at the time it turns. But I believe that the currents of your life are unfolding for your highest good. You have done so well being receptive, yielding to the flow of your life; now is the time to really trust that the river of your life knows where it's going. If your path and Richard's path are no longer crossing, can you trust that something better is on its way?"

"You know, I can see my choices here. I could try to make things different, try to talk to Richard, and make him see how wonderful it could be. But to tell the truth, I've done that in the past and it's not been good to force things."

"It reminds me of what Lao-tzu once said about letting life ripen instead of trying to force things to happen," I told Elizabeth.

We sat in the silence for a few moments, said a prayer, and called it a night.

Later, I thought about the times I had tried to force relationships to work, manipulate situations so I could have the job or the result I wanted, only to be sorry. I also remembered the inexplicable events when, without my intervention, my résumé was chosen over a hundred other applicants, or the love of my life intersected with my path at the exact time when I was ready to open my heart again. Or I walked along the sparkling ocean that somehow found its way through my breath and filled me with its radiance. Whether through despair or wonderment, or some mystery beyond our understanding, we can let go, and the river takes us.

CULTIVATING PATIENCE. Snow falls from the leaf at the exact moment that the force of gravity takes over. The willow bends into the strength of the wind. So, too, are our lives pulled and bent by rhythms of nature. In order to be in harmony with this flow, we must cultivate patience to wait for the right time to act or yield. Lao-tzu writes:

> Do you have the patience to wait
> Till your mud settles and the water is clear?
> Can you remain unmoving
> Till the right action arises by itself?

The Master doesn't seek fulfillment.
Not seeking, not expressing,
She is present, and can welcome all things.

In waiting, the situation can become clear. Sometimes waiting gives time for the mud of ambivalence, confusion, or indecision to settle. Being attentive to the right timing requires patience. Sometimes it is wiser to wait for our lover to come forth and initiate a compliment or kiss before we ask if she loves us. It is wiser to wait to submit a completed manuscript than to submit an unfinished one too early. At the same time it is sometimes wise to initiate a meeting with a person we're attracted to rather than letting that person go on with their lives unaware of our love. The Taoists would say, "Wait for the right time, by trusting your intuitive sense of the right time to act or yield." Often things take longer than our ego-self wants. We can recognize the impatient part of us inside that wants the answer now.

Charlene's Story

I met Charlene in a philosophy class I was teaching in 1979 at the New School for Social Research on the concrete campus of New York City. Her brown eyes sparkled with curiosity and attentiveness as we covered the mysteries of ancient philosophy and Eastern religions. There, in that classroom, began a friendship of twenty years that continues today.

During the years when we both lived in New York City, Charlene expressed over and over her desire for two things: to leave New York City to live in the Southwest, and to be in a loving, intimate relationship.

"All of the concrete doesn't work for me — gray, gray, and more gray. I want to be where things are alive!" Charlene would say, her brown bangs moving like the wind with every gesture.

"So, why don't you move?" I asked.

"I've tried, but I can't seem to make a living except in this gray city."

At this time Charlene was a talented painter who made her living as a scenic artist for *Saturday Night Live*. The money was good but the schedule was brutal, requiring twenty-four- to thirty-six-hour shifts of nonstop, physically demanding work — painting sets, working on ladders, and hauling scenic equipment.

Throughout the years, she had moved temporarily to other cities — Sedona, Arizona and Burlington, Vermont — but always returned to New York for financial reasons. In between, she continued her spiritual work, meditating in Zen temples, singing in gospel choirs, practicing affirmative prayer.

One of her spiritual teachers counseled her about her unfulfilled desires.

"You have to make peace with New York City and wait for the right time to come."

"Wait!" she exclaimed. "I've been waiting for fifteen years. When do I stop waiting?"

"You will know when the right time comes because the doors will open easily."

Finally, after seventeen years of being in New York City, Charlene felt it was the right time to make a trip to Santa Fe to look for a place to live. She had saved enough money to live for six months while she looked for work in Santa Fe. After she found an apartment in Santa Fe, she repacked her suitcases and made her way to the airport for the return flight back to New York City.

While boarding the plane her eye caught a glimpse of a handsome man reading a book. As she got closer to her seat assignment she saw that he was sitting in the assigned seat next to hers. She acknowledged the mutual attraction, but she became annoyed. Why did she have to meet someone now? Wasn't she supposed to concentrate on finding work in Santa Fe?

Their flight to New York was delayed because of snow and the plane was rerouted to Albany. On the five-hour bus trip to New York City, Charlene and Mac fell in love. Four years later, I married them in Santa Fe. They have been married for seven years.

At the wedding Charlene chose a ceremony that honored the magic of life that brought love. In the twinkling of an eye, you can meet someone and your whole life can change.

Charlene smiled at me at the wedding. She said about her new life, "It was worth waiting for."

Challenges and Progress on the Path

One Tuesday night class near the end of the term seemed much more tense than I had anticipated, given the wisdom practice, Go with the Flow. Walt seemed particularly annoyed.

"Yes, Walt?" I asked, attempting to bring the tension to the surface.

"I had a terrible time with the assignment this week. Going with the flow seems so contrary to everything I've learned as a man. I had this inner voice that kept saying, 'What are you, a weakling, just going along with things as they are? Be a man. Take charge.' Okay, I admit it. I don't want to go with the flow. I'd rather be in charge of my destiny." Folding his arms in front of his chest, Walt now seemed more relaxed.

"I can see that you're more comfortable with being in control, Walt. I'm not trying to take that away from you. Yet, can you see some benefit in developing your receptive side as well?"

"Have you been talking to my ex-wife?"

The class laughter broke some of the tension.

Jill spoke quickly, as usual, her light-brown bangs framing a face that personified enthusiasm, "I like it when a man does not always have to be in control and can be receptive to me when I need someone to listen. My challenge was not in being receptive but in taking charge. As I practiced the exercise, 'Is yin or yang needed here?,' I could recognize that I was being called to act, but I kind of fizzled out. At a sales meeting at work, our manager asked me directly what I thought were the benefits of this approach over what we used last year. I froze inside and mumbled something briefly. I realized I was more accustomed to assisting the team rather than being a spokesperson of leadership."

"That's a good realization, Jill," I answered. "It should not be surprising that some of our cultural conditioning would predispose us to favor the yin or yang polarity. What's the benefit and shortcoming of being deficient in either yin or yang? Walt? Jill?"

Walt spoke first, "Well, I must admit, it was more important to me to be right than be receptive to my wife's feelings or requests. At the time, it was too hard to be vulnerable — but here we're saying being receptive is a hallmark of strength rather than weakness. Maybe I would have had more balance in the marriage had I learned the other side of the polarity."

"Good, Walt; it sounds like you're being receptive and vulnerable right now."

Jill came out of her reflective posture. "I can definitely see the advantage of learning how to be more active and articulate. Somewhere inside of me I'm afraid of the power. But the truth is, I contributed to the success of that presentation as much as anyone. I'd feel more complete if I could stand up and speak out."

"It sounds like you're playing the yang role right now. Any other challenges or progress with going with the flow?"

Michael, a handsome man with dark-brown skin and long dreadlocks tied at the neck and resting along his spine, was next to speak. "I can see the value of balancing yin and yang energies and going with the flow within myself. But regardless of how yin I feel, I still have to show up at work at 9:00 AM."

"Yes, we may have parameters to work within, but there is much we can do among these. We can rest when we are tired instead of drinking another cup of coffee or tea to rev up for another cycle of work. We can get up and exercise when our body says, 'Yes, let's go to the gym,' instead of giving in to the habitual mind that bargains for coveted snooze time and one more hit on the alarm clock buzzer," I said.

Grace raised her hand. "I experimented with following the Tao with painting. I had read about how Taoists used the principles of spontaneity with calligraphy and other art forms. On Saturday, when I usually paint, I deliberately cleared myself of all intentions to paint a particular subject. I allowed myself to be empty. I would paint only if I felt moved to do so. I did some chi gong exercises that helped me harmonize with the flow of energy in my body. Then I meditated for quite some time until I felt moved to paint. Without my will, I picked up my brush and dipped into the colors on my palette — first red, then black, in smooth, easy strokes — like a dance of colors moving through me as me. It's hard to explain. It was as if I were the vehicle through which the paint dancing was occurring. I painted for a while and then stopped. Something within me knew the painting was complete. I then bowed to the canvas as my way of acknowledging the Tao. If I say I've touched the experience of wu wei, I know I've already lost it."

"Thank you, Grace. I feel we glimpsed the mystery with you."

❦

Taoism teaches us to live a life of harmony with the invisible mystery woven throughout the matrix of nature. We are invited to learn to have an open posture to life that allows us to intuitively flow with life's ever-changing currents. This way of acting spontaneously and going with the flow gives us a new freedom. Practicing this dance, we learn to cultivate patience, wait for the right time to act or yield, and learn to move with the rhythm of energies as they move between the complementary opposites of yin and yang.

Wisdom Steps

VISUALIZE YOURSELF GOING DOWNSTREAM ON A RAFT. This exercise is designed to give you more self-awareness about your comfort with letting go and trusting the process of life. Feel free to stop the guided imagery exercise at any time by gently opening your eyes and returning your awareness to the present environment. To begin this exercise, you can tape-record the instructions and listen to them as you visualize the process, or you can read the text and then close your eyes to do it:

- Let yourself go to a quiet place and relax, breathing in and out slowly and deeply.

- Imagine that you are walking near a river that is flowing downstream. On the river is a large raft that awaits you. Let yourself take a seat on the raft that has a comfortable place for you to sit down.

- On one of the armrests you have a rope, and on the floor you have foot pedals that allow you to steer the raft. This is the raft of your life flowing down the river of universal intelligence, the Tao.

- The rope is attached to the shore. It is now time to let go of the rope and let the raft take you down the river of your life experiences. Allow yourself to let go.

- Notice how you feel as you let go and let the river take you downstream. Do you trust that the river of life knows its own way and that you are safe? Can you enjoy the ride? Or are you afraid and feel that you are headed for disaster?

You can write down your observations or tuck them away in your awareness about your trust in the flow of life.

PAUSE AND ASK THE QUESTION: IS YIN OR YANG NEEDED HERE? To know whether to yield or act in any given situation, it is wise to pause, turn within, and communicate with a deeper level of wisdom than is ordinarily available to the surface mind. For instance, you are talking to a loved one and you are disagreeing about a particular perception. Sometimes a yin posture of waiting, holding your tongue, and listening with your heart is appropriate. Other times, a more yang approach is needed. You need to boldly state your position, take some definite action, or make a request. How do you know if yin or yang is appropriate? Pause, turn within to your center of wisdom, and receive inner guidance about appropriate action. The question will make room for the answer. Intuitive knowing can come as a bodily sensation, seeing a vision of the appropriate action, or hearing words of wisdom. Cultivating the art of wise action takes practice. Give yourself time. Notice when you hit and when you miss the appropriate action. Learning about our yin and yang responses can sometimes occur in hindsight.

PRACTICE THE ART OF PATIENCE. We live in a culture that supports acting more than waiting. Waiting for the right time to act takes patience. If you are waiting for a doctor's appointment, a bus, or a light to change on your way to work, notice if you are becoming impatient, and catch yourself if you are thinking that things are taking too long. Instead, sink deeper into the present moment. Take a few breaths to slow yourself down and harmonize yourself with the way things are actually flowing. Take time to practice stillness by waiting patiently. Enjoy the tranquility of stillness, which is one of the gifts of patience. By cultivating the art of patience you will have more skill with which to harmonize with the Tao and go with the flow.

CHAPTER EIGHT

ஐ

NEW THOUGHT:
Catch God's Vision of Your Life

*That which distinguishes the new thought from the old
is not a denial of this Divine Reality, but an affirmation
of its immediate availability.*

— ERNEST HOLMES, *THE HOLMES READER FOR ALL SEASONS*

Recovering from the stress of my lifestyle, even for a weekend, gave me moments to pause and ponder the crossroads of my life: should I continue as a minister and dean, or follow my dream to write? I felt restless. I liked much of what I was called to do as a minister — teaching, counseling, directing students in a ministerial program — but something was missing. One of my teachers once called it "divine discontent." Where was it leading me?

Much of my teaching involved helping students in the ministry connect with their authentic calling. We used a technique called visioning, a meditative group process, to help us see God's vision of our lives and ministries. In one class I both facilitated the visioning process and glimpsed God's vision of my own true path.

After fifteen minutes in the silence, I posed a question that opened us to the infinite love intelligence, or God: "What is God's perfect idea of my life and ministry? What does it look and feel like? What is the feeling tone of this vision? We open ourselves to receive this vision."

The first image I received was a scene from my childhood: I was a little girl, maybe five or six, and I was sitting at a table with blue, yellow, and green thick construction paper onto which I had drawn pictures and the words to a story. I was singing a song and making up the words as I went along, as I laced the pages together with strings of red yarn. The vision drew me into the carefree reverie of childhood creativity. I was playing my favorite game with my imagination spinning freely. Then the image changed and I saw myself from behind, in front of a large audience. Lights overhead shone upon me as I looked out into a sea of faces in a darkened auditorium. I was reading from *Wisdom Walk*, a book I longed to write and had been working on for the past several years. I heard gentle, nurturing voices call me affectionately, "Dear one, who makes our heart glad, you are here to write."

Then the image changed again and I saw an amethyst geode. Though deeply embedded in the earth's cavity, the crystals sparkled. It felt like this crystal was inside of me waiting for me to excavate my own inner resources. The luminous quality of this image touched me with its beauty, somehow transporting me to a timeless space. Even so, the next questions for the visioning unfolded effortlessly: "What is God's vision of my transformation at this time? How must I grow? What should I release? What spiritual qualities will help me at this time?"

I saw myself in front of the auditorium again. I could hardly recognize the slim, petite form, standing in a contoured navy suit. My growth included a lifestyle where I would have time to write and finish my book. I was to release self-defeating habits —

overeating, inactivity, and overworking. I needed to cultivate discipline and perseverance.

I felt it was time to close the visioning. Although it seemed like only a few minutes, I knew almost half an hour had passed. A prayer of gratitude ended our session.

In the writing and sharing time that followed, I had several insights. I was struck with the way visioning often opened me to possibilities different from my current reality. During the visioning process, the truth of the vision seems real, as if it has already occurred, even though the current situation may be quite different.

I had tried for years to carve out writing time while working a demanding full-time job. It was difficult to not be consumed by phone calls, emails, student panels, conference calls, meetings, and my other responsibilities as a dean. As far as being slim and petite, I was not this at all; my clothing was full and flowing, not contoured around my body. I was ninety pounds overweight. The vision was calling me to make my writing and health a priority. How could I leave my ministry? How would I reverse lifetime patterns with food?

I continued the process of asking for God's vision of my life and ministry. I facilitated visioning sessions in classes I taught and with a weekly prayer partner on Thursday mornings. Over the period of a year I recorded the visions in a one-inch, white vinyl binder. The visions continued to guide me, not only through the images but through their vibratory frequencies. I saw myself on a trapeze, clutching the bar above me while another bar came toward me. An angel voice said, "Time to let go." In another image I saw myself walking across an abyss on a golden bridge that formed beneath my feet as I took one step at a time. The same inner voice said, "The shining light of faith creates a path over the abyss. It is your fear that creates the threat of falling into the abyss."

In my external life I was a mess. Untangling myself from my position of dean and minister was one of the hardest transitions of my life. I felt overcome with grief and dread. At times I felt scared about being on my own without the security of an institution behind me. I felt guilty about leaving my students. Yet the guidance in the visioning continued to be the same. I saw myself floating safely down a river. The inner voice reminded me about things I knew: "God gives gifts when we surrender. Follow your path, which is unique to you."

The visions were pulling me, although it felt more like they were wooing me. I felt our mutual attraction. Who could resist this combination of unconditional love and soul purpose? Like fated lovers, my soul's purpose and I were destined to meet. The more I felt, remembered, entered the energetic field of the visions, the more I noticed their appearance on the physical plane.

The dominant themes that appeared in the visioning sessions remained consistent. They were always about writing and health. I saw myself nestled inside a sailboat, writing. The quiet solitude felt like heaven. I heard, "Shh!! It's a quiet place. Find a room of your own, a quiet place to write." Without consciously making plans to do so, I felt inspired to experiment with writing times. For several months I awakened at 4:00 AM and wrote for two hours while the rest of the world slept. Next, I borrowed my friend's sailboat and wrote for a few hours on Saturday afternoons. I noticed that when I carved out this time, I felt enriched by the energy field; it matched the original vision in which I saw myself as an author. It was as if a chord in the universe were playing the answer, yes. I felt united with my Beloved.

I watched my physical form change as the images about health continued. In our visioning image, I stepped out of the form of my body as if I were taking off a snowsuit. A younger, smaller me stepped out. I began to take daily walks, joined a weight loss clinic and support group, and weighed and measured cooked vegetables and protein at home. At the end of nine months I had lost eighty pounds.

The visions led me, like crumbs in the forest, down the path of my soul's purpose. Even the parts I couldn't understand at the time are clear now in retrospect. An invisible thread was woven through this canvas that I could not quite see during the process. A divine plan was unfolding. By following this order, I was able to bring into being the book you now hold.

❧

New Thought, a distinctly American movement that began in the mid-nineteenth century, focuses on healing and creating one's own reality through the power of mind and spirit. The founders of New Thought were profoundly practical. They all shared a similar understanding of spiritual reality and a passion for using it practically to create health, wealth, happiness, and most recently, by acquiring a global vision, to assist those in need around the world. New Thought's long line of predecessors include Ralph Waldo Emerson; Phineas Quimby; Mary Baker Eddy, founder of Christian Science; Emma Curtis Hopkins, founder of Divine Science; Charles and Myrtle Fillmore, founders of Unity School of Christianity; and Ernest Holmes, founder of Religious Science.

Getting Our Bearings: New Thought

NATURE OF THE DEITY. Referred to as God, the One, Love, and Presence; God is all-knowing, present everywhere, and all-powerful. This spiritual reality exists in, around, and through each individual.

RELATIONSHIP OF INDIVIDUAL TO THE DIVINE. Each individual can have a personal relationship with God without an intermediary. The individual is to God as the wave is to the ocean. It is believed that we are one with God.

HOW TO WORSHIP. Individuals worship in churches. Affirmative prayer, meditation, and visioning are common modalities of communicating with God. Worship also takes the form of applying spiritual principles in one's everyday life. Developing a consciousness in alignment with attributes of God is a primary focus.

ETHICAL BELIEFS. There is one power in the universe, God, and it is good. Ignorance of the true nature of God is the only sin. Thoughts create reality according to spiritual laws. Individuals can consciously use their thoughts to create the lives they desire. All people have the power to heal and transform their lives as well as conditions in the world at large. Individual lives are instruments of the divine.

THE SOUL AND BELIEFS ABOUT DEATH. Death is a continuation of life on another plane. The soul is eternal and never dies, but ever spirals upward in its evolution and expansion. Death is a transition to another plane of existence and is a time to commemorate and celebrate the life of the deceased.

What Is Visioning?

What if we glimpsed our lives, not through the lens of what happened to us as children, how our parents loved or mistreated us, or how the prevailing culture expects us to be? What if we saw our lives through the eyes of the infinite intelligence and love of God? Visioning, originated and made popular by New Thought leader Dr. Michael Bernard Beckwith, is a meditative process that allows us to see our lives through the mind and heart of God.

Why catch God's vision of your life? Whether we call it our soul purpose, the song we've come to sing, or our service to others, the truth is, we are each here for a purpose. Visioning helps us to connect with that purpose, the divine pattern within us. The visioning process helps us align with a universal intelligence that is greater than, although a part of, our own intelligence. A common New Thought idea is that we are one with God. By putting aside our own individual ideas we can gain access to the ocean of wisdom available to us, not just the small pool of our own individuality.

The visioning process, which begins with meditation and prayer, usually takes place in a group, although one can experience the process alone or with a partner. Visioning is a quest for spiritual guidance that is organized around a common theme — the development of an organization such as a church or theater company, or an arena of an individual's life such as right livelihood, soul purpose, or marriage — anything one wants to manifest in the world. A designated leader facilitates the visioning process.

Participants are asked to be receptive to the content of visioning, which may appear as visual images, auditory responses, or a feeling tone related to specific qualities such as peace, love, or compassion. After jotting down personal notes, members of the group then have an opportunity to share their experiences of the visioning process.

Preparing to Vision

While the act of visioning is a useful and relatively simple way of accessing wisdom, the process requires some mental and spiritual preparation.

IMMERSING YOURSELF IN UNCONDITIONAL LOVE. One of the most profound ways of connecting to God is through love. Unconditional love, unlike romantic love, expects nothing in return. As we open our hearts to the divine frequencies of love, we center ourselves in the heart, which is also the seat of intuition. Visioning is not a mental process. Rather, it is through the intuitive faculty that we hear, see, and feel the wisdom of God. Centering ourselves in love helps us quiet our minds. Immersing ourselves in unconditional love assists us in coming from our hearts, not our heads.

How does one do this? In the meditation period that is usually a prelude to the visioning process, we can evoke unconditional love in different ways. As we turn inward and feel into the meditative stillness, we can remember a time when we have felt love for another. Like basking in the warmth of the sun, we can let that feeling of love fill our bodies, our whole being, and radiate out toward the Beloved. You can imagine your own ways of being enfolded in unconditional love.

SETTING ASIDE ALL PRECONCEIVED IDEAS. It is tempting to impose our own ideas onto the visioning process, especially if we are attached to a particular outcome. For instance, we may have our own agenda about the ideal minister for a spiritual community or a strong preference of what our soul purpose should look like.

We have much to gain by putting our own ideas aside and opening ourselves to God's ideas. Students in classes are always pleasantly surprised when I suggest they use visioning to choose their term papers. Sometimes I have them write down their choices of topics from their surface minds. Then I take them through the visioning process as a way to connect with God's idea of their project. Invariably the subject matter revealed in visioning is deeper, closer to the interests of the student's soul, and thereby more engaging to his or her deeper inclinations. In comparison, the initial subjects, provided from the surface mind, seem flat, reflecting a perfunctory choice rather than a soul-fulfilling one. Being in touch with the revelations of the soul is the potential gift that comes from visioning, whether the focus is a spiritual center, right livelihood, or God's idea of the perfect relationship.

If we find that our preconceived ideas and God's vision coincide, great. However, more often than not, they differ. Often we can see deeper answers revealed in God's vision of a particular situation.

Revelations about Marriage

When meeting with couples to plan their weddings, I often encourage them to come in for a few premarital counseling sessions. Such was the case with Jeremy and Laci, who were planning a June wedding. At first glance the couple who sat before me were nothing out of the ordinary. Laci, about twenty-seven, was blond, with a small frame and wiry demeanor. Jeremy, who was heavyset and talkative, usually preempted with, "I don't want to dominate the discussion, but..."

Sitting on the edges of their chairs hardly looking at one another, they seemed to hope that the session would help them check off a few of the million details that weighed heavily upon them. Laci's mind raced quickly from one thing to another. Juggling a full-time teaching job and finishing her doctorate in economics, she was used to dealing with things quickly. She spoke fast and efficiently, rapidly firing ideas with few words. Jeremy was more laid-back, although he had his Palm Pilot ready to enumerate the details of the wedding plans. Both seemed tense and slightly irritable with each other. Something was off-kilter.

After coming to an impasse about what type of ceremony would best reflect their values, I suggested we vision about their wedding and marriage to catch a glimpse of God's vision of their lives together.

"Before we begin to vision, do you have any cherished ideas concerning your wedding?" I asked.

Laci spoke first, "I've always envisioned red roses atop a two-tier white cake."

Jeremy added, "I've always imagined a mariachi band singing Mexican love songs."

"These are lovely images," I replied. "However, just for now, lay aside any preconceived ideas you may have about your wedding and marriage. It's time now to be empty so that you can receive God's vision of this special occasion." With a clean slate we can more clearly see God's vision and tap into the universal source of wisdom. I explained the visioning process in more depth, and then I invited them to relax, close their eyes, and turn within.

After going through the questions of the visioning process, we discussed God's vision that Jeremy, Laci, and I received. The couple thought they'd receive directions about the ceremony, color scheme, and guest list. Instead, through the images in the visioning, the couple was steered in a different direction that neither of them had anticipated. One of the images Jeremy caught in the visioning pictured both Jeremy and Laci walking quickly, like characters in an old Charlie Chaplin movie. Laci shared that she saw a large image of their hands, their fingers straining to touch one another but failing to meet.

As we continued to talk about the images, the couple realized they'd become so engrossed in the details of the marriage ritual that they were moving away from each other rather than closer. They both felt something was missing, but they'd hesitated to share their feelings. The image of their hands straining to reach one another reminded them about the importance of their connection. With Laci in graduate school and Jeremy in a new job, the couple had drifted apart. But up until this point they'd failed to share their sadness and disappointment about this distancing.

Sharing how they felt about the distance between them and their desire for a deeper connection helped them shift their focus and hone their intimacy skills. The images from the visioning session became a springboard for creative action. They scheduled time with each other. Instead of living together like roommates, passing each other like two ships in the night, they committed to act like lovers again. They remembered earlier times in their relationship, before unexpected bouquets and surprise love notes were replaced by gluing themselves to computer screens late at night. The couple discussed and agreed on times when they would turn off their cell phones and laptops, and reserve time to talk and hold hands. Out of this closeness, they felt confident that the other details concerning their wedding would flow effortlessly.

Visioning helped this couple remember what was important about preparing for their marriage. It was not the details of the ceremony that needed their attention most, but intimacy and time with each other. Although they wondered how they could have forgotten such an important focus, they were also grateful that the visioning process had steered them in the right direction. Beyond their preconceived ideas lay the essential glue that would make their marriage meaningful.

BEING STILL AND KNOWING. The Bible states, "Be still and know that I am God." In the meditative stillness, immersed in love, devoid of preconceived ideas, we can be empty vessels ready to be filled with God's ideas. These may come in visual, auditory, or kinesthetic form. A metaphorical image may come forth. The lyrics to a song may be heard. Some simply feel sensations in their hearts or bodies.

As we practice the art of visioning, we learn to trust what is received. Most significantly, the content of the visioning has a certain vibratory frequency. Catching the vision is synonymous with experiencing a particular content from the visioning process, such as an image, phrase, or instant knowing, which somehow rings true or feels right.

The receptive posture necessary for visioning allows us to access a frequency that is beneficial, satisfying, and healthful. Receiving God's vision lifts us to an awareness that is above ordinary consciousness. Such an experience reminds us that we are heirs to the kingdom and queendom of God. Visioning helps us remember our true, spiritual identity. The vision is an expression of God that is filtering through the container of our individuality.

Gregory, a ministerial colleague of mine, received God's vision for his church as an inner knowing that didn't have a specific content. His knowing of God's vision registered as an inner conviction that love was the atmosphere in which congregants would thrive. Through feeling this love, he could be that space of love for others. Grace, a visual artist and a student in Wisdom Walk classes, received the transmissions from visioning as images. Sometimes these visions became the inspiration for her paintings. Other times, the content of these visual images received in visioning conveyed a clear message that inspired her to action. While visioning about her ministry, she saw people in a building surrounded by abstract paintings. She instantly knew that she was to start a spiritual center that combined spiritual transformation and expressive arts.

WILLINGNESS TO PARTICIPATE IN YOUR OWN TRANSFORMATION. Although we may feel pulled by the vision, we still need to participate in the transformation process that the vision demands. Catching the vision is only the beginning. Bringing the vision into manifestation sets the individual on a course of spiritual transformation. One needs to be willing to be the vehicle for the vision, and this may involve changes in lifestyle, thoughts, and character. It would be easy to think that the real fruits of visioning come solely through the visions, but the real emphasis in visioning needs to be on spiritual transformation. In a meeting I once had with Dr. Michael Bernard Beckwith when I was a minister at Agape International Spiritual Center (in Culver City, California), we spoke about his conception of visioning. As I sat in the cranberry and gold decor of his office, I thought about how the visioning process had prospered as Agape. Starting with twelve people visioning in Rev. Michael's living room, Agape had blossomed into a congregation of ten thousand members. Rev. Michael also was a leader for international world peace, including the Season for Nonviolence and the Synthesis Dialogues with the Dalai Lama.

I remember Rev. Michael explaining, "The real work is

transforming ourselves to be the vehicle for the vision. We are the place where God is being Itself." This usually involves us in releasing habits that do not serve us and cultivating spiritual qualities — such as discipline, perseverance, and patience — that support us and the vision. Dr. Beckwith suggests that members of the group form prayer partnerships. In this way, we can assist each other in the transformational process, but the willingness has to come from each person.

Diane's Story

I witnessed the transformation of a friend and colleague, Rev. Diane Harmony, over many years as she followed the guidance received in visioning to reunite with the one of the children she had given up for adoption twenty-five years earlier. I remember how, before each meeting, Diane had to confront the anguish of her early choices. Would her daughter meet her with disdain, anger, unforgiveness? If she was unhappy, did she blame Diane for it? Did she suffer from feelings of abandonment? Through her doubts and fears Diane continued to return to her original visions of reunion. The intermittent memories always returned her to peace. Her guidance from visioning assured her that she was going in the right direction. But she didn't feel that peace in the process. She prayed for patience; she prayed for strength. She received these in measure, and then she'd face another incline on her journey.

Diane had contacted a person who assisted birth mothers in finding their children. After a year's search Diane had learned that her daughter Polly had grown up in Chicago.

Diane wrote Polly a letter explaining that she thought her to be the daughter she had given up for adoption many years earlier. Diane explained that she was under legal age when she'd given birth, and her parents had made the decision for adoption. Diane proposed that she would call Polly in two weeks at five o'clock, Chicago time.

Diane received no reply to her letter. On the date arranged, she dialed the number and a man answered, "Don't worry, Polly is here. She wanted me to intercept the call because she is nervous. Wait a minute, here she is."

By the time Polly said hello, Diane told me that they were both crying. "I was shaking like a leaf. Even over the phone it felt like we were being pulled together, as if a heart that had been broken into two halves was coming back together again."

Even though Diane reached her goal of finding her daughter, and had gone through initial stages of self-forgiveness, the spiritual transformation required of her was deeper than she had originally conceived. During a family reunion attended by Polly and the three children Diane had later borne and raised, her inner turmoil deepened. Instead of resolution, she felt excruciating pain. She was still drowning in guilt. Why was she in pain when she could be celebrating this reunion? Her children were puzzled and so was Diane. What kind of person gives up her own daughter? She had internalized her own and society's judgments that she was a bad mother. Courageously Diane faced her own self-reproach. Something had to shift. But how? She prayed for emotional freedom, for the self-condemnation to be lifted.

We don't always know the form of answered prayer. It was certainly not Diane's expectation as she sat in church one Sunday morning at Agape. The guest speaker, Iyanla Vanzant, talked about the courage of birth mothers who give their children over to the care of others in the adoption process in order that they may have a better life. Diane could hardly believe her ears. The floodgates of her grief parted through her tears. Yes, she had wanted a better life for her daughter than she could have provided at the age of seventeen. This realization allowed for the deeper level of self-forgiveness she was willing to experience. As Diane healed the emotional trauma associated with the adoption, her healing became the key that unlocked the door to her success and prosperity in the path of ministry upon which she was ready to embark.

Although the path of transformation is challenging at times, it is also tremendously soul-satisfying. When we are aligned with the vision of God, we are aware of the divine pattern within us, which is encoded with a potential that naturally moves toward fulfillment. Like the acorn becoming an oak tree, we feel fulfilled in becoming who we truly are. With visioning, we tap into the larger source.

Principles of Manifestation

An essential concept in New Thought is that we create our lives through the thoughts upon which we dwell. Like a gardener who plants seeds in fertile earth and trusts the law of growth, so can each of us think thoughts and trust the spiritual laws of manifestation. Our thoughts take root and flower, just like seeds in the garden.

Early New Thought contributor Thomas Troward spoke of the creative process in gardening terms in his *Edinburgh Lectures*. With each idea that we plant in our lives, "... we must sow it, and we may also, so to speak, water it by quiet concentrated contemplation of our desire as an actually accomplished fact."

Popular proponent of New Thought principles Wayne Dyer introduced the same principles of the creative process in his book *You'll See It When You Believe It*. This book and others, such as *Creative Visualization* by Shakti Gawain, popularized the importance of visualization as a tool for creating the life you desire. New Thought writers Catherine Ponder and Louise Hay helped readers use these principles in creating wealth and health.

Visioning is sometimes confused with visualization. These are quite distinct. In visualization we use our imagination to conceive a desired outcome. We consciously direct our thought to a particular idea that we would like to see manifest in our lives. For example, we may visualize health, see ourselves with full bank accounts, living with peace of mind, surrounded by beauty. We visualize the life we want to create, and believe it will come to pass.

Visioning is different. Instead of imagination, we utilize the faculty of intuition. We begin by freeing ourselves from any preconceived ideas and letting ourselves be filled by divine ideas, God's ideas, of our lives. This becomes a process of revealing our authentic selves, the spiritual essential self that is one with God. Yet the principle of manifestation is the same for both.

We know that our seeds of thought will manifest according to the spiritual laws of cause and effect, but at what level of the self do we want to conceive the ideas that we will bring to fruition? Is it wise to create from the surface self or from a deeper level of the self and its mystical union with the infinite intelligence of God?

Samantha's Story

I have seen remarkable transformations in people's lives through visioning. Samantha was one of them. An African American pediatrician, in visioning Samantha saw herself adopt a baby girl with grace and ease. Although she was told that the road to adoption for an African American single mother would be long and arduous, she decided to embrace this alternate impression she'd received in visioning. She saw herself united with her adopted daughter in the coming year, and set out on her task of letting go of her fears and cultivating patience (which she knew she would need in child rearing), love, and compassion. About nine months later I was walking down the crowded aisles of a large store when I heard my name being called. I hardly recognized Samantha until she refreshed my memory of her vision of adoption. We hugged and I kept listening to her, but I could hardly take my eyes off her six-month-old companion, dressed in a pink sweater and matching hat. Looking into Samantha's newly adopted daughter's dark-brown eyes and feeling her stillness, I could feel the larger life from which she'd come.

Challenges and Progress on the Path

One evening, I walked into the classroom and lit the dark-cranberry candles that sat in the middle of a blue-striped altar cloth with gold threads running through it. Instead of the usual twenty minutes of meditation, I began this particular Wisdom Walk class by facilitating a visioning exercise with the fifteen or so students. Once I turned on the overhead fluorescents that, despite fore-warning, always shocked us out of the meditative state, we were ready to begin our discussion of the wisdom practice of visioning.

"But how can I trust what I receive in visioning?" Sarah pleaded.

"How do I know what is God's vision and what is my vision?" The random patterns of shadows and light that drifted across her countenance reminded me of the sky before a downpour.

"When I was in college I wanted to be a visual artist," Sarah continued, twirling a strand of almost-black hair that fell down her back. "My parents wouldn't hear of it. 'You have to make a living,' they screamed. 'Painting won't pay the bills.' Then came the stories about their almost starving through the Depression. I was eighteen at the time and frightened. I heeded their warning. Now I'm an accountant, and I can pay my bills, but something is missing. In the visioning I saw large, abstract canvases of breath-taking beauty. I saw myself standing next to them as if I had painted them."

I asked her what it felt like to see the visions of the paintings.

"I felt like they were celestial paintings, as if they were painted by the hand of God."

"What did you get about the transformational journey?"

"When you suggested asking ourselves, 'How must I grow?' I saw a large, green plant that was rising from the earth. The plant seemed healthy, sure of itself. I wondered if I was receiving a message about my own self-confidence," Sarah continued.

"Next, I saw portraits of my family on the walls of my home, and I saw myself taking them down. It was very sad, like I was disowning my family. I wondered if I was being instructed to re-lease my past."

I could see that Sarah was shaken. "How do I know it's not my own wishful thinking about being a painter?" she asked.

I looked into Sarah's large, owl-like, hazel eyes. "It sounds like the experience has also brought up some feelings about the desire to paint and the parental influences that you listened to earlier in your life. Now, you're older and more mature. I suggest you continue to vision and see if the painting images continue."

It's important to distinguish what we experience in the visioning itself and not confuse it with the feelings or thoughts we may have afterward. The fear and doubt usually come later and are more a function of a mental process than the intuitive one that gets activated through visioning. We can think of each visioning experience as a snapshot of a larger picture that is being revealed. Stay with it and see what unfolds. As Howard Thurman, twentieth-century Protestant theologian revered in New Thought communities, said, "It takes time to walk with God."

"What if you fall asleep?" Jill asked. "I'm sorry but I had a hectic week and I heard the questions and then the closing prayer. The middle part was a blank."

"Sometimes people fall asleep during the process. Or they won't get anything even if they stay awake. Don't worry about it. Try the visioning process again in a small group or alone. Keep a notebook next to you. It's great to keep recording them in the same place so you can see the progress or the fuller expression of the visioning that comes in parts."

Beth was often quiet in class. Her face was chiseled, distinguished. Even though she didn't use many words, her attentiveness contributed to class discussions. "I got a strange image of a tree — except I loved it. I got the sense that I was supposed to honor the sacred connection I feel with trees and to revive the lost art of workmanship to carve beautiful doors for people's houses. This is not something I've thought about in this way. But something feels so right about it."

"I resonate with how you and the tree somehow go together," I said. "You certainly light up when you're talking about it. No matter what we receive in visioning, it's important not to judge or evaluate it. Its gifts will reveal themselves as we continue to be open to them."

"Here's something more wild," Beth continued. "I signed up for a woodworking class this week, and I told my husband that I wanted woodcarving tools for my birthday present."

The class sighed in delight.

Donna spoke next, "Thanks, Beth, for sharing how your visioning pulled you into action. I wasn't going to share because I'm afraid of where my vision is leading me. You could say, I've been trying to hide from a vision that I keep seeing, which is my working with homeless kids on the street."

The class listened as Donna continued, repeatedly clearing her throat. Usually a class clown, she seemed fragile today. Her voice, often boisterous and outgoing, was softer. Our attention wrapped around her in support. "I lived on the streets for two years when I was sixteen to escape the abuse of my alcoholic home. I never wanted to go back, but in the visioning, here it was: I was on the streets as an adult helping kids who were living on the street just like I did."

Her voice grew stronger as she continued her story. "This week I called this organization that I had heard about called Kids at Risk. The executive director and I had a long talk and then she asked me to help. She thought that with my background — being sober for twenty years and successful at my job — I could be a real inspiration to these kids."

"What do you think?"

"I'm willing to do this, but, man, it's hard to go back and look at some of the pain of my life back then."

"What qualities did you get in the visioning that could help you?"

"Courage and healing."

The class laughed at the appropriate synchronicity of Donna's situation and the spiritual qualities she chose.

"I know, I know," Donna smiled, knowing she would have to face her fears and heal another layer of her past.

"The good news, Donna, is that you don't have to do this work alone. We're on the transformational journey together and we can support each other. A great tool we can use in class is to support each other as prayer partners. Pray for the qualities that are a part of your transformational journey. What visioning truly opens up for us is our cocreation with God; every step of the way, we are guided and inspired by the infinite intelligence and love of God."

Within each of us is an essential pattern that is a prototype of who we really are, in the same way that an acorn is encoded to be an oak tree. Visioning is a wisdom practice that helps us see our lives according to this essential pattern, which can also be thought of as seeing our lives through the eyes and heart of God. By following the wisdom revealed in these visions and partaking in the spiritual transformation that is required to fulfill the vision, we align ourselves with our authentic essence, which impels us toward fulfillment.

Wisdom Steps

PRACTICE VISIONING BY YOURSELF OR WITH OTHERS. Visioning is usually done in a group. You can also vision alone or with only one other person. Decide on a topic that you want to vision about: life purpose, the development of a creative project, or an existing organization such as a new business. You can pre-record the following instructions or have one member of a group lead the visioning with these guidelines. The guidelines and set of questions will assist you in the visioning process. Remember to empty your mind of preconceived ideas about any given subject and allow yourself to be as empty as possible to allow a divine wisdom source to supply the information.

- Allow yourself to be comfortable and turn within.

- Attune to the silence and the vibration of unconditional love. (Practice being in the silence for at least five to ten minutes. Then ask the following questions, allowing for another five to ten minutes of silence after each set of questions.)

- What is Spirit's vision of _____? What does it feel like, sense like, seem like? (Be receptive to the information as it appears as an image, word, feeling tone, or kinesthetic sense.) (Repeat this question with as many aspects of the topic as you would like.)

- What is Spirit's vision of how I must grow?

- What is it that I must release in order to be a vehicle of this vision?

- What spiritual qualities will assist me during my transformational process?

- End the visioning session by giving thanks for the opportunity to gather in love and receive this guidance.

Give yourself some time to jot down images, impressions, or auditory responses. If you're in a group, share what you each received in visioning. It is very helpful to hear different aspects of sharing from members of a visioning group to see what is unfolding. Every part of what is shared during a visioning session reveals a specific aspect of the divine transmission.

DESIGNATE A REGULAR TIME FOR VISIONING AND KEEP A JOURNAL OF WHAT COMES THROUGH THE VISIONING. Whether you are visioning for the revelation of your soul purpose, a new project, or your ideal mate, a good practice is to set aside a regular period for this visioning activity. You will find it helpful to keep a record of your visioning sessions. Feel free to capture the images and impressions of what is revealed to you. You will find it helpful to review these notes from month to month. It is common to have the vivid images of one month fade by the time of the next scheduled visioning session. Very often, just reading the notes from a journal session will bring back the feeling tone of the energy that is caught during a session. Don't preoccupy yourself with recording the experiences of your visioning sessions in a coherent or logical manner. Rather, stay true to the experience of how the visioning unfolded for you and members of the visioning group.

WORK WITH YOUR OWN TRANSFORMATION. A valuable part of the visioning process deals with spiritual guidance about how you can change, expand, and grow to be able to express the vision. Remind yourself about what you received in visioning: "How must I grow? What do I need to release? What spiritual qualities will assist me during my transformational process?" Then break down the larger scope into manageable baby steps that you can easily accomplish each day. For example, if you want to cultivate the quality of discipline, your baby steps may include a walk along the lake for thirty minutes. Today, if you say you're going to meet your friend for lunch at noon, keep your word. No excuses. If you're starting a new nutritional program, eliminate an item such as sugar or wheat from your day's menu.

Meditation or prayer, whether alone or with a partner, can greatly assist you with your transformation. You can record your progress and reflections in your visioning journal. Your journal will help you mark the expansion of your spiritual journey. Let the spiritual wisdom of your experiences with visioning help you unfold as the spiritual essence of perfection that you are.

◆◆◆

CHAPTER NINE

ALL TRADITIONS:
Offer Yourself in Service to Others

*I don't know what your destiny will be, but one thing I do know,
the only ones among you who will be really happy are those who
have sought and found a way to serve.*

— ALBERT SCHWEITZER, QUOTED IN
SPIRITUAL LITERACY: READING THE SACRED IN EVERYDAY LIFE

In some ways, much of the work I have done in the world — teaching, ministering, counseling, and writing — can be thought of as service. But I notice that sometimes I hit the true mark of service in my work, and other times I don't.

When I lived in the Christine Center, we would begin the day with meditation and a form of calisthenics that included specific breathing practices. In between breakfast and lunch those who lived in the community were expected to practice *karma yoga*, a path to God that involves serving others through work. Each of us was given a list of possible duties we could choose that contributed to the running of the Christine Center. We could cut vegetables in the kitchen and help prepare meals; work in the hothouse cultivating plants, vegetables, and herbs; or sweep walkways and loft spaces as well as do other general-maintenance tasks.

I tried all of these and found boredom — not God. I was still very much preoccupied with myself and interested in getting my own needs gratified. Still, I had to find a place to serve. I loved the library and suggested that I arrange the books into categories to assist the visitors to find books and authors easily. But now, as I look back, I doubt whether this work was true selfless service, because I was motivated primarily by what I could gain from the experience. "What's in this for me?" still loomed larger than my efforts to contribute to the community.

How one moves from self-centeredness toward service is part of the mystery of this practice. For me it occurred over several years as I continued to integrate the wisdom practices discussed in this book. Like an egg hatching, giving way to a new birth, somehow the larger concern for others broke forth in me. Twenty years after failing karma yoga at the Christine Center, I tasted the sweetness of selfless service with Christina, a student in my spiritual practices class.

Christina, an African American woman in her early thirties, was nine months pregnant, and not surprisingly, as the end of the ten-week class grew near, she looked uncomfortable in the straight-back pink-cushioned chairs that we arranged in a circle for our morning classes. The room was often chilly when we convened because the twenty-five-foot ceilings took a long time to heat. I would watch Christina fidget in her chair, two hands on her large belly, blanket around her shoulders, trying to get comfortable. The class claimed that baby as partly ours.

Although she'd been a regular attendee, on the seventh session Christina missed class. She sent a message with Ted, her prayer partner from class. Father of a two-year-old son himself, he had compassion for Christina's situation. "Her water broke and the baby had to be delivered a few weeks early." The class hushed. "But Christina and the baby are fine." Class members, including me, resumed breathing.

However, the next week we had different news. Christina and the baby had to be readmitted to the hospital because of an infection. Although I had never visited a student in the hospital before, I called Christina and asked if she would like me to come. I felt drawn to do this through a force of compassion that came from deep inside me. As I sat with her in the white hospital room, blue curtains drawn around us for privacy, I listened to Christina as she told me how she was going crazy just sitting in this room, holding her baby. Wrapped in white, the baby squirmed. He had one IV in his tiny arm and another one with a large bandage that went into his neck. "Antibiotics," she explained. "If this doesn't work they're talking about surgery, but they say he's too young for the anesthesia." Brow wrinkled, face flushed, she had tears streaming down her face. I just sat with her. Somehow, my heart grew as large as the room. After a while I asked if she would like me to speak a prayer. She nodded. As I sat with her and prayed, I felt this energy softly touch me from inside as if a light mist of spray from a perfume bottle were refreshing my face. Through the comforting words of the prayer and just being with her, my sense of ease was coming from a source greater than myself and deeper than my ordinary awareness.

Christina told me many times how grateful she was to have me sit with her. Her husband worked during the day and also cared for their other children. Other family members lived out of town. My visits, phone calls, and prayers interrupted the endless hours of waiting and became a raft she could ride across the dangerous waters of the unknown during her newborn's illness. Even the tiny infant seemed to fuss less as we prayed in the small hospital room.

Christina and the baby went home from the hospital two weeks later. Surgery was not necessary after all. As I look back, I remember that I felt this experience blessed me, too. Simultaneously I was deeply present yet hardly aware of myself at all. Rather, I was experiencing a larger awareness of what I ordinarily thought of as myself. It felt like a privilege to be of service. I was not doing this for me, nor did I want anything in return. The effects of service lasted longer than my time in the hospital sitting beside Christina and the baby. It changed me. How? It is hard to describe. What comes closest is what twelve-step programs refer to as "freedom from the bondage of self."

❧

The previous practices on our wisdom walk led us to find our inner richness. Our next step is to give it away. Service is giving from the overflow of the abundance of our inner resources, talents, and love. The complement to these, and perhaps even the natural expression of these, is selfless service. The path of service is confirmed by all of the traditions covered in our wisdom walk. Each spiritual tradition brings its own gift to the many dimensions of service.

What Is Selfless Service?

Service is the act of assisting others, giving one's time, energy, and resources to those in need without expectation of receiving anything in return. Examples of selfless service include feeding the homeless, giving blood, donating time in hospitals, fundraising to stop world hunger, and volunteering for ecological programs such as Save the Whales and Greenpeace. Being of service to others can also include random acts of kindness and courtesy — taking the time to give directions to someone who is lost in our neighborhood, helping someone we've never met whose bag of groceries has spilled.

Getting Our Bearings: All Traditions

All the traditions we have explored give service a prominent place in their teachings.

HINDUISM. In this tradition *seva*, or selfless service, is compassion in action. According to the Vedas, this path is called *karma yoga* and is as valuable as the path of knowledge.

BUDDHISM. In the Buddhist teachings, *sunyata* means the inter-relatedness of all things. *Karuna*, or compassion, flows from this recognition of interrelatedness. *Metta*, or loving-kindness, is the attitude that all sentient beings should have toward one another.

ISLAM. One of the five pillars of Islam is Zakat, or almsgiving. Muslims are required to give 2.5 percent of all that they have, including income and possessions, to those who are in need. Muslims also practice *shirk*, doing service in the name of Allah without taking credit for it from an egoistic point of view.

CHRISTIANITY. Christians, like Jews, were concerned with the righteousness of good conduct, exemplified in the Golden Rule: "Do unto others as you would have them do unto you." We also have the teaching, "Faith without works is dead." Jesus Christ's example of healing the sick and serving the poor provides a model of service for Christians to follow. Even the crucifixion is seen as sacrificing one's own life to save others.

JUDAISM. The word *mitzvah* literally means "commandment" but more commonly refers to a good deed. Jews have 613 prescribed commandments, which serve as ethical guides to living. *Tzedakah* is the Hebrew word for charity: giving aid, assistance, and money to the poor and needy.

NATIVE AMERICAN SPIRITUALITY. In Native American teachings there is an ethical imperative to keep the next seven generations in mind when taking any action that will affect the future, especially as it refers to the treatment of Mother Earth. This ethical responsibility is a service to subsequent generations.

TAOISM. In Taoism, service to others emerges from an inner balance that comes from a connection with the Tao. From this starting point, service progressively spills over to the family, community, the world, and the universe. Health procured for the individual in chi gong exercises, in turn, is directed energetically to assist in the healing of others. Reaching out to others in community is a natural progression of living in harmony with the Tao; helping others brings fulfillment. The community — all that is living — is considered a family.

NEW THOUGHT. This teaching espouses tithing as a spiritual practice, giving one tenth of one's income to worthy causes. In recent years, the New Thought movement has developed a more global perspective of service. A Season for Nonviolence, one of the projects created by the Association for Global New Thought, is an educational, community action, and grassroots campaign inspired by the teachings of Mahatma Gandhi and Dr. Martin Luther King Jr. to promote nonviolence as a way to heal and transform the planet. Service projects sponsored by churches, schools, and organizations throughout the United States and eight other countries include candlelight vigils; interdenominational spiritual walks for peace; peace curricula for elementary, middle, and high schools; classes on the nonviolent philosophies of King and Gandhi; and presentations at the United Nations.

Self-Absorption and Selfless Service

We may find times in our lives when selfless service is not our priority. We may be more preoccupied with activities related to ourselves — climbing the success ladder in our careers, raising a family, dealing with a health crisis, or finding out who we are. Sometimes our self-absorption can lead to self-obsession. We become overly concerned with our own plight. Ernest Holmes writes about how service to others can provide the remedy to what ails us when we are overly preoccupied with ourselves:

> When a man's thought rests entirely on himself, he becomes abnormal and unhappy, but when he gives himself with enthusiasm to any legitimate purpose, losing himself in the thing in which he is doing, he becomes normal and happy. . . . Let the one who is sad, depressed, or unhappy find some altruistic purpose into which he may pour his whole being and he will find a new inflow of life of which he has never dreamed.

On the Road to Recovery

After delivering a Sunday sermon in which I talked about service, I spoke to a young blond man in his early thirties who had come up to the podium to share his story with me. Robert identified himself as one-year sober. "I'm in AA and I'm going through a really difficult time. I'm in a relationship. You know, the kind that brings you to your knees?"

I nodded.

"Well, here I am in the middle of this drama with my boyfriend, and I get a phone call from someone in the program asking me to be his sponsor. I think, 'Oh, no, not now.'

But another part of me is telling me, 'Say yes. Your service will help him and you.' Service is a big deal in the program. So I said yes. Then I noticed that helping this newcomer on his journey helped me as well. The act of service replaced the self-obsessive thoughts that sucked me into a downward spiral. It's better for me to not be so preoccupied with myself."

Robert's story may be like our own. We notice that helping another helps us to shift our perspective from self-absorption to selfless service. We are lifted to a different part of ourselves that is connected to a larger source, whether we call it Higher Power or God. As Jack Kornfield describes it in *A Path with Heart*, "We know we are greater than our small story and our small self."

How Shall I Serve?

I saw a video about the biography of Mother Teresa, who devoted her life to helping the poorest of the poor. In one scene, she toured the nursery of the orphanage she'd established for abandoned children. She reached onto a table where about fifteen infants where swathed in white cloths. The baby that she picked up weighed about two pounds. She held the infant tenderly. A first-time visitor to the orphanage looked aghast at the tiny body that fit into Mother Teresa's palms. "Do you think that she will make it?" Mother Teresa looked into the baby's eyes, smiled, and assured the listeners, the visitor, and the viewers, "You can see the life of God sparkle in this child. She's going to make it."

Also known as the Saint of the Gutters, Mother Teresa's heart opened in compassion to all of those abandoned on the streets of Calcutta. "Being unwanted is the worst disease that a human being can experience." When asked how she could bear to see such suffering, she replied, "In every suffering I see the face of Jesus Christ. As he is in need, I help him."

Like me, you may find Mother Teresa's work inspiring. Yet we do not have to be a Mother Teresa to serve others. We may wonder, "How can I be of service to others?" Acts of service come in small and large packages, including common courtesies, thoughtful gestures, simple moments where we lend a hand — assisting another getting off of a bus or helping to boost a heavy suitcase overhead on an airplane. Service can include the helping professions, self-help groups, movements for social change, and voluntary service. We can find hundreds of small ways to assist others in our lives — sisters and brothers, co-workers, neighbors, orphans, and patients in hospitals.

Our call to serve may come spontaneously, such as helping an elderly person cross the street, or it may be a commitment made after years of deliberation when we finally call Greenpeace and ask, "How can I help?"

Meredith Gould points out in her book *Deliberate Acts of Kindness: Service as a Spiritual Practice* that you can trust your call to service by having one or more of the following things happen:

- You are surprised by what you are called to do in areas of service.

- You realize you can use your background, skills, and previous experience.

- You can serve right where you are.

Whether our call to service comes as a compelling inner urge or faint whisper, we can serve wherever we are — both outside our usual routine and within the activities we already perform.

Many Ways to Serve

I was on my way to a Sunday brunch at 26 Beach, a favorite restaurant in Marina del Rey, to celebrate my birthday with friends. As I walked toward the restaurant, a man driving a red truck called to me from his open window, "Sorry to be a bother, but would you please pull your car out of that spot so I can hook up the trailer that is behind your car and transport it to the Valley?" He'd been circling the street for two hours waiting for the driver of the car parked in front of his trailer to move out of the parking space into which I had just driven. Even though people were expecting me at noon, and I was already running a little late, I opened my heart in service to this stranger. He pulled into my spot and then waited for me to circle around the block so I wouldn't lose my parking space. As I parked my car, he smiled back at me, yelling through the open window of his truck, "Thanks a lot, lady. I really appreciate it." However small, this simple act of service rewarded me with a warm glow of satisfaction.

My explanation to my friends about why I was late stimulated a conversation in which they, too, shared their stories of service. Beth, a former student, spoke of her weekly service at a veteran's hospital. Over the course of a year, she'd spent seven hours a week visiting Vietnam vets in a hospice program. Trained as a volunteer with Compassion in Action, an organization that trains individuals to work with hospice patients, Beth shares the fierce commitment of the organization: "No one need die alone." Beth reported that she just visits with these men, listens to their concerns and stories, and walks with them on their journey toward death.

Grace remarked about Beth's modesty, "I think it's amazing that you've spent seven hours a week for the past year assisting in this hospice work. After all, you're working full-time, training for a marathon, and tending to your family."

Curls falling around her dimpled cheeks, blue eyes shining, Beth smiled, "I just love those guys."

A few minutes later, my friend Scott arrived for the celebration carrying bright-pink daisies and a basket of ripe strawberries from the farmer's market. "Happy birthday," he said, leaning over to kiss my cheek.

"How's Wally?" I asked.

"We've had our moments," Scott said, raising his eyebrows and tightening his lips. "He's a headstrong terrier and we have a battle of wills sometimes. I get to work on patience and commitment."

I explained to others at the table that Scott was caring for a terrier that belonged to his friend, Ti Li. Because Scott conducted his bodywork and chi gong classes from home, he felt compassion for Wally, who would otherwise be home alone for long stretches of time while Ti Li worked.

"It's so sweet of you, Scott," I said.

"It's good for me, too," Scott said, slightly blushing.

Throughout the brunch conversation, other acts of service emerged. Scott's friend Harold woke at 5:30 AM on Saturday mornings so he could join others in feeding the homeless at his church. While shopping at the supermarket,

Grace's friend Sandra had taken the time to explain to an elderly Asian woman how to dye Easter eggs.

Kristin, a former student in several of my classes, wrote a play about the nuclear disaster that had occurred in 1986 at the Chernobyl nuclear power plant in Pripyat, Ukraine. The disaster released as much as three hundred times more radioactive fallout than the atomic bomb of Hiroshima, and many children from the region still suffer today. Kristin donated all proceeds from the play to the Children of Chernobyl fund.

When I looked around, service to others was woven into the tapestry of everyday living, with its golden threads of soul radiance shining in dark places. All of these acts of service in everyday life reminded me of something my grandmother used to tell me: "If you want to do something, you'll find a way. If you don't want to do it, you'll find excuses."

LIVING FROM THE HEART. A quote from Lao-tzu has always stuck with me. His words speak of how service spills forth from an inner radiance:

> If there is radiance in the soul, it will abound in the family. If there is radiance in the family, it will be abundant in the community. If there is radiance in the community, it will grow in the nation. If there is radiance in the nation, the universe will flourish.

When we think of the radiance of the soul, traditions point us to the heart. A way to discover the radiance of the soul is to discover the qualities of one's own heart center. Many traditions point to the primacy of living from the heart. The Talmud says,

"God wants the heart." The Dalai Lama said, "The purpose of life is to increase the warm heart. Think of other people. Serve other people sincerely." When we live from the heart center, we become vehicles of compassion, unconditional love, healing, and peace. These unfold into service with others.

I deepened my practice of living from the heart center while attending retreats conducted by Brugh Joy. As we practiced attuning ourselves to the transcendent qualities of the heart center — compassion, innate harmony, the healing presence, and unconditional love — I found myself experiencing more and more of the radiance of the soul about which Lao-tzu so eloquently speaks. Since the heart center is meant to be experienced, not merely understood, I offer these meditation guidelines.

Heart Center Meditation

Reserve about twenty minutes for this meditation. Create a simple altar by arranging four red candles in a circle. Then turn within and focus your attention on the heart center by placing your hand directly on your heart. This will help you embody the transcendent qualities of the heart center — compassion, innate harmony, the healing presence, and unconditional love.

- Lighting the first candle of *compassion*, feel and be this caring about the suffering of others. Allow yourself to speak aloud the word, *compassion*, followed by what this word means to you. Embody compassion.

- Lighting the second candle of *innate harmony*, feel this peace that surpasses understanding. Speak the words aloud and express your understanding of innate harmony.

- Lighting the third candle of the *healing presence*, feel and be the restorative power that moves toward wholeness. When you're ready, say these words aloud, and express what the healing presence means to you.

- Lighting the fourth candle of *unconditional love*, embody this transcendent love that asks nothing in return. Speak out loud the words, *unconditional love*, and what they mean to you.

Notice how you feel when activating these qualities of the heart center. I often feel a change of consciousness that takes me out of my preoccupation with myself, opening me to a much wider field of awareness. My body feels more relaxed, my mind is clearer, and my awareness seems like it comes from the heart. By activating the heart center, I see with the eyes of God and feel with the heart of God. The words to a chant — inspired by Teresa of Avila, sixteenth-century Spanish Carmelite nun and mystic — come to mind, which I've sung while Sufi dancing:

> Spirit has no body on earth but yours
> No hand but yours
> No feet but yours
> Yours are the eyes through which it pours
> Compassion to the world
> Yours are the hands that are blessing me now
> All the praise to the One.

SERVING YOUR FAMILY. I studied psychology when I was in college, and one day I was talking to my father about possible internships to assist others. I was considering working in a pediatric hospital or a group home for wayward teenage girls. After I put forth these possibilities, my father looked at me directly and said, "Why don't you help your grandparents? They need assistance." My grandfather had recently suffered a stroke and my grandmother was his sole caretaker. I remember the shock of my father's proposal. Even though I felt inspired to help others, I hadn't considered being of service to my grandparents.

Although it may seem obvious that we can help those in our family, we may overlook this possibility or have conflicting feelings and resentments toward those we love. Still, families provide many opportunities to serve. If you are a parent you have myriad opportunities every day to share your love and understanding. The mother's kiss on a scraped knee is often overlooked for its power of compassion and healing in action. Family service projects such as recycling and clean-the-beach days can teach children that service is an integral part of living one's life, and can allow families to serve together.

What children observe about service will be more compelling than any message they are told. A seven-year-old girl observed, "When my grandmother got older, she had arthritis and couldn't paint her own toenails. So my grandfather painted them for her, even when he got arthritis. That's what love is."

Burden Turns to Blessing

Anne shared with me her story about selfless service after I gave a talk at her community church. She confessed that when her father had become ill in his later years, she had felt obligated to help him. After all, she was the oldest daughter and how else should she act but kindly toward her father?

Every Sunday she would get up, still tired from the long workweek, and get into the car on Sunday morning. She felt as if she were carrying her two-hundred-pound father on her shoulders as she made the three-hour drive from Ventura to Riverside, California. When she finally arrived she would greet her father with impatience or irritability. When he would ask what was wrong, she would stare at the floor and reply in a monotone, "Nothing is wrong." Anne stayed a few hours and then made the long trudge home, without enthusiasm, grumbling to either herself or her siblings about how unfair it seemed that she had to take care of her father.

Then one Sunday she heard a talk at church on service, and something clicked for her. "Service is an act of love for another. It's not really me who is giving. I am a vehicle of God's love. I am the hands and feet of God." Anne felt stunned. Her legs were like lead pipes. Her face flushed as if she had a fever. She went home from church that day mulling over her thoughts and feelings. Where was her connection with God's love? It was inside of her. But she was also so tired that she felt she had no more to give.

She told me that when she realized that she, not her father, was the cause of her suffering, her experience of service shifted. At this point in her story, her face completely changed. A light was shining through her as she told me about the difference in her experience. "When I visited my father as an act of love and service, my experience, and his, was completely transformed. First of all, I started visiting him every other weekend. I realized that if I was too tired, I had nothing to give him. Second, when I felt like a channel of love, I seemed animated by this sparkling energy that just flowed through me. Even though I didn't want anything from him, I believe I received more than he did. I'm so grateful I found the groove of service that allowed me to be with my father in ways I will never forget."

Anne's story reminds me about the paradox of service. When we engage in service to another without an expectation of getting something in return, we oftentimes feel as though we receive more than we give.

SERVING YOUR COMMUNITY. We have many ways to serve our communities, from assisting with voter registration to donating clothes to battered women's shelters. We also serve our community through work in which we already participate. If you are a teacher you can nurture your students' talents and listen to them respectfully. If you are in business you can provide your clients and customers with excellent products and services. You can treat employees and co-workers with compassion.

I asked Gloria, whom I'd met while she was preparing to become a New Thought minister, what she'd learned about service from the Jewish tradition of her upbringing. She has silver-and-gray hair, cut short about her face, and large blue eyes behind glasses. Gloria was generous with her time, helping new fellow students get acclimated to the program.

"You know," she replied, "I don't remember learning anything specific about Judaism and service. I just assumed it was what everybody did. I grew up watching my mother, who was always engaged in some project. She used to raise money and send it to the children's fund in Israel. Or she would be working with Hadassah, a women's organization, to help feed the poor or tutor children after school."

Rev. Gloria combined her devotion to New Thought and Judaism by founding Mitzvah Makers at the Center for Spiritual Living in Santa Rosa, California. The group is involved with a clothing and food drive that collects up to six truckloads of goods that they disperse to those in need. "We get a tremendous response from the community. People are hungry to give."

SERVING IN THE WORLD. We may wonder, "How can I, as one person, change the world?" We may feel such a task is impossible and therefore give up because we think our efforts are inconsequential. Margaret Mead reminds us, "Never doubt that a small group of thoughtful committed citizens can change the world. Indeed, it is the only thing that ever has." An example of this is World Wall for Peace, a nonprofit organization created by Carolyna Marks. She travels around the world helping people in communities to identify emotions and religious and cultural differences, transmute conflict into creativity, and use art as a way to express peace. Through her workshops she gathers tiles created by participants in the workshops and, from them, constructs walls of peace.

We can also serve in the world by responding to natural disasters such as hurricanes, wildfires, and earthquakes by providing monetary contributions, blanket funds, and gifts from the heart. Websites such as Church World Service Emergency Response Program have "How to Help" links for people who want to contribute time and money.

Fear of Service

Saint Augustine reminds us, "Fill yourself first, and then only will you be able to give to others." This makes sense. How can you give from any empty cup? Yet in many instances, service can lead to burnout. We give to others beyond our capacities and wind up feeling depleted, with nothing left to give. It is essential to balance service with self-care.

I once noticed that I was particularly sensitive to the importance of not letting service take a toll on my physical and psychological health. I felt ambivalent about service. I wanted to help, yet I also shied away from overextending myself. I felt that I was in the middle of some inner conflict that needed resolution. Since I encourage students to explore rather than ignore such material, I resolved to move forward into the tangled nest of mixed feelings. This led to memories about my grandmother.

Can You Give Too Much?

Watching my grandmother give so much of herself to others at the cost of depleting herself left me with a mixed message about service. Service was a wonderful gift to others, but it seemed to cause pain and suffering to the one who sacrificed. Somehow the thought of losing myself to only help others seemed like a dim prospect. Did I not understand service as my grandmother did?

I was in my mid-twenties when I lived with my grandmother during one summer when I was in graduate school. I hadn't been in such close proximity to her since my childhood experiences of lighting the Sabbath candles. Her apartment in Long Beach, New York, overlooked the ocean, and in the mornings I would join her on the balcony, where she would cut vegetables and I would peck out thoughts on my electric typewriter. My father had died early, at the age of forty-nine, from a sudden heart attack, and spending time with my grandmother helped both of us assuage our inconsolable grief. Although we didn't talk about him very much, we found comfort in each other's company, as if our being together were a substitute for being with him.

The Jewish holidays fell early that year, right after Labor Day, which allowed me to witness my grandmother's preparation of the Rosh Hashanah holiday dinners that would take place in a couple of days.

On the eve of that Jewish New Year, I remember turning over in bed in the middle of the night while gathering the cotton quilt around my shoulders to shelter myself from the cool, salt air coming through the windows. Eyes blinking with sleep, I saw my grandmother fully dressed in a sleeveless, black-and-white polyester-print dress carrying trays of baked bread and placing them under the windowsill to cool. Although it was three o'clock in the morning, my grandmother looked vibrantly awake. She moved quickly and efficiently, making use of her predawn time, free from the questions of nosy, though well-meaning, neighbors.

Framed by her white hair and her gold-rimmed glasses, her eyes were wide and shining. As our eyes met, I felt the passion that ignited her, propelling her, lifting her, at least temporarily, from the limitations that her arthritic body usually placed on her. She was infused with a great love and nothing could stop its expression — her service to our family whom she loved.

"Grandma, do you need any help?"

"No, *querida*, dear one, you go back to sleep," she whispered, her voice dripping with honey. I never saw her happier than when she was giving.

My grandmother was an artist in the kitchen. The holiday tables were works of art: There were two fish appetizers — halibut sautéed in garlic, fresh tomatoes, and olive oil; and gefilte fish for Aunt Dottie's husband, Uncle Irv, the only Ashkenazi Jew amid our Sephardic clan. There were condiments of roasted red peppers in garlic and olive oil; baked triangles of bread with sesame seeds, *biscohos*, which tasted like cake; and pickled eggplant and olives. The main courses were whole turkey, with assorted light and dark meat on a platter; roast beef; white rice and red rice; string beans with onions and tomatoes; baked okra with lemon, tomato, and parsley; zucchini, tomatoes, and green peppers stuffed with chopped meat, rice, and spices; *keftekas*, chopped meat mixed with leeks hand-fried on the stove; and coleslaw. The list went on, as the twenty-five of us — aunts, uncles, cousins — laughed, shared, and consumed course after course, receiving this great love in every bite.

In my early adult years I saw the aftermath of her acts of service. Her arthritic body would hurt for two to three weeks after the holidays, often confining her to bed. It was difficult to witness her pain. Maybe I felt guilty that my enjoyment was somehow responsible for her pain. Did love and service have to be such a sacrifice? Did selfless service imply self-neglect? I was left with a lot of questions. I even wondered if I had unconsciously talked myself out of being so giving because it seemed to cost my grandmother so much.

Now I see things differently. My grandmother's expression of love in service to her family was not only her gift to us, but it was also God's gift to her. It was natural for her to give. She embodied unconditional love, without even knowing what that was. Her faith and spiritual practice opened the door to the service that graced her with the freedom to express her love. She knew she would pay a price for her service and she chose love and service anyway.

Could she have taken better care of herself? Yes. In fairness to her, cultural awareness about exercise and nutrition was not as high as it is today. Part of her legacy is to show the importance of taking care of the body temple, an imperative for being of service. Was she also influenced by the paradigm of women who cared only for others and little for herself? Yes. Still, the true value of her example was to see how great a love can be that even physical pain could not deter. Love finds expression in service, transcends barriers, and bestows gifts upon the giver and receiver.

Challenges and Progress on the Path

One Tuesday evening, our Wisdom Walk class gathered for a discussion on service. Marla, a tall woman in her early sixties with short blond hair cut close to her head, seemed to pale and squirm in her chair as we spoke about service. I asked her, "Is anything wrong, Marla? You seem uncomfortable tonight."

"I want to scream. Every time I hear the word *service* I cringe. It reminds me of a painful experience I had at church a few years ago when I got really burned out on service. In the beginning I really wanted to help, but the more I gave, the more I was asked to give. I didn't know how to say no. It seemed like every waking hour was accounted for by a project at church."

Marla continued her story, describing the increasing role that she took on at her church. Because there were many needs to fulfill and because Marla was an excellent leader, they called upon her to assume many responsibilities. However, Marla had over-committed herself. She fed the homeless on Saturday mornings, prayed for people in crisis on Thursday afternoons, helped set up the Sunday service, and then taught in children's church. She served her spiritual community while keeping a full-time job.

"Marla, why did you take on so much?" I asked.

"At first it seemed manageable. I loved helping when I could. But then I crossed the line and I felt increasingly overwhelmed. After two years, I left the community. I couldn't take it anymore. I ran away with my life."

I understood Marla's concern and used it as a springboard to address the class. "Perhaps you've heard about or experienced what Marla is talking about. Several issues are intertwined here. First, with regard to service, setting limits and taking care of one-self are essential; without these, burnout is inevitable. Can you see any others?"

Azita interjected, her chestnut-brown hair falling below her shoulders, framing her Middle Eastern beauty, "I've also felt overwhelmed by overcommitting myself by saying yes to projects at my church. For many years I thought that I couldn't maintain a balance for myself. What I realized years later was that I didn't have a life outside of church and that on some level I was expecting my service to fill my needs of belonging and feeling appreciated. The lines of selfless service and expecting my needs to be filled got mixed up for me. Because I have developed friendships and have stronger skills for self-care, I think I'd now be better at serving others."

"Thank you, Azita; I find your sharing very insightful."

"I do, too," Marla added. "I'll have to think more about this. Thank you."

Another hand went up when I asked about other challenges. Sarah's face flushed and her eyes closed, as she turned inward to gather her thoughts. "How do I say this without sounding insensitive? I'm afraid to get involved in other people's suffering. I feel like I will get swallowed up. I went to a hospital to volunteer on the children's ward and I saw children in pain, children who were bald from chemotherapy. I went home every night and cried. It was very difficult to endure people's suffering. I felt caught in a dilemma. It's hard to look at suffering but also excruciating to live with myself if I look away because the suffering is too hard to bear."

I told Sarah that it is not always easy to face the suffering of others. Sometimes others' suffering brings us face-to-face with our own pain and fear. "Sarah, I'm glad you've brought up this important issue about confronting suffering. You are not alone."

Addressing the class, I continued, "Let me share with you Pema Chödrön's description of *tonglen* practice, a method for connecting with suffering.

- We begin this practice of taking on the suffering of another by breathing in their pain, fear, or helplessness, so they can be well and have more space to relax.

- We continue by breathing out, sending them peace, relaxation, or whatever we think will bring them relief or happiness.

- If in the process we encounter our own fear, tightness in our chest, or suffering then we can use the tonglen practice toward ourselves and the many others like us in the world who may have the same suffering.

- Then we continue to breathe out, sending ourselves and others the peace or courage that will bring relief from this suffering.

"Pema Chödrön teaches us an important lesson," I continued. "She says that, 'To the degree that we have compassion for ourselves, we will also have compassion for others.' When we use the tonglen practice, we can dissolve the armor of self-protection that keeps us separate from others. This can open us more to our fellow human beings with whom we share a relationship."

Sarah thanked me for sharing the tonglen practice and said she would try it when she returned to the children's hospital the following week.

Jim asked to speak next by raising his forefinger when I glanced in his direction. A tall, blond man of medium build in his sixties, he laced his fingers through his hair repeatedly. "Since we've been dealing with service, I've been feeling guilty about not thinking about others as much as I could. I feel guilty that I'm so self-absorbed and always thinking about myself. I've been so programmed to get ahead and succeed that I've closed myself off from others."

I nodded in response to Jim's sharing, as did others in class. "I can relate, Jim, and maybe there's another way of dealing with service that can be more responsive to you than guilt."

"Like what?" Jim asked, the clouds in his eyes parting a bit.

"Compassionate action. Is there some act of service that you might try in order to see how the wisdom practice of service might enhance your wisdom walk?"

Jim agreed that he would work on it in the coming week.

The next week Jim came back to class with sparkling eyes.

"Yes, Jim?" I asked.

"Okay, I did some homework. Not a lot, just a little." The class laughed. "I've felt an impulse to volunteer at this hospital I pass every day when I go to work. Last Wednesday, the day after class, I pulled my car into the driveway and asked if I could speak to someone in charge of pastoral care. I'd helped my mother recover when she had a stroke. I thought if I could help anyone who is convalescing, I would be happy to do so. Sister Barton thanked me for coming in and asked me to fill out an application. She said they train volunteers once a month and that she'd be calling me. I can't explain why I feel so excited, but I do."

I told Jim that he was on his way to experiencing compassion in action. "Let that thought for all of us be the segue for this evening. Goodnight, everyone."

꩜

We all have something to offer others in our families, communities, and the world. Living from the heart, as a vehicle of compassion, healing, harmony, and love — in service to others — is a gift we give and one we receive. We are invited to be what Mother Teresa said of herself: "I am a pencil in the hand of God, who is writing a love letter to the world."

Wisdom Steps

ASK FOR INNER GUIDANCE ABOUT YOUR PERSONAL CALL TO SERVICE. If you are not sure about how you may serve others, or if you'd like to discover ways to expand your service commitments, you can receive inner guidance. Here are some suggestions:

- Turn within for five to ten minutes of meditation. (I highly recommend the heart-center meditation described previously in this chapter.)

- Next, become aware of selfless service — assisting others in need while wanting nothing in return.

- Sitting quietly, ask yourself the question, "How am I called to serve others and how shall I begin?" Let the answers come in whatever forms they arise: a visual image or symbol, an auditory response, a feeling in your body.

- When you're ready, write down or draw your answers to these questions. Let the content of this meditation lead you to the activity of selfless service in your family, community, and the world.

ENGAGE IN ONE ACT OF COMPASSIONATE SERVICE TO A FRIEND OR FAMILY MEMBER. You may find that this wisdom practice is one that you do already. However, you may find that the awareness of compassionate service adds an extra dimension of loving-kindness that you consciously express in your ordinary act. Be aware of a need that a friend or family member has, and decide how you can be of service to that person. Your service act could be going to a store on the other end of town to get a remedy for your spouse who has the flu; it may involve driving a friend to the hospital to visit her ailing grandmother. Whatever acts you perform, check your intention. Rather than merely fulfilling an obligation or repaying a favor that you feel too busy to do, it is wise to incorporate compassion and loving-kindness into your intention. This will positively affect both the giver and receiver of service. Give yourself and others the gift of compassionate service and notice the changes you experience as you do this. You may wish to jot down the effect of your wisdom practice or discuss your insights with a friend.

SEE ONE NEED IN YOUR COMMUNITY AND CONTRIBUTE TO ITS FULFILLMENT. What pulls on your heartstrings is usually an invitation of where you need to serve. Whether it is a battered women's shelter, a pound for stray animals, or a homeless breakfast served at a local church, when you feel compelled to open your heart to a cause, a service opportunity is calling you. Take the time to answer the call. Contact the organization — spiritual, social service, or neighborhood watch — to which you would like to contribute. Find out how you can volunteer your time and talents. See if an orientation or any previous training is necessary. Make a commitment to participate and give your time and talents as compassionate service. Don't be surprised if you feel that you receive more than you give.

EPILOGUE: *Acquiring a Taste for Wisdom*

*Peace cannot be kept by force, it can only be achieved
by understanding.*

— ALBERT EINSTEIN

lato describes the journey of the soul. Before entering
the body the soul knows all things. But just before it enters an earthly existence, the body is dipped into the
River of Forgetfulness.

I find comfort in this story. The myth reveals the mystery
inherent in our wisdom walk. Our lives are about remembering
what we already know. In one moment we remember that we
have access to a banquet of spiritual wisdom; then in a blink, it's
gone and we forget our spiritual legacy.

I do this all the time; both forget and remember, neglect to
apply wisdom in my life and then — sometimes quickly, sometimes not — remember the benefit of using the wisdom practices
in my life. Recognizing the mystery contained in our wisdom walk
helps us accept this elusive cycle. Whenever we get swept away by

forgetfulness, we can simply remind ourselves of what we already know. We don't need to berate ourselves. Forgetting is part of the process until the wisdom practices become a way of life. Compassion, not self-criticism, is what we need when we slip into old patterns — as I, myself, did toward the end of writing this book.

One Friday night I found myself crispy around the edges, not totally burned out but sufficiently seared to have a mini-meltdown. I felt tired, edgy, and off center. I can always tell when my wisdom walk is slipping: the grounded serenity I feel when I engage in the wisdom practices dissipates.

I'd received word from my assistant that my computer system had crashed before every file had been backed up. Reacting from depleted reserves, I felt as if I myself were crashing. In a flash, an old part of me took the driver's seat, and as if it were a sane choice, I dialed the phone to order a pizza. I had not had pizza in a year, since I'd lost eighty pounds. Yet I stood there, one finger in the yellow pages, the other dialing the number. I called two restaurants: One pizza place wouldn't deliver; the other had a phone problem and I couldn't get through even though I dialed the phone several times. It was enough of a time delay to return to another part of myself.

With good inner counsel, I took myself to a small gym in the marina that is often empty. I pounded out a few rounds on the stationary bike, skipped the treadmill, and after a long, hot shower, went straight to the sauna.

In the dry heat I felt my shoulders drop, my breath slow down, and my racing mind switch from work matters to soul nourishment. I began to review the wisdom practices that always bring me sanely back to myself.

1. CREATE A HOME ALTAR. I took off my red stone bracelet and shaped it into a circle to remind myself of the unity of

life. I placed my wedding band in the center of the red beads and claimed that at my center I was connected to the infinite. I laughed to myself, *If I can create an altar while wearing only a towel in a sauna, anyone can create an altar anywhere.*

2. MEDITATE AND FIND PEACE. I closed my eyes and began to watch my breath, focusing only on breathing in and out. I felt my mind begin to quiet down like a clock winding down.

3. SURRENDER TO PRAYER. I whispered audibly, "Thank you for these moments of great peace as I pause in a busy week."

4. FORGIVE YOURSELF AND OTHERS. I said to myself aloud, "I forgive you for overworking this week and getting out of balance."

5. MAKE TIME FOR THE SABBATH. I committed to really take Monday off, including putting down my pen. I would suggest a family Sabbath walk and give myself extra sleep in the morning.

6. LET NATURE BE YOUR TEACHER. The heat of the sauna was conducive to inner work. I closed my eyes and saw a deer walk across my inner awareness. "Walk gently," the deer counseled. I took this as a reminder to slow down and be kind to myself.

7. GO WITH THE FLOW. "Okay, I've been going too fast," I admitted. Not resisting, I let myself pull back to get into balance. After a lot of yang, I need more yin activities. I would give myself the weekend to rest as much as I could.

8. CATCH GOD'S VISION OF YOUR LIFE. Closing my eyes again, I saw myself at a book signing — published author. An inner voice said, "Keep working on the book. You need to continue writing as a priority."

9. OFFER YOURSELF IN SERVICE TO OTHERS. I decided to
   call my brother and lend an ear to his challenges with his
   teenage sons. I would keep in touch with family.

   In less than an hour, I had reviewed some essentials from the
wisdom practices of *Wisdom Walk*, and I felt much better.

My Wisdom Walk Journey

It has been my experience that the wisdom walk deepens with
time. My early altars were perfunctory but later became places of
beauty where I could sit in front of them and really feel a shift
of consciousness that connected me with the divine. It used to
take me a long time to get into a groove of meditation that had my
mind quiet down with fewer runaway thoughts. Now I can reach
a place of inner peace much more quickly, even in the midst of a
chaotic day.

   Some practices drop off only to reappear with more vigor. If
my schedule gets demanding and I skip making time for the Sabbath, the absence of such time creates a greater fire and commitment for me to put that wisdom practice back into my life. It's
obvious when I'm missing Sabbath time: I don't feel as well as
when I've taken time to enjoy a day off from work.

   I've also learned to recognize situations that can threaten my
wisdom walk — an overly busy schedule, stress from deadlines,
or traveling that disrupts the groove of my practice. During times
like these I've learned to increase the wisdom practices rather than
decrease them. Packing less into my work time, preplanning to
meet deadlines, and mentally rehearsing how wisdom practices can
integrate with travel have helped me deal with these challenges.

   What I love about my wisdom walk is the balance I feel
within my soul when I use these tools. I find that I need regular

doses of wisdom practices throughout the day and week to keep my balance and connect with the larger source of spiritual radiance of which I am a part. In the same way that I've learned to maintain an even blood sugar level by eating nutritious meals at regular intervals throughout the day, I maintain a serenity of soul as I engage in wisdom practices — as I create a sanctuary with an altar, meditate, pray, forgive myself and others, go with the flow, connect with God's spiritual vision of my life, and offer myself in service to others. In the same way that we feed our bodies to reap the nutritional benefits, we have to feed our souls. Eating well, walking, resting, and nourishing the soul are the components of living wisely.

I know when I am hitting the bull's-eye of my wisdom walk, because my life sings. Yet even when I miss the shot, I have the tools to try again and again. Every time I participate in a wisdom practice, I, and the people around me, benefit.

The Banquet

I always find the final class of Wisdom Walk to be bittersweet. It's time for the group to say good-bye after sharing our intimate journey; it's also a delight to be at the end of class, aware of insights and wisdom gained along the way. We're different as a result of our wisdom walk together.

I was mulling over these thoughts as I walked into the room of one Wisdom Walk class where we'd met for the past ten weeks. This night was different: The seminar tables upon which we'd usually scattered class handouts, notes, water bottles, and coffee mugs had been transformed into a banquet of multiethnic foods. Strewn upon every corner of the purple tablecloth trimmed in gold was a different delicacy representing the spiritual traditions

we'd studied. Samosas, tofu stir-fry with snow peas, Middle Eastern hummus and tabbouleh, potato latkes, blue-corn chips and
fry bread, pad thai, vegan tofu loaves — all welcomed us to a delicious feast.

I had always marveled that so many people enjoyed ethnic
foods, but when it came to the spiritual traditions from which
these foods derived, they were less inclined to take a bite. Not so
with those who'd taken a wisdom walk. Now, the banquet table was
not only about feeding our bodies; because we'd also acquired a
taste for wisdom, we'd learned the benefits of nourishing our souls
as well. Combining body and soul made the journey complete and
satisfied a deeper hunger that food alone could not satiate.

As class continued we delighted in tasting dish after dish,
laughing and joking as we reflected on the highlights of our wisdom walk. Grace spoke first, purple highlights in her hair framing
her face. "I brought the Indian delicacy, samosas, representing
the Hindu tradition. Aren't these deep-fried triangles filled with
peas and potatoes yummy?" she said, popping the last bite of one
into her mouth. "I love that so many traditions offer us wisdom.
My favorite practice is creating an altar. I delight in bringing a
sense of the sacred into my living and working environments."

Sarah was next. "Well, I thought I knew about these cultures,
but seeing them all together has been profound. In different ways
these spiritual traditions are saying the same thing."

Walt interjected, "Even I can see that."

"Tell us more, Walt, about what you see," I instructed.

"Well, I felt that a oneness permeated the traditions. All spiritual traditions talk about God in some way or another, how our
lives are part of something larger than going to work every day,
managing sales accounts, and figuring out the bottom line for that
day. There's more to life than the day-to-day things. There's a
larger sense."

"Great, Walt — well stated," I said.

Donna wiped her mouth and swallowed a last bite. "For me, it's the Sabbath. Did everyone taste the potato latkes I brought? They're sometimes called potato pancakes, and they're great with sour cream or applesauce. Getting back to the Sabbath, now my friends understand that on Friday nights my phones are off. I've gotten a lot of complaints, but I'm not budging; I love and protect my Sabbath time."

Renee picked up a tray of noodles and passed it around the table for anyone who wanted a second helping. "I brought my favorite, tofu pad thai — noodles, spicy peanut sauce, and scallions topped with chopped nuts. Since many in Thailand practice Taoism, my dish represents that tradition. Here's my version of going with the flow: Before this class, I turned my back on most spiritual traditions because I didn't like their treatment of women. What's different for me is that now I realize I don't have to reject the wisdom the traditions offer. I can appreciate the Jewish Sabbath, the Muslim devotion to prayer, and Christian forgiveness *and* still think there's room for improvement in how these traditions can honor women and their contributions." Renee's smile filled the room. We smiled with her.

Victoria wore a beige and maroon flowing skirt and matching blouse. The silky fabric shone under the overhead fluorescents as she stood up. "The dip you're scooping up with those blue-corn chips is hummus, garbanzo beans mixed with tahini and garlic, a food from the Middle East, where many follow Islam and Judaism. In order to really convey what I have benefited from studying the world's great spiritual traditions, I want everyone to join me on the dance floor." Victoria pointed to the wooden floor area on the other side of the room.

As we walked across the gray carpet to the shellacked planks, Victoria continued, "All around the world people are forming circles and dancing for world peace. These dances draw from all spiritual traditions around the world and celebrate their under-lying unity. Don't worry, you don't need musical or dance experience. Everyone is welcome."

According to Victoria's instructions, we held hands and walked clockwise in a circle. "As we walk together in this circle, we join the timeless tradition of sacred dance, in which people throughout the ages have celebrated seasonal changes and life passages through movement, music, and song."

We continued to circle at a quickened pace, singing the names of the divine from diverse spiritual traditions in this universal dance of worship. Then Victoria had us stand still and extend our hands toward the center of the circle, singing the chant several times, "Toward the One, toward the One, toward the One."

I realized that our wisdom walk together was culminating in this dance that honored and celebrated all traditions. Since each person in class brought to the banquet food that represented a different spiritual tradition, it was as if our dance placed Hindu next to Muslim, Jew next to Christian, Taoist next to Buddhist, Native American next to New Thought, and so on. Were we a microcosm of a world that could appreciate the wisdom that ran through diverse spiritual traditions? If others around the world took this wisdom walk, could we look forward to a universal dance of peace? We had done so in this class. We worked out our disagreements, looked within ourselves to see our part in the conflicts, listened to views divergent from our own, and then came to a banquet where we appreciated the food and spiritual nourishment each tradition brought to the table.

Our dance ended as we faced each other, looked into each other's eyes, and bowed to each other, hands clasped together as if we were praying. "*Namaste*," we told each other. "May the spirit in me honor the spirit in you — *namaste*."

"Let's close out our class with the peace song," I offered. Then, glancing over at Renee, I added, "With the gender-neutral lyrics."

As Victoria led us in the song, I looked around the circle at people of different shapes, races, and faiths holding hands and singing, "Let there be peace on earth and let it begin with me."

I thought about Gandhi's courage to be a peaceful presence in the world and his invitation to us: "You must be the change you want to see in the world." I prayed that our wisdom walk would lead us to peace.

⧉

APPENDIX 1: *Tools for the Journey*

long your wisdom walk you may read a chapter that inadvertently triggers an inner land mine by provoking intense feelings. This section offers you additional tools to help you navigate through what might feel like difficult material. In what follows, you will receive:

- A definition and some examples of dealing with charged material

- Specific journal questions to use as you explore your own spiritual origins and confront beliefs or prejudices about other spiritual traditions

- Wisdom Steps to help you discover your feelings, share your story with others, and cultivate a nurturing inner voice

Dealing with Charged Material

Charged material refers to unresolved or partially unconscious issues, usually rooted in your personal history or in attitudes you were taught early in life. When encountering a specific word (for example, *God* or *Jesus*) or reading about a particular tradition (for example, Islam, Judaism, or Christianity), you may find yourself experiencing resistance, anger, or defensiveness. Such a reaction may prevent you from taking in the wisdom available in the practice.

From dealing with my own charges and assisting my students in Wisdom Walk classes, I know that this process is challenging but rewarding. As you become aware of your "charge," you may initially want to avoid it or deny it is happening. You may prefer any distraction to dealing with the uncomfortable feelings or memories that the charge evokes. However, I urge you to stay present with these feelings and let them lead you to remembered events. The process of deactivating the charge will set you free, help you heal some misunderstandings about the original situation, and offer you an opportunity to reclaim and appreciate your own or another's spiritual tradition.

Sometimes we are not aware of charged material, and other times we want to gain more awareness about our own beliefs and attitudes. These tools can satisfy all of these accounts.

Using the journal tools and Wisdom Steps in the sections that follow will help you deactivate your charges. You may find the following format helpful:

1. Acknowledge that you have been triggered by the material and that you are experiencing a charged reaction.

2. Identify whether the charge pertains to your own spiritual origins (Tool #1), another spiritual tradition (Tool #2), or to having been raised with no spiritual tradition (Tool #3).

3. Read the directions and write the answers to the journal questions in the appropriate section.

Tool #1: Exploring Your Spiritual Origins

PURPOSE. Take this journey to explore beliefs about the spiritual tradition in which you were raised. Examining these ideas may bring up charged material as well as new perspectives about your own, or your family's, cherished values. Reexamining your beliefs can give you a renewed appreciation of what your own tradition offers you.

JOURNAL QUESTIONS. The following questions can assist you in exploring unresolved feelings and unexamined beliefs about your own spiritual origins, including having been raised with no spiritual tradition.

1. To begin, read the question and let yourself remember and reflect for five minutes before writing.

2. Then reserve a block of time, fifteen to twenty minutes, to write your answer to one or two questions.

3. Repeat this process until you answer all questions. Feel free to adapt the process to your own needs.

IF YOU WERE RAISED
WITH ONE OR MORE SPIRITUAL TRADITIONS

1. How do you describe the spiritual tradition(s) in which you were raised (for example, conservative, liberal, one tradition, or exposure to many traditions)?

2. What benefits have you derived from the spiritual tradition of your birth?

3. What experiences within your spiritual tradition elicit strong feelings or reactions (for example, anger, fear, guilt, or sadness; as well as joy, reverence, health, or spiritual inspiration)?

4. What disadvantages, if any, have you experienced from your own religion of origin? What negativity, if any, do you feel toward your religion?

Making Peace

I did not always appreciate my Jewish heritage. While living in New York City, I never had to come to terms with having or not having a Jewish identity. Participating in holiday dinners with my Jewish relatives seemed sufficient to qualify as being Jewish. Simply living in New York City seemed Jewish enough since Jewishness was included in the culture. Local radio stations guided travelers home through traffic reports on the High Holy Days. "If you want to arrive home before sundown for Rosh Hashanah, give yourself extra time. Happy New Year, everyone." Being Jewish had a place in the multicultural pulse of the Big Apple. I often stated, "I was born into Judaism." In the meantime, I was exploring yoga, meditation, and the wisdom of Eastern traditions, and I identified more with these than with Judaism as an organized religion.

It wasn't until my first teaching job, at the University of Kentucky, that I had to confront not having a Jewish identity. One Christmas in 1982 I was driving to dinner with a new friend I'd met on campus. Courtney, a native of Kentucky and returning adult student, was a dark-haired beauty with cobalt-blue eyes and a deep southern drawl. As we drove past a house with an electric-red candelabra and white candles, I felt joyful. "Oh, look, a Chanukah menorah. Isn't that nice?"

My friend shook her head, "Oh, no, those are Christmas candles. Believe me, no one would put out a Jewish symbol on their front porch."

I looked at her with surprise, "Why is that?"

She said, "The South doesn't look kindly at Jews. Many people still think that Jews killed Jesus and have horns on their head. No, you're not going to see outwardly displayed signs of Judaism in Lexington. Maybe at the U, but not on the streets."

Her words made my stomach churn. Was it my responsibility to defend the Jews? No, Jews don't have horns. We are physically like everyone else. But I'd never felt this "we" with Judaism. My identity wasn't tied to the religion of my birth. I just went to holiday dinners to please my grandmothers, whom I loved.

I missed that radio announcers in the Bluegrass State didn't mention the High Holy Days. I felt sad that I hadn't heard a friendly "Happy New Year" in September or the familiar Hebrew sounds of Rosh Hashanah or Yom Kippur. And now, there were no menorahs on windowsills to celebrate Chanukah. I had taken for granted the inclusivity of being a Jewish minority, and now its absence felt terribly lonely.

As we rode down the street my head began to pound as heat blushed my cheeks. *What about the six million Jews who died in the gas chambers? If I say nothing, am I like the ones who turned their heads to these atrocities? But I can't pretend to feel Jewish if I really don't; that's crazy.*

My friend sensed the wreckage of World War II sitting next to her. "Are you okay?"

"No, not really," I answered. "I feel like I might be getting sick." We ended that evening early and I found refuge in falling asleep before 8:00 PM.

I lived with this conflict for months, going back and forth in my mind about the moral obligation of being Jewish. If I identified as Jewish, I had integrity with a long line of discriminated-against people. If I didn't identify as a Jew, I had integrity with myself, because I really didn't feel Jewish.

The conflict subsided in the busyness of academic life — grading papers, teaching classes, preparing lessons — until one day I heard some students laughing as we walked out of class. I couldn't believe my ears. They were laughing at an anti-Semitic joke. I waited a moment and cleared my throat.

"I don't find anti-Semitic jokes funny," I said over my shoulder as I walked past them on the way to my next class. I could at least give anti-Semitism the same respect as I gave sexism and racism. But my conflict was still not solved.

Years passed as I pondered the question. In 1986 I attended a writer's group while teaching at the University of Wisconsin. I'd begun to research some material on Sephardic Jews, as a way to learn more about my own heritage. I also phoned my grandmother, my cousin Fran, and Aunt Dottie. Yet despite lengthy conversations about struggling with Jewish identity, I still did not feel Jewish.

It wasn't until 1992, when I was preparing to teach a class on Judaism in a Wisdom Walk class, that I was startled by a realization: I knew less about Judaism than any other religion. Why was that? In a certain class, I gave students some direction on how to heal their particular charge about the material we had discussed in class. I realized that my charge took the form of cool distance to the point of indifference. I proceeded with my own healing in the same way that I guided my students. As I answered some of the journal questions on the handout, I saw how I had let disappointments solidify into resentments, distancing me from my heritage. My list of injustices had gotten longer through the years: My brother received Hebrew training and had a bar mitzvah, but I did not. I asked the rabbi questions, but I did not feel satisfied with the answers. The services at temple were in Hebrew, a language I didn't understand, which made sitting in services tedious and boring. The women sat separated from men.

By bringing these to the surface, I was able to confront my anger and sadness. Initially, I'd buried these feelings, but they'd accumulated. I allowed myself to receive help to clear them away, as if I were opening a cell and freeing the prisoners held captive for years. To all of my indictments I found an alternative. I could choose to educate myself in Judaism and even pursue a bat mitzvah as my cousin Fran had done. I could find answers to my questions that satisfied my desire to know, and I could attend Jewish services that were conducted in English by women rabbis if I chose to seek them out. Now, my previous attitudes lost their charge and seemed less significant than they'd once felt. My unresolved issues had distorted my view. I had projected my own displaced anger onto a religion that had much more breadth than I had previously explored.

The real turning point for me was remembering my connection with Judaism through my grandmother. I remembered how we lit Sabbath candles together and how she loved each of us deeply. These memories opened my heart, revealing to me that my connection to Judaism was inextricably woven into the love of my family. Although the cultural practices of my family did not represent all of the tenets of the Jewish religion, I could allow myself this connection with Judaism through the heart, and learn more about the religion as I continued my wisdom walk. Despite my disappointments and hurt, I could also open the door to this love and let myself heal, accept, and forgive.

Today I am grateful that I trudged through the conflict of my inner turmoil, so I could reclaim what was dear to me about Judaism. I can say today, without ambivalence, that I appreciate the richness of my Jewish heritage. I also love the wisdom from many spiritual traditions.

Robin's Story

When Robin heard the word *Jesus* or *Christianity*, she felt cold inside. These charged words triggered a memory of her born-again mother, who, in the name of Jesus, sent her unwanted Christian literature to save her from her homosexuality. Despite Robin's repeated requests to not send her these pamphlets, the next letter from her mother always contained some anti-gay propaganda.

As we listened to Robin discuss her frustration in class,

I watched her ordinarily smiling blue eyes turn steel gray, as if her anger submerged her in a deep freeze.

"I know my anger is hurting me more than my mother or the pope, but I feel outraged by my mother's lack of respect for me. Whenever I hear the word *Jesus* or *Christianity*, I feel livid."

We could see the anger rise like an elevator that hit her chin but then went back down. "It's not about spirituality. I've been practicing the steps of AA for twenty years and I feel connected to a higher power, who, by the way, loves me exactly as I am."

Robin agreed to tackle the journal questions and was able to get in touch with her feelings. She knew in her heart and from involvement with her twelve-step program that harboring resentments would threaten her sobriety.

"To make matters worse, my best friend told me that she wants to be a minister and is asking for my support. Anything that has to do with church makes me want to run the other way. But now, my best friend wants me to witness her in a church ordination ceremony and I'm conflicted about it. If I condemn her, if I reject her lifestyle, I'll be just like my family, who don't accept me."

Since class was coming to an end, I suggested that Robin give herself some time in the upcoming week to honor her feelings, share her story, and cultivate an inner nurturing voice, while answering the journal questions.

The next week in class Robin was back, and was eager to share about working with the wisdom steps.

"When I first started writing the journal questions I felt uncomfortably angry. It helped that the first wisdom step encouraged me to acknowledge my feelings. I never realized before how much I suppressed these feelings. Then in the middle of getting into these feelings I'd hear a harsh voice contradict this process. 'Why do you have to be so dramatic and make a big deal over a few pamphlets? It's not the end of the world, you know.' Ordinarily, I'd push down my feelings. But this time I asked myself, 'What would an inner, nurturing voice say?' I heard, 'Robin, you're entitled to have feelings. It takes courage to feel. You're doing great.'

"At the crossroads of the two different paths these voices offered, I decided to travel the path of compassion and support toward myself, for once.

"Here's what I realized: I have found my spiritual path and it's not Christianity. The AA program works better for me. I realized I wasn't angry at Christianity or Jesus but at my mother, who is trying to change me in the name of religion. The best my mother and I can do right now is to just drop the topic and try to focus on other things.

"I'll just have to work on tolerating her zealous approach to religion since I'd like her to accept my lifestyle. This also goes for my friend, the minister. I can support her choice even if I don't convert to her denomination. What's different is that I don't have a charge about it, which makes everything easier."

Tool #2: Uncovering Your Beliefs
about Other Spiritual Traditions

PURPOSE. Take this wisdom-walk side trip to uncover charged material, to explore your beliefs about other traditions, or work with feelings of prejudice toward a specific tradition. Use this time as an opportunity to see what beliefs you currently hold about other traditions, even if they are divergent from the attitudes with which you were raised.

When evaluating your attitudes and beliefs about traditions other than your own, be especially aware of the cultural lens through which you may be viewing another's tradition. Our own values may not be shared by others. Consider the merits of cultural relativism, which encourages us to understand that an individual's beliefs should be interpreted within his or her own culture, rather than our own. It is wiser, for instance, to respect differences in prayer practices, traditional dress, and various approaches to understanding the divine, than to judge these as inferior because they may be different from our own. Difference does not mean deficiency. Examining your charged material can widen your perspectives.

In Wisdom Walk classes people are often surprised by their answers to these questions. Many students have encountered family, institutional, and media beliefs in the past that are quite different from the ones they hold as adults. For example, Mark realized that his charge regarding Buddhism was related to his father's prejudice toward Asian people; Mark had absorbed his father's bitterness from fighting in World War II but realized it was not his own. Helene was less angry about the Christmas holidays after she uncovered her grief about her parents' suffering during the Holocaust. Holly realized that her resentments about being excluded from Native American ceremonies was more about her own judgments toward her neighbors on the reservation than their attitudes toward her. Even after exploration we may wonder: How am I still affected by these cherished beliefs of my family, institution, or media? Or maybe I had early beliefs about others' religions that I've forgotten, yet still can reclaim.

JOURNAL QUESTIONS. The following questions can assist you in exploring unresolved feelings and unexamined beliefs about other spiritual traditions.

1. To begin, read the question and let yourself remember and reflect for five minutes before writing.

2. Then reserve a block of time, fifteen to twenty minutes, to write your answer to one or two questions.

3. Repeat this process until you answer all questions. Feel free to adapt the process to your own needs.

REGARDING YOUR BELIEFS
ABOUT OTHER SPIRITUAL TRADITIONS

1. What spiritual traditions elicit strong feelings of anger, fear, sadness, guilt, mistrust, or estrangement, and what is the source of this dissonance?

2. Have you had a close relationship with someone from a different religion? How was that?

3. What did your own spiritual tradition, family, friends, or coworkers convey about spiritual traditions other than your own?

4. What value have you derived, or think you can derive, from exploring spiritual traditions other than your own?

Blood Brothers

My best friend, Richie, lived downstairs in our Brooklyn apartment building that housed four families. Richie looked like a young Richard Gere, dimple-cheeked, handsome, almost pretty. He was closer than a brother; he was a blood brother by childhood ritual. We'd made small cuts on our fingers to mingle our blood. This meant we'd be bonded for life.

During the winter holiday Richie always had a Christmas tree in his living room with red, blue, and gold lights; colored balls; peppermint candy canes, and presents piled high. While standing at the door waiting for him to come out to play, I'd glimpse the tree and feel the dazzle of blinking lights and tinsel.

When I asked my father why we didn't have a tree, he'd said, "Because we're Jewish and Richie's family is Catholic." I'd replied, "Oh." But I concluded in my nine-year-old wisdom that religion must be a game of make-believe that adults play. It was like when we'd play stickball and Richie and I were on opposite teams in the schoolyard. It was just a game. In truth we were one blood, one life, which was obvious to us as we'd lace arms around each other on our walk back home.

Remembering this conclusion of my youth made me aware of my early appreciation of spiritual diversity, an attitude that continued to shape my adult life as well. Remembering this story has also led to appreciating my childhood environment, which was broad-minded and tolerant of differences.

Scott's Story

Scott, the youngest of six children, said that his family did not stress any particular spiritual tradition, that they hadn't had strong beliefs about God one way or the other. When Scott was seven, his oldest sister, then sixteen, became involved in a church close to their home. She wanted Scott to join her in Sunday school, and after repeated requests, Scott conceded.

In the small classroom adjacent to the sanctuary, Scott sat with a room full of children ages six to sixteen. The topic of the day was "What is God to you?" Scott had never heard about God very much, and he remembered that the initial discussions he had heard seemed interesting. When the teacher called on him to answer the question under discussion, Scott stood next to his chair as other students did. "I think God is in the trees that stand in the backyard, in the moon at nighttime, and in the flowers." Scott was about to continue when he noticed the teacher frown and pucker her lips as if she had tasted a lemon.

"Scott, we believe that God is our heavenly Father, who sacrificed his only son, Jesus, the Christ, that we may be saved from eternal damnation." The sting of her words froze Scott in his tracks, even though his face felt flushed from the other children's giggles. Although the class continued, Scott stood frozen in that moment in which he decided, "I hate church and I don't believe in God."

As Scott grew up he identified himself as an atheist, although he continued to enjoy being in nature. It wasn't until adulthood that he learned about other spiritual traditions and realized that he'd shut down from exposure to a narrow perspective at an age when he had been too young to debate different points.

It wasn't until Scott's father died that he revisited the

idea of spirituality. The portal of death opened him to consider the existence of God in a way that was larger than he'd conceived it.

Looking back at the earlier experience, he realized that his Sunday school teacher had acted according to her spiritual beliefs. Although he would have preferred a larger container for his beliefs, he didn't have to close the door on religion and God from the feeling that his belief had not been respected. He didn't have to condemn her beliefs as he felt the Sunday school teacher had condemned his early experiences of spirituality in nature.

Tool #3: Exploring Beliefs about Being Raised with No Spiritual Tradition

PURPOSE. Take this wisdom-walk journey to explore how having been raised without a spiritual tradition affected you. Pay special attention to how you may have felt being a minority in school or social settings.

In Wisdom Walk classes those students who were raised outside of a spiritual tradition are often glad this subject is discussed. Being in environments that assume religious preference — from the Pledge of Allegiance in grade-school classrooms to the Christmas-Chanukah majority during the holiday season — individuals not raised in specific traditions can feel left out or awkward in school and social settings.

JOURNAL QUESTIONS. The following questions can assist you in exploring unresolved feelings and unexamined beliefs about having been raised with no spiritual tradition.

1. To begin, read the question and let yourself remember and reflect for five minutes before writing.

2. Then reserve a block of time, fifteen to twenty minutes, to write your answer to one or two questions.

3. Repeat this process until you answer all questions. Feel free to adapt the process to your own needs.

IF YOU WERE RAISED WITH NO SPIRITUAL TRADITION

1. How did you feel about peers who had religious traditions?

2. How did you feel when religion was mentioned in school, movies, or conversations?

3. Did you have spiritual experiences, and if so, what did you tell yourself about them?

4. In what, if anything, were you encouraged to have faith?

The Pledge of Allegiance

Jill, a petite woman in her forties with deep-blue eyes, spoke in a quickened cadence one Saturday afternoon in class, "Whenever I heard the word, *God*, I'd feel shame — not because I'd done anything wrong, but because I'd feel nothing. I felt embarrassed that I had no frame of reference for understanding God when I thought almost everyone else did. As I explored some of the journal questions I remembered my days in elementary school. I mouthed the words, 'One nation, under God' during the Pledge of Allegiance, but I couldn't imagine what that meant. I felt embarrassed. I thought I was missing something I was supposed to know

— like multiplication tables. I never told any of my friends because I didn't want them to think I was weird. They often assumed I was Christian, so I let them. It was too complicated to explain my father's argument that the existence of God couldn't be proved or disproved, and his advice that I'd be better off relying on reason and scientific proof for the truth. But in fifth grade or even high school, I wasn't about to say, 'My family's agnostic.' It was more important to me to fit in.

"But now, looking at things again as an adult, I think, 'Jill, honey, there's nothing wrong with you because you were raised without a specific spiritual tradition. So you were different from your classmates. Different does not mean deficient.'"

Wisdom Steps

ACKNOWLEDGE YOUR FEELINGS. I learned a lot about exploring my feelings from Laurel Mellin's book *The Pathway*. It takes practice to feel anger, sadness, fear, and guilt. You may choose to journal about your feelings or sing these feelings out loud. Whichever way you choose, keep your sentences short.

"I feel angry that _____."

"I feel sad that_____."

"I feel scared that _____."

"I feel guilty that _____."

It's amazing how checking in with our feelings can be extremely liberating. Just by acknowledging our feelings, we are liberating ourselves from the burden of carrying around unexpressed feelings.

SHARE YOUR STORY. Whether you speak to a friend, therapist, or clergy, telling a trusted person about your feelings can help set you free. There is a great power in remembering what happened. The charge leads you to emotions, which in turn lead to memories of unresolved incidents. When you share your story, you discover your thoughts, attitudes, and beliefs about the incident, which may not coincide with your current ones. In this confrontation between old and new ideas, you have great opportunity to witness and participate in your own transformation.

CULTIVATE AN INNER, NURTURING VOICE. You demonstrate courage when you share your story. However, you may also feel vulnerable doing so. It's important to be aware of your internal dialogue at this time. Be on the lookout for the harsh, critical voice that may want to minimize or criticize you for sharing your story: "Don't be such a baby. That happened a long time ago, so get over it." It is not wise to let the harsh voice be in charge. Rather, tune in to the compassionate voice inside of you that listens and supports you as would a good friend. Listen for the qualities of understanding and encouragement in your internal dialogue: "Good job for taking a risk and sharing a difficult time in your life. Good for you for being brave and facing, rather than running away from, your feelings." By taking this side trip, you are giving yourself a chance to view consciously what you have carried around unconsciously like a heavy ball chained around your neck.

You most likely will feel a sense of relief as you get in touch with your feelings, share your story, and show compassion for yourself. Often, wisdom walkers claim they feel much freer. Claim that feeling of liberation for yourself. Acknowledge that your wisdom walk journey has been worthwhile.

~<del>o</del>~

APPENDIX 2:
Reflections on Your Wisdom Walk

t the end of a trip it's often a delight to review the high-lights. As you have reached this last portion, you may think that your wisdom walk is over, but actually, para-doxically, the end of a journey is also a beginning. Reserve some time, ten to fifteen minutes, with pen and paper handy, and reflect on your wisdom walk so far.

BACKWARD GLANCE

- What has changed in your life as a result of your wisdom walk?

- Which wisdom practices have given you the most satis-faction?

- Are there wisdom practices that you had set aside for another time that you'd like to try now, or are there those with which you'd like to spend more time?

FORWARD GLANCE

- Which wisdom practices do you commit to on a daily basis? Weekly? Monthly?

- What situations challenge your wisdom walk?

- What solutions can you envision that would help you during these challenges?

APPENDIX 3: *Wisdom Walk Checklist*

ince my commitment is to integrate all of these practices into my life, I created a checklist to remind me of all the wisdom steps that lead to fulfillment on this journey. You can use this checklist as an evening or weekly inventory, or on an as-needed basis. The checklist provides a way to continually integrate the wisdom practices into your life to assure that you continue to benefit from these practices. Here are some questions to ask yourself from my own Wisdom Walk Checklist. Remember, we cannot be nourished today by yesterday's meals or yesterday's wisdom practices.

1. Hinduism: Create a Home Altar

- Have I created an altar in my home or work area?

- Have I sat in sacred space in front of an altar today?

- Do I recognize the inner sanctuary that I carry with me throughout the day?

2. Buddhism: Meditate and Find Peace

- Have I meditated in the morning, afternoon, and/or evening?

- Have I expressed my insights in my meditation journal?

- Am I practicing mindfulness in my daily activities, such as walking, washing dishes, or raking leaves?

3. Islam: Surrender to Prayer

- Have I attuned myself to the frequency of prayer as I arise, at meals, and before I retire?

- Have I created and glanced at my portable prayers or spontaneously given thanks for things I appreciated in my life today?

- Have I danced my prayers today?

4. Christianity: Forgive Yourself and Others

- Have I visualized people in my life walking down the corridors of my heart and feeling safe, surrounded by love rather than condemnation?

- Have I taken the time to release myself from resentment by affirming, "I fully and freely forgive _____ for _____. I wish this person all the blessings of life."

- Is there anyone on my forgiveness list, including myself, with whom I can move toward resolution by writing in my journal?

5. Judaism: Make Time for the Sabbath

- Have I taken Sabbath time this week?

- What activities am I enjoying, or would like to enjoy, during Sabbath time?

- As part of my Sabbath time, have I spent time appreciating the many blessings of my life?

6. Native American Spirituality: Let Nature Be Your Teacher

- Have I walked in nature today and enjoyed my solitude?

- Have I opened myself to an animal-wisdom teacher through meditation or walking in nature?

- Have I spent any time this week touching the earth and life cycles through gardening or tending to houseplants?

7. Taoism: Go with the Flow

- In the situations that I face today, can I visualize myself floating downstream, letting go and trusting the flow of life?

- When I'm undecided about how to best interact with another person or with a situation, have I paused to ask, "Is yin or yang needed here?"

- Have I practiced patience while waiting? Have I harmonized myself with the flow of life?

8. New Thought: Catch God's Vision of Your Life

- Have I visioned, or planned to vision, with myself or others this week?

- Have I reviewed my visioning journal to keep the visions and guidance from visioning foremost in my mind?

- Am I taking baby steps today in the direction of the spiritual growth indicated through visioning?

9. All Traditions: Offer Yourself in Service to Others

- Am I acting on inner guidance I've received about how I can be of service to others?

- Have I been of service to a friend, member of my family, or community?

- Am I too preoccupied with myself, or am I also aware of others in my life?

NOTES

Introduction

xiii *"Wisdom is better than rubies..."*: Prov. 8:11 (King James Version).

Chapter 1. Hinduism: Create a Home Altar

18 *suggests that we create nine different altars...*: Denise Linn, *Altars: Bringing Sacred Shrines into Your Everyday Life* (New York: Ballantine Wellspring, 1999), 88–95.

Chapter 2. Buddhism: Meditate and Find Peace

25 *"Be lamps unto yourselves..."*: Gautama Buddha, quoted in Philip Novak, *The World's Wisdom: Sacred Texts of the World's Religions* (San Francisco: HarperSanFrancisco, 1994), 61.

27 *account of Buddha's awakening...*: Huston Smith, *The Illustrated World's Religions* (San Francisco: HarperSanFrancisco, 1994), 68.

29   *"One of the things that meditation teaches us..."*: Dalai Lama, *The Path to Tranquility: Daily Wisdom* (New York: Penguin Group, 1998), 121.

31   *"Kindness is my religion..."*: I heard the Dalai Lama say this when I attended a conference in the early 1990s called "East Meets West," in Newport Beach, CA. The Dalai Lama, who had recently been awarded the Nobel Peace Prize, was the keynote speaker. His Holiness also develops his ideas on kindness in his *Ethics for the New Millennium*, (New York: Riverhead Books, 1999) 68–73.

34   *"Our true home is in the present moment..."*: Thich Nhat Hanh, *Touching Peace: Practicing the Art of Mindful Living* (Berkeley, CA: Parallax Press, 1992), 1.

37   *"I have arrived..."*: Thich Nhat Hanh, *The Long Road Turns to Joy: A Guide to Walking Meditation* (Berkeley, CA: Parallax Press, 1996), 27.

38   *"When you discover in meditation..."*: ———, This is my recollection of an experience at this conference on mindfulness, Santa Barbara, CA, approx. 1998.

39   *"Far out, jealous rage..."*: Ram Dass, *Journey of Awakening: A Meditator's Guidebook* (New York: Bantam Books, 1990), 158.

40   *"Music does it for me..."*: Anugama, *Shamanic Dream*, Open Sky Music B00005TZOE, 2000.

44   *"There are documented studies..."*: Ann Hayes, "Meditation and Health: An Annotated Bibliography," *Reference and User Services Quarterly* 44, no. 1 (fall 2004): 18–25.

Chapter 3. Islam: Surrendering to Prayer

49   *"The Lord is my shepherd...."*: Ps. 23:1–5 (KJV).

51   *"There is no god but Allah..."*: Koran, reprinted in Huston Smith, *The Illustrated World's Religions* (San Francisco: HarperSanFrancisco, 1994), 160.

54   *The emphasis on surrender or submission...*: Ibid., 148–149.

54   *"Proclaim your Lord is wondrous and kind..."*: Koran 96:1–3.

57   *recited his morning prayers out loud...*: Jim Castelli, editor, *How I Pray: People of Different Religions Share with Us That Most Sacred and Intimate Act of Faith* (New York: Ballantine Books, 1994), 78.

59   *we came whirling out of nothingness...*: Jalal al-Din Rumi, Daniel Liebert, translator, *Rumi: Fragments, Ecstasies* (Santa Fe: Source Books, 1981), 11.

62   *describe the five times of prayer...*: Coleman Barks and Michael Green,

The Illuminated Prayer: The Five-Times Prayer of the Sufis as Revealed by Jellaludin Rumi and Bawa Muhaiyaddeen (New York: Ballantine Wellspring, 2000), 45–58.

Chapter 4. Christianity: Forgive Yourself and Others

75   *learning to apply the principles of Alcoholics Anonymous...:* More information is available at www.alcoholics-anonymous.org.

76   *I attended Al-Anon meetings...:* More information is available at www.al-anon.alateen.org.

77   *"Forgiveness List..."*: Catherine Ponder is a leading New Thought author on prosperity, love, and forgiveness. More information is available at www.CatherinePonder.com.

80   *"Forgive them, Father..."*: Luke 23:34 (KJV).

80   *"I give you a new commandment..."*: John 13:34 (New Revised Standard Version), quoted in Philip Novak, *The World's Wisdom: Sacred Texts of the World's Religions* (San Francisco: HarperSanFrancisco, 1994), 242.

81   *"Let the one who has not sinned..."*: John 8:4–6, 7, 9–11, quoted in Novak, 243.

81   *"There is no difficulty..."*: Emmet Fox, *Power Through Constructive Thinking* (New York: HarperCollins, 1940), 267.

84   *"if another member of the church sins against me..."*: Matt. 18:21–22 (KJV).

86   *"The truth shall set you free..."*: John 8:32 (NRSV).

97   *"Forgiveness is a pleasant inner act..."*: Attributed to Catherine Ponder, specific source unknown. Compare her thoughts on forgiveness in *The Dynamic Laws of Prosperity* (Marina del Rey, CA: DeVorrs Publications, 1962), 384–411.

Chapter 5. Judaism: Make Time for the Sabbath

101   *"the heights of the earth..."*: Is. 58:13–14. (NRSV).

103   *The Ten Commandments...*: Exodus 19:3–6, 20:1–14, quoted in Philip Novak, *The World's Wisdom: Sacred Texts of the World's Religions* (San Francisco: HarperSanFrancisco, 1994), 187–188 (reprinted from *The Tanakh: The New JPS Translation According to the Traditional Hebrew Text* [Philadelphia: Jewish Publication Society, 1988]).

104   *"As a doe longs for running streams..."*: Ps. 42:1, quoted in Frederic and

Mary Ann Brussat, *Spiritual Literacy: Reading the Sacred in Everyday Life* (New York: Scribner, 1996), 506.

105   *"Just to be is a blessing..."*: Abraham Joshua Heschel, *The Sabbath: Its Meaning for Modern Man* (New York: Farrar, Straus and Giroux, 1951), 123.

105   *"Come, my beloved, to meet the bride..."*: Solomon Alkabetz of Safed, 1550, quoted in Daniel Matt, *The Essential Kabbalah: The Heart of Jewish Mysticism* (San Francisco: HarperSanFrancisco, 1995), 54.

106   *"The Sabbath is a bride and its celebration is like a wedding..."*: Quoted in Wayne Muller, *Sabbath: Finding Rest, Renewal and Delight in Our Busy Lives* (New York: Bantam, 2000), 54.

107   *a sanctuary in time...*: Heschel, *The Sabbath*, 7.

110   *In a film I show to students...*: Dr. Pinchas Peli, sixth-generation rabbi, interviewed by Ronald Eyres, *The Long Search*, v. 7, "Judaism: The Chosen People." 1977 Video Series produced by the BBC in association with Time Life Books, R.M. Production (New York: Ambrose Video, 1987), 13 videos.

Chapter 6. Native American Spirituality: Let Nature Be Your Teacher

126   *approximately 2.4 million people...*: Stuart M. Matlins and Arthur J. Magida, *How to Be a Perfect Stranger: The Essential Religious Etiquette Handbook*, 3rd ed. (New York: Jewish Lights Publishing, 2002) 216–217.

128   *"Earth, teach me stillness..."*: Quoted in Philip Novak, *The World's Wisdom: Sacred Texts of the World's Religions* (San Francisco: HarperSanFrancisco, 1994), 369–370.

130   *"The sea does not reward those..."*: Anne Morrow Lindbergh, *Gift from the Sea* (New York: Pantheon Books, 1992), 11.

133   *"Examining your life..."*: Denise Linn, *Quest: A Guide for Creating Your Own Vision Quest* (New York: Ballantine Books, 1997), 103.

138   *We may gently remove a spider...*: Sue Monk Kidd, *The Secret Lives of Bees* (New York: The Penguin Group, 2003), 173.

Chapter 7. Taoism: Go with the Flow

154   *Lao-tzu, the old master who founded Taoism...*: Huston Smith, *The Illustrated World's Religions* (San Francisco: HarperSanFrancisco, 1994), 124.

162   *"We must let ripen..."*: This rhyme refers to the wisdom of Lao Tzu,

Tao Te Ching, ch. 48. Compare a different translation in Lao Tzu, Tao Te Ching, trans. Stephen Mitchell (New York: HarperCollins, 1988), 54.

173 *"Do you have the patience to wait ..."*: Lao Tzu, Tao Te Ching, trans. Stephen Mitchell (San Francisco: Harper & Row, 1988), ch. 15, quoted in Philip Novak, *The World's Wisdom: Sacred Texts of the World's Religions* (San Francisco: HarperSanFrancisco, 1994), 151.

Chapter 8. New Thought: Catch God's Vision of Your Life

194 *"Be still and know that I am God ..."*: Ps. 46:10 (KJV).

199 *"...we must sow it ..."*: Thomas Troward, *The Edinburgh and Dore Lectures on Mental Science* (Los Angeles: DeVorss and Company, 1989), 37.

199 *principles of the creative process ...*: Wayne Dyer, *You'll See It When You Believe It: The Way to Your Personal Transformation* (New York: Harper Paperbacks, 2001), 220.

199 *visualization as a tool for creating the life you desire....*: Shakti Gawain, *Creative Visualization: Use the Power of Your Imagination to Create What You Want in Your Life* (Novato, CA: New World Library, 2002), 11.

202 *"It takes time to walk with God ..."*: Howard Thurman, *For the Inward Journey* (New York: Harcourt Brace Jovanovich, 1984), 34.

Chapter 9. All Traditions: Offer Yourself in Service to Others

210 *"freedom from the bondage of self ..."*: Excerpt from a larger quote, which is part of the Third Step prayer that is central to the recovery process. "God, I offer myself to thee—to build with me and to do with me as Thou wilt. Relieve me of the bondage of self, that I may better do thy will..."*Anonymous*, Alcoholics Anonymous (New York, Alcoholics Anonymous World Service, 2001), 63.

211 *"Do unto others ..."*: Luke 6:31 (KJV).

211 *"Faith without works is dead ..."*: James 2:26 (KJV).

213 *"When a man's thought rests entirely on himself ..."*: Ernest Holmes, *Science of Mind* (New York: Jeremy P. Tarcher/Putnam, 1997), 440.

214 *"We know we are greater than our small story ..."*: Jack Kornfield, *A Path with Heart: A Guide Through the Perils and Promises of Spiritual Life* (New York: Bantam Books, 1993), 29.

215 *You are surprised by what you are called to do....*: Meredith Gould, *Deliberate Acts of Kindness: Service as a Spiritual Practice* (New York: Image Books/Doubleday, 2002), 29.

218   *"If there is radiance in the soul ..."*: Attributed to Lao Tzu, Tao Te
      Ching, ch. 54. Compare another translation of Lao Tzu, Tao Te Ching,
      trans. Gia-Fu Feng and Jane English (New York: Vintage Books,
      1972), 104.

219   *"God wants the heart ..."*: The Talmud, quoted in Frederic and Mary
      Ann Brussat, *Spiritual Literacy: Reading the Sacred in Everyday Life*
      (New York: Scribner, 1996), 530.

219   *"The purpose of life ..."*: Attributed to the Dalai Lama, specific source
      unknown. See also the Dalai Lama's discussion of the warm heart in
      The Art of Happiness (New York: Riverhead Books, 1998), 189.

220   *"Spirit has no body on earth but yours ..."*: Teresa of Avila, Sufi dance
      song (adapted), quoted in *Spiritual Literacy*, 325.

224   *"Never doubt that a small group of thoughtful committed citizens ..."*:
      Attributed to Margaret Mead, specific source unknown.

224   *"Fill yourself first ..."*: Saint Augustine, quoted in Kathryn Spink,
      Mother Teresa: A Complete Authorized Biography (New York: Harper-
      Collins, 1997), 181.

230   *We begin this practice of taking on the suffering of another ...*: Pema
      Chödrön, *When Things Fall Apart: Heart Advice for Difficult Times*
      (Boston: Shambhala Publications, Inc., 1997), 95–96.

231   *"To the degree that we have compassion for ourselves ..."*: Ibid., 80.

232   *"I am a pencil in the hand of God ..."*: Mother Teresa, quoted in
      Frederick and Mary Ann Brussat, *Spiritual Literacy: Reading the
      Sacred in Everyday Life* (New York: Scribner, 1996), 285.

Epilogue: Acquiring a Taste for Wisdom

243   *"Let there be peace on earth ..."*: Jill Jackson and Sy Miller, *Let There Be
      Peace on Earth*, copyright 1955.

243   *"You must be the change ..."*: Attributed to Mahatma Gandhi, specific
      source unknown.

Appendix 1: Tools for the Journey

261   *I learned a lot about exploring my feelings ...*: Laurel Mellin, *The
      Pathway: Follow the Road to Health and Happiness* (New York:
      HarperCollins, 2003), 183.

BIBLIOGRAPHY

Chapter 1. Hinduism: Create a Home Altar

Knipe, David M. *Hinduism: Experiments in the Sacred*. San Francisco: HarperSan Francisco, 1991.

Linn, Denise. *Altars: Bringing Sacred Shrines into Your Everyday Life*. New York: Ballantine Wellspring, 1999.

Narayanan, Vasudha. *Hinduism: Origins, Beliefs, Practices, Holy Texts, Sacred Places*. New York: Oxford University Press, 2004.

Streep, Peg. *Altars Made Easy*. San Francisco: HarperSanFrancisco, 1997.

Chapter 2. Buddhism: Meditate and Find Peace

Collier, James Lincoln. *The Empty Mirror*. New York/London: Bloomsbury, 2004.

Dalai Lama. *The Art of Happiness*. New York: Riverhead Books, 1998.

————. *Ethics for the New Millennium*. New York: Riverhead Books, 1999.

————. *The Path to Tranquility: Daily Wisdom*. New York: Penguin Group, 1998.

Dass Ram. *Journey of Awakening: A Meditator's Guidebook*. New York:
Bantam Books, 1990.

Kornfield, Jack. *After Ecstasy, the Laundry: How the Heart Grows Wise on the
Spiritual Path*. New York: Bantam Dell Publishing, 2001.

———. *A Path with Heart*. New York: Bantam Books, 1993.

Nhat Hanh, Thich. *The Essential Writings*. Edited by Robert Ellsberg.
Maryknoll, NY: Orbis Books, 2001.

———. *The Long Road Turns to Joy: A Guide to Walking Meditation*.
Berkeley, CA: Parallax Press, 1996.

———. *Peace with Every Step*. New York: Tarcher/Putnam, 2002.

———. *Touching Peace: Practicing the Art of Mindful Living*. Berkeley, CA:
Parallax Press, 1992.

Novak, Philip. *The World's Wisdom: Sacred Texts of the World's Religions*.
San Francisco: HarperSanFrancisco, 1994.

Smith, Huston. *The Illustrated World's Religions*. San Francisco:
HarperSanFrancisco, 1994.

Suzuki, Shunryu. *Zen Mind, Beginner's Mind*. Boston: Weatherhill Books, 1973.

Chapter 3. Islam: Surrender to Prayer

Barks, Coleman, and Michael Green. *The Illuminated Prayer: The Five-Times
Prayer of the Sufis*. New York: Ballantine Wellspring, 2000.

Castelli, Jim, editor. *How I Pray: People of Different Religions Share with Us That
Most Sacred and Intimate Act of Faith*. New York: Ballantine Books, 1994.

Liebert, Daniel, trans. *Rumi: Fragments, Ecstasies*. Santa Fe: Source Books,
1981.

Roth, Gabrielle. *Sweat Your Prayers*. New York: Tarcher/Putnam, 1997.

Shannon, Maggie Oman. *The Way We Pray: Prayer Practices from Around the
World*. Boston: Conari Press, 2001.

Smith, Huston. *The Illustrated World's Religions*. San Francisco: HarperSan-
Francisco, 1994.

Chapter 4. Christianity: Forgive Yourself and Others

Enright, Robert. *Forgiveness Is a Choice: A Step-by-Step Process of Resolving
Anger and Restoring Hope*. Washington, DC: American Psychological
Association, 2001.

Ferrini, Paul, and Pia MacKenzie. *Twelve Steps of Forgiveness: A Practical Guide
in Transforming Fear to Love*. Greenfield, MA: Heartways Press, 1991.

Fox, Emmet. *Power Through Constructive Thinking*. New York: Harper-Collins, 1940.

Ponder, Catherine. *The Dynamic Laws of Prosperity*. Marina del Rey, CA: DeVorss Publications, 1962.

Chapter 5. Judaism: Make Time for the Sabbath

Brussat, Frederic and Mary Ann. *Spiritual Literacy: Reading the Sacred in Everyday Life*. New York: Scribner, 1996.

Heschel, Abraham Joshua. *The Sabbath: Its Meaning for Modern Man*. New York: Farrar, Straus and Giroux, 1951.

Matlins, Stuart M., and Arthur J. Magida. *How to Be a Perfect Stranger: The Essential Religious Etiquette Handbook*. 3rd ed. New York: Jewish Lights Publishing, 2002.

Matt, Daniel. *The Essential Kabbalah: The Heart of Jewish Mysticism*. San Francisco: HarperSanFrancisco, 1995.

Muller, Wayne. *Sabbath: Finding Rest, Renewal, and Delight in Our Busy Lives*. New York: Bantam, 2000.

Chapter 6. Native American Spirituality: Let Nature Be Your Teacher

Kidd, Sue Monk. *The Secret Lives of Bees*. New York: The Penguin Group, 2003.

Lindbergh, Anne Morrow. *Gift from the Sea*. New York: Pantheon Books, 1992.

Linn, Denise. *Quest: A Guide for Creating Your Own Vision Quest*. New York: Ballantine Books, 1997.

Matlins, Stuart M., and Arthur J. Magida. *How to Be a Perfect Stranger: The Essential Religious Etiquette Handbook*. 3rd ed. New York: Jewish Lights Publishing, 2002.

Novak, Philip. *The World's Wisdom: Sacred Texts of the World's Religions*. San Francisco: HarperSanFrancisco, 1994.

Sams, Jamie and David Carson. *Medicine Cards: The Discovery of Power Through the Ways of Animals*. Santa Fe: Bear & Company, 1988.

Chapter 7. Taoism: Go with the Flow

Lao Tzu, Tao Te Ching. Translated by Stephen Mitchell. New York: HarperCollins, 1988.

Novak, Philip. *The World's Wisdom: Sacred Texts of the World's Religions*. San Francisco: HarperSanFrancisco, 1994.

Oldstone-Moore, Jennifer. *Taoism: Origins, Beliefs, Practices, Holy Texts, Sacred Places*. London, Oxford University Press, 2003.

Smith, Huston. *The Illustrated World's Religions*. San Francisco: HarperSanFrancisco, 1994.

Chapter 8. New Thought: Catch God's Vision of Your Life

Dyer, Wayne. *You'll See It When You Believe It: The Way to Your Personal Transformation*. New York: Harper Paperbacks, 2001.

Gawain, Shakti. *Creative Visualization: Use the Power of Your Imagination to Create What You Want in Your Life*. Novato, CA: New World Library, 2002.

Holmes, Ernest. *The Holmes Reader for All Seasons*. Marina del Rey, CA: DeVorrs Publications, 1993.

Hopkins, Emma Curtis. *Scientific Mental Practice*. Marina del Rey, CA: DeVorrs & Company, 1974.

Morrissey, Mary Manin. *Building Your Field of Dreams*. New York: Bantam Books, 1997.

———. *New Thought: Practical Steps to Living Your Greater Life*. New York: Tarcher/Putnam, 1996.

Thurman, Howard. *For the Inward Journey*. New York: Harcourt Brace Jovanovich, 1984.

Troward, Thomas, *The Edinburgh and Dore Lectures on Mental Science*. Los Angeles: DeVorss and Company, 1989.

Chapter 9. All Traditions: Offer Yourself in Service to Others

Brussat, Frederic and Mary Ann. *Spiritual Literacy: Reading the Sacred in Everyday Life*. New York: Scribner, 1996.

Chödrön, Pema. *When Things Fall Apart: Heart Advice for Difficult Times*. Boston: Shambhala Publications, Inc., 1997.

Cousins, Norman. *The Words of Albert Schweitzer*. New York: Newmarket Press, 1990.

Dalai Lama. *The Art of Happiness*. New York: Riverhead Books, 1998.

Dass, Ram, and Mirabai Bush. *Compassion in Action: Setting Out on the Path of Service*. New York: Three Rivers Press, 1995.

Dass, Ram, and Paul Gorman. *How Can I Help: Stories and Reflections on Service*. New York: Alfred A. Knopf, 1986.

Gould, Meredith. *Deliberate Acts of Kindness: Service as a Spiritual Practice*. New York: Image Books/Doubleday, 2002.

Holmes, Ernest. *Science of Mind*. New York: Jeremy P. Tarcher/Putnam, 1997.

Kornfield, Jack. *After the Ecstacy, the Laundry: How the Heart Grows Wise on the Spiritual Path*. New York: Bantam Dell Publishing, 2001.

———, *A Path with Heart: A Guide Through the Perils and Promises of Spiritual Life*. New York: Bantam Books, 1993.

Lao Tzu. Tao Te Ching. Translated by Gia-Fu Feng and Jane English. New York: Vintage Books, 1972.

Nhat Hanh, Thich. *The Long Road Turns to Joy: A Guide to Walking Meditation*. Berkeley: Parallax Press, 1996.

Spink, Kathryn. *Mother Teresa: A Complete Authorized Biography*. New York: HarperCollins, 1997.

Appendix 1: Tools for the Journey

Mellin, Laurel. *The Pathway: Follow the Road to Health and Happiness*. New York: HarperCollins, 2003.

Sources for the Wisdom of World Religions

Borysenko, Joan. *The Ways of the Mystic: Seven Paths to God*. Carlsbad, CA: Hay House, 1997.

Brussat, Frederic and Mary Ann. *Spiritual Literacy: Reading the Sacred in Everyday Life*. New York: Scribner, 1996.

Fox, Matthew. *One River, Many Wells: Wisdom Springing from Many Faiths*. New York: Tarcher/Putnam, 2002.

Matlins, Stuart M., and Arthur J. Magida. *How to Be a Perfect Stranger: The Essential Religious Etiquette Handbook*. 3rd ed. New York: Jewish Lights Publishing, 2002.

Novak, Philip. *The World's Wisdom: Sacred Texts of the World's Religions*. San Francisco: HarperSanFrancisco, 1994.

ABOUT THE AUTHOR

 Sage Bennet, PhD, is a frequent speaker and presenter at spiritual centers, colleges, and universities throughout the United States. She offers seminars, retreats, counseling, and coaching to those exploring the deeper mysteries of their spiritual journeys. She is currently on the faculties of Loyola Marymount University, Los Angeles Harbor College, and Holmes Institute. Sage has been an educator for more than twenty-five years. She has a master's degree and a doctorate in philosophy from the New School for Social Research in New York City, as well as a bachelor's in psychology from Long Island University. Sage is also an ordained minister. She was a minister and dean of Holmes Institute–LA at the Agape International Spiritual Center for eight years. For the past decade she has performed sacred ceremonies such as weddings, memorials, and elegant transition rituals.

She has a private practice in Marina del Rey, California, where she offers spiritual counseling and coaching, in person and by phone, to individuals throughout the world. She lives with her partner and Portuguese water dog on a boat in Marina del Rey. Her website is www.sagebennet.com.